NO LONGER PROPERTY OF
ANYTHINK LIBRARIES/
RANGEVIEW LIBRARY DISTRICT

HOLDING THE LINE

HOLDING
THE LINE

INSIDE
TRUMP'S
PENTAGON
WITH
SECRETARY
MATTIS

GUY M. SNODGRASS
COMMANDER, US NAVY (RET.)

SENTINEL

SENTINEL
An imprint of Penguin Random House LLC
penguinrandomhouse.com

Copyright © 2019 Guy M. Snodgrass
Penguin supports copyright. Copyright fuels creativity, encourages diverse voices, promotes free speech, and creates a vibrant culture. Thank you for buying an authorized edition of this book and for complying with copyright laws by not reproducing, scanning, or distributing any part of it in any form without permission. You are supporting writers and allowing Penguin to continue to publish books for every reader.

Photo credits: Insert p. 1 (top), p. 8 (middle), photos by Navy Commander Guy M. Snodgrass; p. 1 (bottom), photo by Ashley Taylor; p. 2 (top), official US Naval War College photo; p. 2 (middle), DOD photo by US Air Force Staff Sergeant Jette Carr; p. 2 (bottom), p. 3 (top and bottom), p. 4 (top and bottom), p. 7 (bottom), p. 8 (top) DOD photos by US Army Sergeant Amber I. Smith; p. 5 (top and bottom), DOD photos by Navy Mass Communication Specialist 1st Class Kathryn E. Holm; p. 6 (top, middle, bottom), p. 7 (top), DOD photos by Tech Sergeant Vernon Young Jr.

Most Sentinel books are available at a discount when purchased in quantity for sales promotions or corporate use. Special editions, which include personalized covers, excerpts, and corporate imprints, can be created when purchased in large quantities. For more information, please call (212) 572-2232 or e-mail specialmarkets@ penguinrandomhouse.com. Your local bookstore can also assist with discounted bulk purchases using the Penguin Random House corporate Business-to-Business program. For assistance in locating a participating retailer, e-mail B2B@penguinrandomhouse.com.

Library of Congress Cataloging-in-Publication Data
Names: Snodgrass, Guy M., author.
Title: Holding the line: inside Trump's Pentagon with Secretary Mattis / Guy M. Snodgrass.
Description: [New York] : Sentinel, [2019] | Includes bibliographical references.
Identifiers: LCCN 2019031023 (print) | LCCN 2019031024 (ebook) |
ISBN 9780593084373 (hardcover) | ISBN 9780593084380 (ebook)
Subjects: LCSH: Mattis, James N., 1950– | Snodgrass, Guy M. | Trump, Donald, 1946– |
United States. Department of Defense—Officials and employees—Biography. |
National security—United States—History—21st century. | United States—Military policy. |
United States—Foreign relations administration. | United States—Foreign relations—2017– |
United States—Politics and government—2017–
Classification: LCC E897.4.M37 S66 2019 (print) | LCC E897.4.M37 (ebook) |
DDC 355/.033573—dc23
LC record available at https://lccn.loc.gov/2019031023
LC ebook record available at https://lccn.loc.gov/2019031024

Printed in the United States of America
1 3 5 7 9 10 8 6 4 2

Book design by Lauren Kolm

All statements of fact, opinion, or analysis are those of the author and do not reflect the official positions or views of the U.S. government. Nothing in the contents should be construed as asserting or implying U.S. government authentication of information or endorsement of the author's views. This material has been reviewed by the U.S. government to prevent the disclosure of classified information.

This book is dedicated to the men and women of the Department of Defense. Thank you for holding the line—twenty-four hours a day, seven days a week, 365 days a year.

CONTENTS

FIRST PRINCIPLES

I, James Norman Mattis, do solemnly swear that I will support and defend the Constitution of the United States against all enemies, foreign and domestic; that I will bear true faith and allegiance to the same; that I take this obligation freely, without any mental reservation or purpose of evasion; and that I will well and faithfully discharge the duties of the office on which I am about to enter. So help me God.

—JANUARY 20, 2017, THE WHITE HOUSE

We in the Department of Defense recognize that there are a lot of passions running about in our country, as there ought to be in a vibrant Republic. But for those privileged to wear the cloth of our nation, to serve . . . you stand the ramparts—unapologetic, apolitical, defending our experiment in self-governance. And you hold the line. ●

—SECRETARY JIM MATTIS, MAY 27, 2017,
WEST POINT, NY

AUTHOR'S NOTE

For more than twenty years, I served proudly in the United States military alongside men and women from all walks of life. Despite our wide-ranging experiences and backgrounds, we shared a belief in core values that can sound clichéd in today's highly polarized environment: duty, honor, integrity, commitment, mission, country.

These values are why we serve. These values are why we sacrifice time away from home and our families. These values are what make the US military the most admired institution in our country, and perhaps one of the only institutions to retain the respect and trust of the vast majority of the American people.

That trust is precious. It is fragile.

If lost, it may be gone forever.

For seventeen months of my final years in uniform, I worked directly for a man who understood that danger.

Secretary of Defense James Mattis joined the administration with a reputation as one of the most storied living leaders in our armed forces. He saw it as his job, his duty, his mission, not only to restore America's military might but to protect the military's reputation for independence and nonpartisanship.

Mattis sought to strengthen alliances wherever he could find them. He joined forces with like-minded world leaders and a handful of senior administration officials widely considered to be the "adults in the room."

In May 2017, Mattis addressed the graduating class at the US Military Academy at West Point, telling them to "hold the line, confronting our nation's foes with implacable will . . . to hold the line, living by a moral code regardless of who is watching . . . and to hold the line, loyal to the country and Constitution as we defend our fundamental freedoms."

For nearly two years, Secretary James Mattis—along with millions of men and women serving in the Department of Defense—did just that. They held the line during the most challenging and unusual times the military has faced in generations. They held the line with an administration in Washington, DC, willing to challenge, question, and sometimes undermine the long-standing traditions and views of America's military leadership, and those of our friends and allies abroad.

Then, on December 20, 2018, Mattis resigned.

INTRODUCTION

Marines don't know how to spell the word *defeat.*

—GENERAL JAMES MATTIS

Thursday, December 20, 2018—The White House

Secretary of Defense James Norman Mattis exited the West Wing, climbing into the lead vehicle of his motorcade to speed back to the Pentagon. He would not be coming back.

He'd had enough. He was done.

His resignation—and its blunt manner—launched shock waves through a town that by now seemed impervious to the seismic blasts regularly exploding throughout the Trump administration.

Officially, Mattis had gone to the Oval Office to reverse the president's tweet-born announcement of a precipitous troop pull-out from Syria. He failed, and when that happened, he informed Trump he was leaving.

But that wasn't the whole truth. There's precious little whole truth in Washington. Mattis's outrage over Syria, while real, was only a pretext to announce a decision he had made months before to cut his losses and move on.

And why not? To survive in Washington, you need alliances. One by one, what administration allies Mattis once had vanished into the night: Secretary of State Rex Tillerson, National Security Adviser H. R. McMaster, and now Trump's chief of staff, John Kelly, had one foot out the door.

Trump later tweeted that Mattis was "retiring." He wasn't.

Arriving at the Pentagon, Mattis immediately distributed copies of his previously composed resignation letter to defense reporters. The letter minced few words. Its key section highlighted the disparity between a president and his secretary of defense, saying:

"My views on treating allies with respect and also being clear-eyed about both malign actors and strategic competitors are strongly held and informed by over four decades of immersion in these issues. We must do everything possible to advance an international order that is most conducive to our security, prosperity and values, and we are strengthened in this effort by the solidarity of our alliances.

"Because you have the right to have a Secretary of Defense whose views are better aligned with yours on these and other subjects, I believe it is right for me to step down from my position."

James Mattis, the quintessential Marine, had learned some valuable and painful lessons while serving the Trump administration. Prime among them was how to spell a new word: *defeat*.

And, to be honest about it, so had I.

ONE

SERVICE BEFORE SELF

Right now, somewhere around the world, young men
are landing high-performance jet aircraft on the
pitching decks of aircraft carriers . . . living on
the edge of danger so the rest of us need not think
about, let alone experience, danger.

—GEORGE WILL

Tuesday, April 22, 2003

I was in a tight left turn, flying at 16,000 feet over a training range in California at full afterburner, when my airplane suddenly shuddered.

What the hell was that?

A second later the headphones in my helmet crackled to life. "Engine fire, right . . . engine fire, right."

Oh crap.

Flying behind my aircraft, the flight instructor I'd just been dogfighting with saw something I couldn't: a fifteen-foot stream of fire pouring from the exhaust of my right engine.

Only seconds away from possible death, my first thought was to stop the fight. I carefully leveled the wings of my F/A-18C Hornet fighter, my right hand nudging the control stick as my left hand pulled both jet engine throttles back into a midrange position. What next?

Aviate. Navigate. Communicate.

Every naval aviator knows these three major functions of flight in descending order of priority.

First, aviate. Ensure the aircraft's safety along with the lives of everyone on board. As a single-seat fighter pilot, the only life in immediate danger was my own. Luckily, I was over a remote part of California, so there was no risk of crashing into a populated area.

Second, navigate. A basic principle of flying is the ability to arrive safely at your destination, even under the most extreme circumstances.

Third, communicate. Never use the radio until after accomplishing the first two steps, as it's by far the least critical of the three rules. Many pilots have lost their lives because they focused on unimportant tasks—like talking on the radio—instead of concentrating on the most important function: safe operation of the aircraft.

Priorities matter.

I scanned the instruments by my left knee: my right engine had flatlined at zero rpm. The right fire warning light also was glowing bright red. A right engine fire is one of twenty emergencies so deadly that every pilot is required to memorize a list of steps called "immediate action items." Failure to recite the list verbatim meant you were grounded. Failure to execute each step in the correct order could be the difference between life and death.

Something in me clicked.

Set each throttle to the minimum power setting practical. *Check.* Slowly pull the right engine lever all the way back to turn it off. *Check.* Lift the protective cover and press the FIRE button, cutting off fuel that could cause an explosion. *Check.* Press the button for the fire extinguisher before moving on to the last step: putting the handle for my arresting hook down. *Check . . . and check.*

I needed to make an emergency landing at the nearest airfield, using the plane's "tailhook" to catch a wire across the runway. This would bring the plane to a quick halt so firefighters could spray foam on the jet after shutting off the remaining engine.

An arrested landing is part of every Navy fighter pilot's training. It's who we are. When we deploy to sea, our runway becomes an aircraft carrier floating in the middle of the ocean. An aircraft carrier's landing area is only slightly longer than the length of a football field, so a tailhook becomes the only way to bring an aircraft to a complete stop. One second before landing you're flying along, then *wham,* you're thrown violently forward in your seat as the wheels touch down, the hook catching as you slow from 150 mph to a standstill in less than two seconds.

I was now out of immediate danger but the aircraft was slowly and steadily losing altitude. It was obvious I wouldn't make it back to the military airfield at my home base in Lemoore, California, so I banked the plane to the right and pointed straight toward Naval Air Weapons Station China Lake, a much closer military airfield.

My wingman flew his plane over to my right side to take a closer look. "Raider 21, it looks like the fire is out." *Well, at least I'm not about to explode.*

I reached over next to my right hip where my green flight bag was located. Made of a fireproof cloth and relatively thin, it had the same rough dimensions as a pizza box. I unzipped the top and rummaged through the contents. Finally feeling what I wanted, I pulled out my pocket checklist to prepare for my upcoming emergency landing.

A few minutes later we finished the last step. I keyed the mic. "China Lake Tower, this is Raider 21, emergency aircraft."

There was a brief hiss of static before the control tower answered. "Raider 21, China Lake Tower, we copy your emergency. Go ahead." I took a deep breath. No matter what was happening inside the cockpit, you had to sound calm, cool, and collected on the radio. A calm demeanor was contagious and led to better decision-making.

"China Lake Tower, Raider 21. I had a right engine fire and need an immediate arrested landing. One soul on board. Thirty minutes of fuel remaining. Fire is out." The tower answered right back. "Copy all, Raider 21. No traffic between you and the airport. Fire trucks are rolling."

Twelve minutes later I spotted the airfield, located just to the right side of the airplane's nose. I had never been happier to find a place to land. "Tower, Raider 21. Field in sight."

"Raider 21, you are cleared for landing runway three. Arresting gear is in battery," a radio call letting me know that my hook would catch a wire they had raised on the runway. My landing gear was already down, so I gently banked the F/A-18 to the right and started my descent.

Flying with a single engine is challenging. The plane has half the power you're used to, making it harder to gain altitude if you find yourself in a bad position. Since the right engine was shut down, the thrust from the left engine kept pushing the plane's nose farther to the right. It felt like trying to drive a car along an icy road—you never quite knew what you were going to get.

About five minutes later I touched down, small puffs of smoke appearing as the wheels hit the runway, the hook catching to bring me to an abrupt stop. I quickly shut down the left engine. Only then did I notice that both my legs were trembling—the most obvious sign of all the adrenaline coursing through my body. I unstrapped my harness and made my way out of the plane as firefighters ensured the fire was out.

Walking around to the right side I could see obvious damage: oil splashed up the right side of the aircraft, all the way to the nose. *What the heck happened here? How can oil be this far forward on the jet when I was moving at hundreds of miles an hour?* The firefighters assured me there was no danger, so I climbed into the engine's intake on the right side of the plane to take a look. Using my fingers, I slowly rotated the fan blades of the engine. It sounded like someone had poured a can of marbles into the engine. After a quarter turn the blades seized. They would never move again.

The engine was trashed.

Two weeks later I received results from the official investigation: someone had left a small rag in the engine as it was being rebuilt. By sheer dumb luck I'd been the first pilot to fly the plane after the engine was installed. The rag had popped loose inside the oil system, causing a catastrophic overpressure in the engine, which is why oil sprayed all over the right side of the jet. The temperature got so hot that titanium bolts inside the engine warped and melted. A $70 million aircraft had nearly been lost because one person hadn't done their job.

Proper procedure. Remaining calm under pressure. Every member of the military knows these are important. But now I knew the importance of these rules—this way of life—in a way that wasn't purely academic. Usually the least sexy part of any job, adhering to proper procedure develops the trust required to operate during stressful and oftentimes chaotic situations.

I would see this principle at play over the next fourteen years, but it wasn't until 2017 that I learned just how important these traits are when operating under pressure at the highest levels of our government.

My family and I were just getting settled—only three months into our ninth move in the spring of 2017—when the military wanted us to make another. We were unpacking moving boxes in Norfolk, Virginia, where I was stationed as an executive assistant to a two-star admiral, when a member of Secretary of Defense James Mattis's personal office called. The person on the other end had a question: Would I be interested in working as a speechwriter for the new secretary?

Being asked to serve with Mattis was a rare opportunity. We had met briefly once before, ironically as I waited to interview for another speechwriting job, that one with then–Chief of Naval Operations Admiral Jonathan Greenert in 2012. I could think of no other military officer more universally respected by members of the armed services than Mattis was. Military scholars regard him with near reverence, a combat-hardened general who at one point owned more than seven thousand books in his library—the modern-day embodiment of a warrior scholar.

Mattis managed to cross over into American popular culture, acquiring a status as the toughest of tough guys. In fact, memes circulated with sayings such as "Mattis once won a staring contest . . . with the sun" and "When Chuck Norris goes to sleep, he checks under the bed for Mattis." Someone even started a Facebook-based "Draft Mattis" campaign during the 2016 presidential election. I noted with interest as word spread rapidly within military circles—heck, I'd even found myself wishing that he'd answer the call to run for office.

Was I interested in joining his team? Absolutely. But the decision required some soul-searching. I'd put my wife, Sarah, through a lot, ever since our first year of marriage when I'd been deployed to the Middle East and away from home for nine months. Since then, we'd managed several years of sporadic separation, including two tours to Japan. So far, she and I were loving the change of pace in Norfolk, in part because we were finally able to see each other on a daily basis. I had recently completed a job as commanding officer for the *Dambusters,* a two-and-a-half-year overseas tour in charge of an F/A-18E Super Hornet squadron based in Japan, a group of 220 sailors—pilots, maintenance staff, and support personnel—responsible for twelve fighter jets, worth around $1.1 billion in taxpayer dollars. I was living my dream—a dream that had taken hold in high school while watching fighter jets fly during Boy Scout fund-raisers at an Air Force base in North Texas.

While in Japan, Sarah and our three children enjoyed sushi and sightseeing while I was busy flying missions from an aircraft carrier patrolling Pacific waters. I was out at sea or away for training more than seven months each year, leading the family to joke that even though they were forward deployed with me in Japan, I merely visited them. Sarah was always a tireless supporter of my military career, supporting me with a dignity and grace that still amazes me to this day. But at some point, she had every right to suggest that her needs—our family's needs—had to come first.

In Norfolk, we had a beautiful home in a great neighborhood. Our kids had just started in a new school. As a naval officer and fighter pilot, I was in line for a leadership role as the commander of either an air wing or a nuclear-powered aircraft carrier (only naval aviators can command a carrier). In my case, the Navy decided to position me for command of an air wing— a collection of some seventy fighter planes and electronic attack jets, propeller-driven surveillance planes, and helicopters that deploy around the world while embarked on board an aircraft carrier.

Commanding an air wing was the better of the two paths for my family, giving us a chance to stay in one place for the next four years. Moving to Washington, DC, would put my path at risk. Plus, after a decade of running hard in my career, it was nice to finally have some downtime to let my family recharge their batteries . . . and my own.

Then there was the question of politics. I had been on board an aircraft carrier in the Pacific waiting to take off when some sailors began jumping up and down in excitement: Trump had won the election. His desire to strengthen America's economy and military seemed laudable, and his outside-of-government perspective was refreshing. But like so many people, I found his ethics and character appalling, watching aghast at the negative headlines that dominated television news every day. Our Japanese friends thought his candidacy was merely entertainment. For a while, we all did.

Men and women in uniform are trained to be strictly nonpartisan—lives depend on our ability to carry out orders regardless of the president's political party. But this job would not be as separate from politics. Despite wearing a uniform, I was aware that working for the secretary of defense would effectively be a political job in the Trump administration. As a military officer, I wasn't quite sure how I felt about the arrangement. But the job meant working directly for Mattis, not Trump, so I was willing to consider the opportunity. As for Mattis, I knew next to nothing about what he'd be like as a boss.

After discussing the opportunity with Sarah, I reached out to Commander Ryan Stoddard, a classmate from the US Naval Academy who had worked for Mattis before. His verdict?

"If you want the good life, stay put. Mattis tends to burn out his staff. But if you're up for the challenge, I doubt you'll ever find a job more rewarding than this one. In fact, I've been asked to consider joining the team as aide de camp," a position akin to a personal assistant to Mattis.

An interview date was scheduled, and I set out to devour

everything I could find on what Mattis had said or written. I watched online interviews and speeches, read remarks that he delivered throughout his military career, and started reading books that I knew he enjoyed. Articles online described how Mattis carried a copy of *Meditations* by Roman emperor Marcus Aurelius wherever he went, so that was my first stop. I already could see the parallels: a strict adherence to stoicism, his belief that "there's nothing new under the sun," and the importance of taking things as they come without overreacting. He was my kind of leader.

Two weeks later, I drove to the Pentagon.

Situated on a parcel of land almost twice as large as Disneyland, the Pentagon is the most massive office building in the world, a five-sided, five-ringed, five-storied behemoth to support twenty-six thousand uniformed and civilian employees. There are also two basement levels for good measure, a full-sized gym, numerous restaurants, and enough parking for nine thousand cars. It's gargantuan, though constructed in such a way that you can move from one point inside the building to the farthest point on the other side in less than seven minutes.

Navigating my way through the building, I met with Mattis's action group, the military's equivalent of a planning and deep-thinking team. The secretary's deputy chief of staff, Tony DeMartino, led the interview. A retired US Army colonel, Tony spent time with a consulting group before joining the secretary's team. His primary role as deputy chief of staff was leading the personnel search and conducting vetting for senior positions in the Department of Defense.

Tony was gregarious and easygoing, the kind of guy that

wants you to call him by his first name despite his seniority. "Hey man, it's great to have you here. I've read your résumé and, look, I get it. You've done well in your military career and it's a plus that you've already been a speechwriter. We're shorthanded and we could really use your help." We discussed my career and my concerns that joining Team Mattis might alter my path in the Navy. Tony assured me that I'd be fine: the team would have my back. Overall it was an enjoyable, low-threat interview. Tony was obviously a strategic thinker and a team builder. I liked him immediately.

Tony leaned back in his chair and stared at me for a few seconds. "I've seen everything I need to see. Hang out here for a minute. I want to go get the chief of staff."

Tony walked out, returning about five minutes later with Kevin Sweeney, a retired rear admiral who worked for Mattis at US Central Command. I knew Sweeney only through his reputation, a tough-as-nails surface warfare officer who commanded a Navy destroyer before topping out as the commander of a carrier strike group, a large collection of ships and aircraft that usually went to sea together. He chewed through his staff during that tour. More than a few officers had warned me to be cautious around him, so I wasn't sure what to expect.

Of average height and slender build, Sweeney had white hair, glasses with thin black rims, and a hurried demeanor that I took to mean that he was incredibly busy. His handshake was odd, as he extended his hand out horizontally, palm facing down. He never uttered a word. He just looked at me, shook my hand, patted me on the shoulder, and then walked out.

I think Sweeney just wanted to put eyes on me to size me

up, as he didn't ask a single question. The silence seemed like a bad sign to me. Tony, however, seemed to think it went well. He turned to me and said, "That was great. I think he really liked you."

I headed back to Norfolk the same day, calling Sarah during my four-hour drive back home. She was happy that the meeting went well and enthusiastic about the opportunity. Better yet, we were due to head to North Carolina's Outer Banks for our children's spring break.

A few days later, Tony called. "Congrats man, you got the job. Get here as soon as you can." I was a little surprised, as I never interviewed with Mattis. However, the Navy's a tight-knit community, so I figured it was likely because senior officers recommended me for the job. Plus, I knew Mattis lived a packed schedule.

I accepted.

I felt compelled to serve. The past ten years had borne witness to the military's slow decline in readiness as budgets tightened, spare parts dried up, and our best and brightest service members decided to seek greener pastures elsewhere. Despite the hardship of yet another move and more time away from the family, this was my opportunity to make a difference, to help Mattis restore America's military to fighting trim.

In what may be the land speed record for getting redirected to a new duty station, the Navy needed only two days to produce the paperwork that would normally take several weeks, if not several months, to complete. It was easy, I was told, when you could just tell everyone that "the secretary of defense wants this guy in the Pentagon right now."

Sarah and I decided that it made sense for me to spend the first four months with Mattis as a geographic bachelor, military slang for keeping the family in Norfolk while I found a short-term rental in Washington, DC. This would give the kids a chance to finish their semester before shifting to yet another new school, their second in six months.

With Sarah's blessing, I packed my suitcases, jumped in the car, and headed up to Washington, DC, ready to begin a new adventure with Mattis and the team.

TWO

WARRIOR MONK

It is not the critic who counts. . . . [It's] the man who
is actually in the arena . . . [who], if he fails, at least
fails while daring greatly, so that his place shall
never be with those cold and timid souls who
neither know victory nor defeat.

—THEODORE ROOSEVELT

Holy crap, it's "Mad Dog" Mattis.

It was April 2017, and I was seeing my new boss—Secretary of Defense James Mattis—for the first time.

Standing by the copier in the long corridor that runs the length of Mattis's office suite, I heard someone coming around the corner. I looked up and caught sight of him just five feet away. Head low, reviewing the stapled document in his hands, Mattis glanced up just as he was about to pass.

He smiled and stopped. "Good morning. Who are you?"

"Sir, good morning. I'm Commander Snodgrass, call sign

'Bus,' your new speechwriter. I arrived last week while you were in the Middle East."

"It's good to have you aboard, Bus. Can you make these changes to my remarks for this morning's town hall?" He handed his speech to me. "I need them back right away."

I had no idea where the speech's file was or even which specific event he meant. Still, I managed to cough up the right answer: "Yes, sir, I'll take care of it."

He turned and headed toward his office, already focused on his next thought.

———

I had plenty of reasons to admire Mattis. So much about him was different. He wasn't descended from admirals or generals, didn't attend an Ivy League school or come from a wealthy family. But he did have two distinct advantages: a mother and a father who instilled in him a love of learning—and who refused to have a television in the house.

Mattis grew up in Richland, Washington, where his father was a merchant mariner before joining the World War II–era Manhattan Project at the Hanford nuclear laboratory. His Canadian-born mother also took part in the war, serving in Army Intelligence in South Africa and working in the unfinished Pentagon during the spring of 1942.

Mattis attended Central Washington University, a former teachers' college located 110 miles east of Seattle. He majored in history, a discipline that served him well in studying wars, alliances, strategies, leaders, and tactics of the past. It also taught him what to do—and not do—on today's battlefields. "A real understanding of history means that we face nothing new under the sun," Mattis once said. "We have been fighting on this planet for five thousand years and we should take advantage of their experience. Winging it while filling body bags as we sort out what works reminds us of the cost of incompetence in our profession."

I liked the answer he gave as secretary of defense, when a young Marine asked about how he stays fresh as a leader: "You stay teachable most by reading books, by reading what other people went through. I can't tell you the number of times . . . I was engaged in a fight somewhere and I knew within a couple of minutes how I was going to screw up the enemy. I knew it because I'd done so much reading."

Mattis might have ended up teaching "Western Civilization" at some high school in Spokane or back in his hometown except for one small, very late 1960s matter: the draft. Mattis did not want to be drafted into the army.

Instead, as a freshman in 1969, he enlisted in the Marine Corps Reserves. Upon graduation in 1972, he commissioned as a second lieutenant in the Marine infantry. Though he never did serve in Vietnam (things were winding down), his three years as an enlisted Marine still made him a grunt's grunt, a distinction that garnered extra appreciation from the thousands of enlisted Marines he would later command.

He may have missed Vietnam, but name a Middle Eastern hot spot in the 1990s or 2000s, and Mattis served in the thick of it. He commanded troops during the First Gulf War and was among the first on the ground in Afghanistan. In late 2001, a twenty-four-year-old Marine lieutenant named Nathan Fick noticed an extra head in a nearby foxhole. It was Mattis. "No one would have questioned Mattis if he'd slept eight hours each night in a private room," marveled Fick, "to be woken each morning by an aide who ironed his uniforms and heated his MREs (meals ready to eat). But there he was, in the middle of a freezing night, out on the lines with his Marines."

He played a key role in Saddam Hussein's overthrow in the Second Gulf War. During that campaign, Mattis raised eyebrows by relieving Colonel Joe D. Dowdy from his regimental command. Firing a commander in the middle of combat is rarely done anymore. But Dowdy was moving his troops too slowly for Mattis's comfort, and Mattis ingloriously sacked him. "We're doing it in the Marines," he argued in one of his rare discussions of the incident. "Even Jesus of Nazareth had one of twelve turn to mud on him."

Yes, Mattis could be brutally ruthless in combat, but there are just as many stories of his thoughtfulness, either in visiting a wounded Marine corporal at Bethesda Naval Hospital, consoling a leatherneck drill instructor at Quantico laid low by post-traumatic stress disorder, or, as he traveled cross-country, quietly visiting the parents of service members who perished under his command.

Friends told me about how General Charles Krulak Jr., former commandant of the Marine Corps, had once arrived at the Combat Development Command Headquarters at Quantico, Virginia, on Christmas Day to visit Marines on duty. When Krulak asked a young enlisted Marine, "Who is the officer standing guard with you?" he replied "Sir, Brigadier General Mattis." Confused, General Krulak asked again, pointing to the cot in the corner. "Well, who slept in that cot as the officer of the day?" The Marine again replied, "Sir, it was Brigadier General Mattis."

At that point, Mattis walked around the corner and explained to Krulak that a young officer with a family was originally scheduled for duty on Christmas Day. Mattis, who never married, thought the Marine should be with his family—and stood watch in his stead.

It was stories like this one—along with numerous other examples of Mattis's selfless service—that made me want to work for him in the first place.

Mattis also had a well-known reputation for embodying the "warrior's ethos" with his quotability—a great quality in your boss if you're a speechwriter.

In 2006 he said, "The first time you blow someone away is not an insignificant event. That said, there are some assholes in the world that just need to be shot," while addressing two hundred Marines in al Asad in Iraq. Or when he held forth with "You go into Afghanistan, you got guys who slap women around for five years because they didn't wear a veil. You know, guys like that ain't got no manhood left anyway. So it's a hell of a lot of fun to shoot them." He continued: "Actually it's quite fun to fight them, you know. It's a hell of a hoot. It's fun to shoot some people. I'll be right up there with you. I like brawling." On the gentler side were words of wisdom like, "Be polite, be professional, but have a plan to kill everybody you meet," or "Engage your brain before you engage your weapon."

There are more Mattis quotes—a lot more. Here are just some of them:

"There is only one 'retirement plan' for terrorists."

"There are hunters and there are victims. By your discipline, cunning, obedience and alertness, you will decide if you are a hunter or a victim."

"If you can't eat it, shoot it, or wear it, don't bring it."

And one of my personal favorites: "Always carry a knife with you. Just in case there's cheesecake, or you need to stab someone in the throat."

As secretary of defense he added to that repertoire. When CBS News's John Dickerson asked, "What keeps you awake at night?" he responded, "Nothing, I keep other people awake at night." In a politically correct world, Mattis seemed empowered to say exactly what he thought and still get away with it—and the troops loved him for it.

Don't misconstrue his confidence, as Mattis is the furthest thing from a braggart or boaster. He's actually extremely modest and self-effacing. But when the occasion calls for it—when the situation demands it—he's not shy about doing his duty. And if that duty requires dispensing inspiration, well, he'll provide that too.

The press caught on, giving Mattis the moniker "Mad Dog" based on his many "Mattisisms" and his ruthless style in combat zones. He privately hated the nickname. Instead, as Mattis explained at the 2017 Air Force Association symposium, the nickname he actually preferred was "CHAOS," an acronym that stands for "the Colonel Has An Outstanding Solution," a tongue-in-cheek reference to Mattis's habit of always coming up with "bright" ideas. Of course, Mattis's bright ideas had usually translated to a lot of extra work for the Marines he led. But the Marines thought it was hilarious and the call sign stuck.

A big part of the reason I respected Mattis was his reputation for taking honorable stands throughout his military career, a fact underscored by the "Tailhook certification" letter he submitted to the Marine Corps as a lieutenant colonel.

The 1991 Tailhook scandal centered around ninety allegations of sexual assault that occurred during the annual symposium for Navy and Marine Corps tactical aviators. Plastered on the front pages of newspapers nationwide, the scandal was a public relations nightmare, sparking a witch hunt to determine who'd attended the symposium. Like most naval officers at the time, Mattis was asked to confirm two items before he could be promoted to his next rank: whether he, or anyone under his charge, had attended Tailhook '91.

Mattis wasn't anywhere near Las Vegas at the time. He could have answered 'no' to both questions and continued on with his career. But he didn't.

Instead, he composed a two-page response, citing the beliefs put forth by the Founding Fathers, of his right against "unreasonable search and seizure" and protesting the lack of due process stemming from a demand to "incriminate (or not incriminate) myself regarding attendance." He wrote that he was submitting his answers under protest, only then confirming that, no, he had not attended Tailhook '91.

Mattis's last tour of duty was a three-year stint as the commander of US Central Command, a role where he was accountable for all American military operations in Iraq and Afghanistan. His command spanned four million square miles across twenty nations and 550 million people. In 2013, Mattis retired following a forty-four-year military career.

He turned reflective two years later, discussing his core beliefs during a speech to the Marines' Memorial Club in San Francisco. His remarks, later reprinted in *The Wall Street Journal,* evoked Abraham Lincoln's call for Americans to "listen to their better angels" and stated that "we are masters of our character, choosing what we will stand for in this life."

His speech, and the career that preceded it, was a road map for understanding who Mattis was as a leader in the Trump administration—a man of conviction who believed deeply in the long-standing values that make the United States unique among the world's nations.

A week after crossing paths with Mattis by the copy machine, we convened our very first speech preparation session. We were getting an entire hour, an eternity for Mattis, who had just recently returned from a trip to the Middle East.

Bill Rivers and I were the first new speechwriters brought onto Mattis's staff. I was an active-duty Navy commander taking the role of chief speechwriter. Bill was a political appointee whose previous job had been at the US Senate working for Senator Deb Fischer (R-NE). A Delaware native, Bill was young, talented, and ambitious, with boyish looks that made him appear several years younger than he was. Playing on this theme, Mattis nicknamed him "Old Man" Rivers.

Located down the hall from Secretary Mattis's front office, Bill and I occupied prime real estate by Pentagon standards. The speechwriting team traditionally was located down with public affairs, about a four-minute walk from where the secretary worked. Mattis, however, wanted his speechwriters attached to him. We received individual offices so we could close the door and write without distraction. It worked well, affording Mattis the ability to see us when he wanted to drop something off or check on us.

"Hey, Bill, you ready to head over?" We needed to get moving if we wanted to make it to Mattis's office with a few minutes to spare before the meeting started. Bill popped around the corner of my doorway. "All set." We were excited. Bill had interviewed with Mattis, but other than my two quick run-ins with our new boss, this would be my first extended session with him.

As a student of history, I enjoyed the walk to Mattis's office. Located in the outermost, or "E" ring, of the Pentagon, you can tell when you've hit the secretary's corridor, as nondescript white drywall located throughout the building gives way to an immaculately maintained, wood-paneled hallway festooned with large oil paintings of previous secretaries.

Bill and I passed through the secretary of defense's reception area and through another door leading to the hallway connecting to his personal office. There we joined Justin Mikolay, the third and most senior member of the early speechwriting team. He had the distinction of being the only speechwriter on staff for the first few months of Mattis's tenure, a Herculean task by any measure. A Naval Academy and Princeton graduate, Justin previously served as a speechwriter for Mattis at US Central Command and then for Defense Secretary Leon Panetta, a Democrat. Easygoing and great to work with, Justin had been running hard for months and was grateful to see us on the team.

Joining us were members of Mattis's personal staff, including

Senior Adviser Sally Donnelly and Chief of Staff Admiral Kevin Sweeney (ret.).

Donnelly, senior adviser to Mattis during his first year in office, had run a DC-based consulting firm with DeMartino prior to joining the administration. Previously a reporter for *Time* magazine, she was a consummate DC insider who possessed a knack for gaining entry to any organization. Sally was the only person in our office with a deep knowledge of the inner workings in Washington. She possessed a sixth sense about potential issues that could cause headaches, enabling us to get out in front of a crisis to inoculate Mattis or the military against negative headlines. She was energetic, upbeat, and one of the few people willing to correct Mattis when she thought something was wrong, a trait I would come to appreciate.

The first thing I noticed when stepping into Mattis's office was its enormity by Pentagon standards. It could easily be divided into a cubicle farm seating twenty people.

My eyes fixed on a large oil painting of General George Marshall in his Army uniform. It was a fitting portrait, as Marshall was the only other retired general to serve as secretary of defense.

The National Security Act of 1947, as amended, created the Department of Defense. It also requires the secretary of defense to be a civilian who has been out of uniform for at least seven years. Mattis had been out for three years and, like Marshall, required a congressional waiver.

Mattis's waiver cleared by a wide margin, in the Senate by 81-17, and in the House 268-151. The Senate then confirmed Mattis 98-1 later the same day. It wasn't lost on me that even then, both sides of the aisle embraced Mattis as a moderating influence on an unproven president. The sole dissenting vote was Senator Kirsten Gillibrand (D-NY), a fact that Mattis was privately proud of, as he didn't think much of her apparent disdain for the military.

Mattis kept his desk—"Black Jack" Pershing and George Marshall's old desk—immaculately clean, with just a few mementos on the front edge along with some binders and books currently on Mattis's docket. Wooden in- and out-boxes adorned the side of his desk. A few folders occupied the out-box. Nothing cluttered Mattis's in-box, reflecting his penchant for devouring paperwork.

Justin waved Bill and me to a small round table with four chairs placed around it, located just to the left of where the large Pershing desk stood. Justin whispered to avoid disturbing Mattis's train of thought. "This is where he takes most of his meetings. This round desk belonged to General William Tecumseh Sherman during the Civil War, who 'acquired it' from a plantation on his way to burn Atlanta."

I noticed a third, normal-sized desk placed against the office's back wall. Justin followed my eyes. "That desk belonged to Ulysses S. Grant when he was a general, but before he became president." Sitting on Grant's desk were two computer monitors, a pair of reading glasses, and a large phone with one-touch buttons designed to reach other senior leaders. A singularly large button rang directly to President Trump's office.

Large windows on both sides of Grant's desk afforded a commanding view of the Pentagon's parade field and the Potomac beyond. There was one other desk, positioned just in front of the window to the left. Mattis noticed me looking at it as he walked over to us. "That's Rumsfeld's standing desk," Mattis said, "where he worked throughout the day as he wrote his 'snowflakes' to the staff." "Snowflakes" denoted the sheer volume of small white paper memos Donald Rumsfeld had routinely sent, sometimes frustrating staffers inundated by a blizzard of incoming messages. While Mattis sent far fewer memos, I'd soon learn that his demand for information certainly rivaled that of Rumsfeld.

Justin, Bill, and I took our seats, joining Mattis as he took a seat at the small round table. Leaning back, Mattis began to tell us how he wanted his speeches to sound. He wanted an unobtrusive speaking style "focusing on the essence of the job" while shunning any spotlight for himself. "That's what I'll ask you to do. I am lighthearted to the point of irreverence about myself, but I'm dead serious when it comes to my job." He asked that we use history. It could be hundreds of years old or just from last week, but either way he wanted to have good stories.

This was a great start to our first speech prep meeting. Some senior leaders expect speechwriters to try to figure things out as they go, but Mattis wanted to give Bill and me a very clear road map.

To aid us in learning his voice and finding quotes that he was partial to, Mattis offered access to his office closet. There, he kept many years' worth of meticulous notes in black Moleskine notebooks from his time in uniform. Each page included a small printout of his daily schedule, along with handwritten notes. Lined up on the shelf above them were three special journals in old, worn three-ring binders. These he referred to as his "Books of Wisdom."

He shared with us that the idea for the books came from a

youthful encounter. "I once hitchhiked to San Francisco to meet Eric Hoffer, a philosopher and longshoreman who wrote the book *True Believer.* Eric was the one who told me, 'Make sure you write down everything interesting you find,' and I have ever since." This treasure trove held decades of his personal thoughts, plus correspondence from his mother, friends, and colleagues.

Mattis emphasized his apolitical stance. He expected all of us to follow suit. When it comes to Congress, "We will consider both left wing and right wing to be winnable constituencies. We are not liberal or conservative. Whoever wants to fight for America, come on board."

I'd lived my military career with the same worldview. Why distance yourself from half the nation? National security benefited all Americans, not just the political majority. Plus, with elections taking place every two years, you never knew where the political winds would blow.

Sweeney spoke up, speaking to Mattis. "You used to be a military officer. As secretary, one of the themes has to be you reinforcing the president and his agenda. You've never before endorsed a political side. Now, you are by definition."

Mattis thought for a moment, chewing on his lip. "This is why we need to get something meaty out of the White House. There can be no daylight between us. People are getting tired of hearing one thing out of this administration and then the opposite. It's got to be aligned."

That was an understatement. The administration seemed caught in a game of catch-up with the press, entangled in constantly changing stories or different versions of events depending on who was being interviewed. It would be difficult for any administration to gain traction without maintaining credibility, either at home or abroad. And to maintain credibility, we had to make sure that our story was the same as theirs.

Over the next year, speech prep like this became some of my favorite time with Mattis. It wasn't just my opportunity to receive guidance for upcoming events. It worked as safe space on his calendar so he could relax a bit and provide deeper background than most people on his staff or in the Pentagon ever heard.

One story he shared with us was how he'd come to find himself serving as the secretary of defense in the first place. He'd been busy volunteering at the Tri-Cities Food Bank in Washington State after the 2016 election when his cell phone rang. Setting down a crate of food, he answered the call.

"Hi Jim, this is Mike Pence. Do you have a minute to chat?" Mattis wasn't in a place where he could talk, responding, "No, not at the moment. I'm right in the middle of something. Can I call you back?" Finishing his tasks, Mattis returned the call, discovering that his name was on a short list for consideration for secretary of defense. Pence wanted to know: Would he make the trek to Trump National Golf Club in Bedminster, New Jersey, on November 19 to meet the president-elect?

Mattis said he would and got to work preparing. He organized copious notes and spoke with friends and family for their thoughts. Then he traveled east to meet with Trump.

The interview process turned into Trump's latest version of *The Apprentice*, with reporters lingering outside to ambush candidates as they departed. It made for great theater the day of Mattis's interview. Vice President–elect Pence opened the door for Trump and Mattis, and they stepped outside for a quick photo op. The press shouted incoherent questions. "He's the real deal," said Trump. "He's just a brilliant, wonderful man. What a career."

Despite Trump's words, the interview hadn't instilled much confidence in Mattis about his chances. His conversation with Trump was friendly enough, but he had "disagreed with the president-elect on every one of the main points that he raised."

Their most memorable exchange occurred when Trump told Mattis that he supported the use of waterboarding on prisoners of war. Mattis disagreed, saying, "I've never found it to be useful. Give me a pack of cigarettes and a couple of beers and I do better with that than I do with torture." Having disagreed so much with the president-elect, Mattis told us that he thought, *Well, thanks for the invite,* as he pretended to dust his hands off. *I certainly won't be hearing back from those guys.*

Nonetheless, Trump's appreciation for Mattis appeared to increase in the weeks following his interview. Having decided to select Mattis as his nominee for secretary of defense, he teased the announcement at a December 1 victory rally in Cincinnati, the first stop on his "Thank You" tour around the country after the election. "We are going to appoint 'Mad Dog' Mattis as our secretary of defense," Trump announced to raucous cheers, "He's the closest thing to General George Patton we have."

In retrospect, the disagreements between Mattis and Trump presaged a fundamental chasm, one that would only widen with time.

But as a staff we were off to a great start. I was newly arrived, optimistic about my role, and team morale was high. But our own survival would depend on the endurance of a much more powerful team than the one Mattis oversaw.

The media called them "the adults in the room."

THREE

THE ADULTS

There is only one thing worse than fighting with
allies, and that is fighting without them.

—WINSTON CHURCHILL

"Shhh! Bus, keep your voice down!"

I was still in my first few weeks with the team and learning the ropes. It was a steep learning curve. I had ducked in to say hello to Mattis's scheduler, one of two people who sat in a small room just outside his office, not realizing that Mattis was in the middle of an important phone call.

The door to Mattis's office usually remains open during meetings and phone calls, so I needed to be more cautious in the future. The scheduler put a finger to her lips and pointed toward his door: I could clearly make out the voices of Secretary of State

Rex Tillerson and National Security Adviser H. R. McMaster coming from his speakerphone. I quickly learned that they were two of his closest associates in the administration.

Few things mattered more to Mattis throughout his military career than allies, a point he drove home during his confirmation hearing.

Allies make difficult tasks possible, whether winning friends, taking bullets on the ground, or easing logistical bottlenecks. As Mattis told me, "In my past, I fought many times, and never in a solely American formation; it was always alongside foreign troops." Put simply, nations with allies thrive—an approach to security and prosperity that has served the United States well for decades.

Nations without them end up waiting for the cavalry that never arrives.

Now returned to Washington, DC, Mattis was embarking on a task as treacherous—though not as deadly—as what he had previously faced during combat abroad, finding himself at ground zero of an administration outright startled to have won election in the first place.

The nation needed reassurance. As secretary of defense, Mattis was a welcome addition to what was widely considered by the media to be a largely inexperienced team.

A political junkie, I read with interest a December 2016 *Politico* article expressing the relief felt when Mattis was tapped to head the Pentagon:

"For many, and even for self-proclaimed progressives, Donald Trump's pick [of] retired Marine Corps Gen. James Mattis is a light in the darkness—a kind of oasis in the midst of a vast reactionary desert. And so it seems, all of us can now breathe a sigh of relief: After all these weeks, there's finally an adult in the room."

The prevailing sentiment held that Mattis would bring decades of experience to bear, guiding Trump's use and understanding of the military while dissuading Trump from any needless adventurism. And if he couldn't, he'd be the one you would want in charge to roll up his sleeves and finish the job.

But while the nation needed reassurance, Mattis needed allies. Not the Saudis or South Koreans or Brits he'd previously relied on as a military commander, but other Trump administration heavyweights who could help steer an untested organization.

Assembling a cabinet is a difficult task during the best of times, and the pieces don't always fit neatly together. The jobs are big, and so are the egos.

Lincoln assembled a "Team of Rivals"—uniting men from various factions of the Republican party who fought one another and often with him. Franklin Roosevelt coasted to victory in 1932, but to bring the nation together he enticed Republicans to join his original cabinet—and did it again as war neared. Warren Harding isn't remembered as a Lincoln or a Roosevelt, but as a new president he vowed to hire "the best minds," and in many cases he actually did so. But, as his critics charged, he also hired his "best friends," and they were often dismally woeful. A few even went to jail.

Like Harding, Trump brought some of his best friends (and family) with him into the administration. He also had his version of the best minds, a collection of heavyweights whom he felt came straight from central casting to plug critical vacancies.

The media popularly referred to them as the "adults in the room," a small group of key—and necessary—allies joining Mattis in the administration.

At the top of the list was Secretary of State Rex Tillerson.

Tillerson was certainly an adult, but questions remained regarding how much he knew the room, as he possessed no familiarity at State or in government at all. His experience as a businessman, however, meant he knew how to run a multinational corporation and get things done.

Tillerson is a multimillionaire oil man, but he didn't come from money. He waited on tables, swept floors, and even picked cotton to fund his education at the University of Oklahoma. Starting at Exxon in 1975 as a production engineer, he stayed there the entire length of his career, reaching the firm's presidency in 2004, becoming the quintessential American success story. Along the way he negotiated oil deals in such key nations as Yemen, Russia, Saudi Arabia, Qatar, Syria, and Kurdistan. He knew his way around the international block.

And he was respected. The list of persons who recommended Tillerson to Trump is really an all-star team and quite diverse: Condoleezza Rice, Robert Gates, Steve Bannon, and Trump's son-in-law, Jared Kushner.

To say the least, Tillerson didn't need the job. He was making $40 million a year, with a retirement package of $180 million. I respected that he walked away from both to join Trump—and, more to the point, serve his nation. He is a patriot and a man of great gravitas.

I had a chance to interact with him during a few meetings. Although of average height, Tillerson's stoic demeanor, thatch of silver hair, discerning eyes, and deep voice made him seem taller and helped give Tillerson presence. He was the only member of the cabinet Mattis seemed to trust implicitly and they talked regularly.

Mattis appreciated Tillerson's "steady as she goes" approach to international diplomacy, a logical approach for a longtime CEO of a flagship corporation. He served as a natural foil to President Trump's instincts to challenge preexisting norms and relationships under the presumption that America had been persistently "ripped off" or taken advantage of by our friends and allies. Tillerson knew that strengthening alliances required steady, personal relationships—not public finger-pointing or rash decisions.

Mattis's affection for Tillerson came through loud and clear during our visit to the US European Command in Stuttgart, Germany. While there we held an "all hands call" for all command personnel in a large gymnasium on base.

While Mattis took questions from the audience, a young Army sergeant walked up to a microphone and asked, "How do you work with senior leadership? Do you and the secretary of state work well together?"

Mattis praised his partner within the administration. Tillerson was well prepared for the job because he'd "conducted a twenty-five-year international listening tour" during his time with Exxon Mobil. Tillerson's international relationships were a distinct competitive advantage.

Mattis noted there was a roughly forty-year period when the secretary of state and secretary of defense just didn't get along, a point he told us several times in private. Unfortunately, "Marines wound up catching mortar rounds in the chest because of it," a reference to conflicts that could have been avoided had the two top cabinet members worked better together. That lesson stuck with Mattis, driving his desire for a close working relationship. Mattis ended his response simply, saying he "enjoys an excellent relationship with 'Saint Rex of Texas.'" They remained in constant communication, even breakfasting together every Thursday when both were in town.

From the outset, however, Tillerson was hamstrung by Trump's mandate to shake up the state department. Trump believed long-serving federal employees were a shadow government, a "deep state" of insular, corrupt DC insiders. This wasn't my experience. Rather, long-serving employees provide the momentum and knowledge to keep federal agencies running smoothly during otherwise invariably awkward administrative transitions.

Unfortunately, employees at State didn't seem to mind venting their low opinion of their new chief executive with the press, bolstering Trump's often-overheated claims of sabotage and sedition within administration corridors.

Despite Trump's efforts to remake the state department, Mattis and Tillerson were partners, intent on maintaining not only their own alliance, but the web that united America both formally and informally to dozens of nations—big and small—around the world. Both knew that this alliance structure enables the US to accomplish far more with our friends than we ever could alone.

Mattis also required an ally at the White House itself, and he had one in National Security Adviser H. R. McMaster. Sort of.

An active-duty Army three-star general who had served in Afghanistan and both Iraqi conflicts, McMaster earned a silver star for valor during the Battle of 73 Easting in the Persian Gulf

War, commonly referred to "as the last great tank battle of the twentieth century." Both leaders enjoyed a scholarly reputation: Mattis as a voracious reader, McMaster as the author of a highly praised critique of our Vietnam involvement, *Dereliction of Duty: Lyndon Johnson, Robert McNamara, the Joint Chiefs of Staff, and the Lies That Led to Vietnam.* McMaster is revered in the Army, the rare officer who spoke truth to power and still managed to get promoted to general. He also holds a PhD in military history from the University of North Carolina at Chapel Hill.

Unlike Mattis, McMaster was Army and a product of West Point, one of America's prized military service academies. He also wasn't Trump's first choice for the job he would ultimately hold. That choice was the controversial Lieutenant General Mike Flynn, an Army general who served as an adviser to Trump during the 2016 campaign. How Mattis and Flynn might have interacted, we'll never know, though Mattis had little use for the way Flynn had politicized his former rank.

Mattis told us that he feared a threat to the apolitical tradition long followed by American generals and flag officers. He cited Flynn's chants of "Lock her up" at 2016's Republican National Convention and Marine General John Allen's public endorsement of Hillary Clinton at the Democrats' 2016 gathering. Mattis counted both as friends, but felt the impartiality of the military wobbled on a slippery slope when retired senior officers took overt political positions. I knew General of the Army Omar Bradley would have agreed, having said, "The best service a retired general can perform is to turn in his tongue along with his uniform and mothball his opinions."

Flynn, however, almost instantly departed the administration after having admitted to misleading both Congress and Vice President Pence regarding his contacts with the Russian ambassador. It was a harbinger of turmoil to come within the administration.

Mattis had himself been blindsided by Trump's insensitivity to using the military as a backdrop for political—or, at least, nonmilitary—issues.

Trump had sprung a bombshell during Mattis's ceremonial swearing-in ceremony at the Pentagon, taking an action that Mattis later confessed had grated on him. Seated in the Pentagon's Hall of Heroes, with an oversized version of the Medal of Honor inscribed with the word "valor" as a backdrop, the president signed Executive Order 13679, titled "Protecting the Nation from Foreign Terrorist Entry into the United States." Most know it as the controversial Muslim ban.

Fiercely apolitical throughout his Marine career, Mattis was convinced that the military should avoid involvement in political stunts to the maximum extent possible. Military members certainly have their own strongly held beliefs, but every uniformed leader I've worked with publicly preserved an apolitical stance. We serve the president regardless of political affiliation, a practice foundational to the sustained high level of trust and confidence that the US military has enjoyed for decades.

Besides going against general military values, Trump's provocative action could be considered a calculated insult to Mattis himself. Just six months earlier, speaking at Stanford, Mattis specifically critiqued then-candidate Trump's proposed "ban" as a menace to our often-delicate system of global alliances. "This kind of thing is causing us great damage right now," Mattis had said, "and it's sending shock waves through the international system."

But on this day in January 2017, Trump was now using both Mattis and his department's hard-earned credibility to announce, in the Hall of Heroes no less, the travel ban, one of his first of many controversial actions as president.

McMaster and Mattis both desired to rein in Trump's disruptive and often unpredictable proclivities in foreign affairs. As such, both were "adults in the room," but adults don't always have to like each other, and the Mattis-McMaster partnership was strained from the start.

First, there was the difference of military rank. Mattis was a retired four-star general now running the defense department while McMaster remained an active-duty three-star general. In the military, the difference between three and four stars is significant. Mattis would always treat McMaster as the far more junior partner.

Second, there was the difference in personality. As senior adviser to the president for national security affairs, McMaster's ability to wield power derived from his proximity to Trump and his own force of personality. But sometimes McMaster's personality was too forceful. Mattis was reserved and stoic. McMaster was excitable and prone to lecture people. McMaster's style also wasn't very compatible with the president he served, as he preferred to present information with military-like precision rather than the freewheeling, conversational style Trump preferred.

Increasingly, Mattis found one thing impossible to be stoic about: McMaster.

McMaster simply grated on him as few people could, routinely calling over to the Pentagon in a panic because of turmoil in the West Wing. I had been shot at—and the shot missed—during combat in the skies over Iraq. It changes your perspective on life. The woes I heard described during numerous phone calls from McMaster, while significant, didn't warrant the agitation his voice conveyed. McMaster, however, was the closest to the White House's daily operations. He had conducted a lifelong study of how the interagency system should best work, and his sense of urgency was a strong indicator that it wasn't working to his satisfaction.

Ultimately, Mattis and Tillerson cemented themselves into a "coalition of two" between the state and defense departments, undercutting McMaster's authority over key administration decisions.

An unlikely—but key—Mattis ally was Director of the National Economic Council Gary Cohn. Whereas Tillerson was Mattis's diplomatic ally in the administration, Cohn partnered with Mattis on an area of supreme importance to Trump: the economy.

A Democrat, Cohn achieved great wealth at Wall Street's Goldman Sachs. His severance package on joining the administration was $285 million. But he was a free trader. Aside from fearing the economic effect of Trump's protectionist policies, he was concerned about the possibility of fraying the often-tenuous bonds of America's international alliances. In this, Cohn and Mattis (who always emphasized that a strong US military rested on the shoulders of a strong US economy) shared common cause. Both appeared to get along well with each other, though

Mattis's day-to-day interactions with Cohn were far less than with Tillerson and McMaster.

The last "adult in the room," and the third "general in the room," was General John F. Kelly, Trump's pick for director of Homeland Security. Like Mattis, the 6'1" Boston-born Kelly joined the Marines in order to avoid the draft and served in both Iraqi wars. Again, like Mattis, Kelly dreaded any premature withdrawal of US forces from global hot spots and warned that our war against terror would not be easily or quickly concluded. "If you think this war against our way of life is over because some of the self-appointed opinion-makers and chattering class grow 'war weary,' because they want to be out of Iraq or Afghanistan," he said in 2014, "you are mistaken. This enemy . . . will fight us for generations."

Cementing his status with Trump, Kelly, as Homeland Security chief, fully supported construction of Trump's campaign promise, the border wall, as well as imposing further restrictions on illegal immigration.

It seemed that the Trump administration had brought in well-respected leaders to fill key administration roles. The "best minds"—Mattis, Tillerson, Cohn, McMaster, Kelly—were in positions of significant influence, able to temper the designs of Trump's "best friends" and his family.

But, as I heard Mattis say many times during my tenure with him: "No war is over until the enemy says it's over. We may think it over, we may declare it over, but in fact, the enemy gets a vote." Unfortunately, we'd learn soon enough that the "best friends" within the administration had more votes than any of the "best men" knew.

FOUR

EARLY DAYS

Those who enjoy their work become totally
absorbed in it, often forgetting to eat and
drink and seek other forms of enjoyment.

—MARCUS AURELIUS

I rang the buzzer on the control box outside the door to the secretary's action group, the name for the planning team that served as the nexus for most information coming into the front office. The camera in the box whirred, swiveling slowly upward to bring my face into view. "Come on in," said the voice from the control box, accompanied by a sharp metallic click as the door's latch unlocked.

I pushed on the heavy oak door and stepped into a narrow hallway leading to a small office space with four desks. Sitting alone at one of the desks was The Reader.

Will Bushman grew to become one of my favorite people on our team. The action group's deputy director, he was in his late thirties—a West Point graduate and former Army Ranger who had left uniformed service to pursue a law degree. Of average height and build, he was wearing a small pair of glasses as he sat in front of his desk. *Huh,* I thought, *this is what a middle-aged Harry Potter would look like.* It was late in the day and Will's eyes looked tired.

Will was known as The Reader because his primary job was to read everything. News articles, congressional testimony, think-tank reports—you name it—and Will was expected to read it, highlight the relevant sections, and then distill everything into a single sheet of paper for Mattis. It was a time-consuming but critical task.

As a team, we were moving forward at a steady clip. It was now May, and Bushman was busy at his desk working on the plan for the remainder of the year.

One of the things I noticed early on was that our team had a plan. This sounds like an obvious expectation: it's the US government, of course there's a plan. But the defense department was relatively unique during the Trump administration's first year. While the White House was busy responding to the day-to-day headlines, we knew what we wanted to strategically accomplish, and knew how to get there. This gave us an early opportunity to drive the national security agenda.

Driving the agenda was made possible in part because Mattis remained remarkably consistent with his ideas. He was well thought out, meticulous, and unwavering in his approach. The material I'd studied to prepare for the job aligned with what we were working on now. This steadfast approach also held for what he hoped to accomplish as defense secretary.

During his nomination hearing Mattis had listed three priorities for the department: restore the readiness and lethality of America's military, strengthen alliances and build new partnerships, and reform the department to deliver better performance and affordability.

"Everything we do must contribute to the lethality of our military." This deeply held belief underpinned Mattis's thoughts. The other two priorities, while incredibly important, were secondary to this. Lethality and readiness drove all his actions. I'd be sitting in a meeting when a senior official would bring up the latest "great idea." If the briefer couldn't tie it to the increasing lethality of the armed forces, then we weren't going to invest the time, energy, or precious limited resources to pursue it. Mattis expected departmental leadership to remain laser-focused on his three priorities—period.

These three priorities never wavered, affording us the stability we needed to remain consistent. I told a friend that Mattis was like a cargo plane: steady, dependable, and you knew you'd arrive safely at your destination. Trump, on the other hand, was like a fighter plane: maneuverable and capable of fast speeds, but you were always hanging on for dear life.

As a team, we set out to codify Mattis's priorities and share them within the department. I worked with Will and other members of the action group to create slides and memos to convey his vision for the department. All we needed now was Mattis's approval.

Of course, that's easier said than done. The reality is that there's no easing into the role of secretary of defense. The defense department is easily the largest "company" in the world. The secretary leads more than two million personnel across more than six thousand locations in 146 countries. Phone calls with government officials, consultations with international counterparts, and meetings with senior leaders are just one part of a complicated daily schedule. The US military has global responsibilities and, as Mattis put it, "the world gets a vote."

He couldn't be more right: in any given week we were fighting the war on terrorism, managing North Korean belligerence, addressing a rise in global instability, and contending with an administration having trouble finding a consistent message. There were also congressional engagements, bilateral meetings with Mattis's counterparts visiting from nations around the world, and myriad other issues.

I'd listened for years as military leaders dispensed pithy sayings like, "remember, it's a marathon . . . not a sprint." Perhaps in a normal job. When it came to working for Mattis, however, it felt more like a marathon at a sprinter's pace. We were notorious for packing each day's schedule as tightly as we possibly could, then marveling a month or two down the road that we couldn't seem to catch our breath.

But our team had a few internal issues to address along with our overseas ones, with several lasting throughout Mattis's tenure: the hiring process for senior defense department positions, and front office staff interaction with Pentagon leadership at large.

Hiring personnel proved a challenge for Mattis. First, the administration banned the "Never Trumpers," a large group of Republicans united in opposition to Trump's run for the presidency.

I felt the president should have claimed victory and rallied the finest professionals he could find to his flag. Instead, he seemed captivated by retaliating against those who had spoken out against him. Anyone associated with the "Never Trump" movement was barred from the administration, regardless of qualification.

As if this wasn't enough, another power struggle was playing out between the White House and the Pentagon.

As in every administration, Trump's Presidential Personnel Office wanted to dole out rewards to loyal campaign staffers. This included select positions within each federal agency, including senior roles at the Pentagon, a move Mattis resisted. Unfortunately, the president hadn't attracted large numbers of national security professionals to his team while running. The talent pool was shallow.

Sweeney sprang into action, leading the effort to help Mattis bring in the personnel he wanted, rather than acceding to the personnel list dictated by the White House.

The White House pushed back.

Personalities matter in politics and tend to have long-lasting implications. The White House's transition team for the Pentagon included Mira Ricardel, a former Boeing executive and assistant secretary of defense under President George W. Bush, and Mike Duffey, executive director of the Wisconsin Republican Party and a former defense department liaison to the Bush White House. Ricardel worked out of the Eisenhower Executive Office Building next door to the White House. Duffey, on the other hand, was positioned at the Pentagon on the other side of the Potomac to help onboard personnel.

Unfortunately, Ricardel and Sweeney never learned how to

get along. Duffey soon found himself caught up in their feud, as Ricardel was forcing Trump loyalists toward the Pentagon while Sweeney was resisting her.

Mattis wanted the best people he could find, regardless of political affiliation. This placed Duffey in an awkward position early on. In reality, he was merely a middleman lacking the authority to resolve disputes. Things rapidly came to a head, and Ricardel was invited to the Pentagon to clear the air.

The meeting grew heated and things didn't end well.

Mattis, it turns out, was blocking Ricardel from the senior policy position she coveted at the Pentagon. For her part, Ricardel did not agree with a recently retired general occupying the position of defense secretary. She hardly helped her mission by talking down to Mattis, leading him to grumble afterward, "I never want to see that little girl again." She was subsequently labeled persona non grata at the Pentagon, their relationship in tatters.

Ricardel stayed at the White House a bit longer before finding a job at the commerce department. But, before leaving, she managed to place senior leaders throughout the Pentagon, including fellow Boeing executive Pat Shanahan as deputy secretary of defense, the number-two job.

Success in politics requires good—or at least workable—relationships. Ricardel had tried, and failed, to impose her will on Mattis and the team. The fractured relationship seemed to be of little concern now that Ricardel was out of the picture. But you never know where folks will ultimately end up . . . and it wouldn't be the last we'd see of Ricardel.

There was, however, one very bright spot on the personnel

front. Mattis and the Pentagon were seen as a safe haven for establishment Republicans to serve without taking too much risk to their subsequent careers. Many a political appointee confided to me that they harbored significant reservations in joining an unproven Trump administration. Working alongside Mattis was viewed as a safe place to land.

If Trump was successful, well, a rising tide lifts all boats. If things went poorly, they could serve their country and the administration, knowing that in the end they would be able to claim they had joined to support Mattis. It was a cold political calculation, but it helped the Pentagon attract higher-quality people.

Additional systemic internal issues arose in the early months.

The first centered around information flow within the Pentagon. Or, more to the point, how Sweeney and Rear Admiral Craig Faller, the senior military assistant, interacted with Pentagon employees. An active-duty two-star Navy admiral, Faller was an "admiral's admiral": tall and thin, a head full of white hair, with a commanding presence. I overheard on more than one occasion, "That's exactly what I thought an admiral would look/be like." These two admirals would have outsized influence during Mattis's tenure.

Mattis believes there are only two types of organizations: one where the leader directs and assigns tasks, or a second variation, where the staff informs the leader of where to go and what to do. A longtime military commander, Mattis was clearly in the first camp. Using his staff, he would direct the Pentagon. The Pentagon would never direct him.

America's military is a behemoth, and Mattis enjoyed telling audiences that if it were a country, the military would represent the seventeenth-largest economy in the world. Feeling that he needed to take charge at the Pentagon to move quickly forward led Mattis to seek his comfort zone, largely surrounding himself with military personnel of two predominant flavors: those who served with him at US Central Command (the majority of the office) and officers from the Navy and the Marine Corps (myself included). The argument went that since we came from a shared background, we'd know how to get the job done to his satisfaction.

Although our team could move fast, I was concerned about the ripples we created in our wake. Civilians in the Department of Defense were largely accustomed to a more collegial organization, although long-serving career civilians recalled the use of such aggressive top-down leadership during Donald Rumsfeld's second tenure in the Pentagon. It was still a shock to the system when Mattis's front office team began issuing orders and demanding results, circumventing the flow of information in the building that had taken hold during the past decade.

Senior staffers throughout the Pentagon, especially in the policy shop, saw their products marginalized and shunted aside in order to react to pointed questions from the front office. This concern came up repeatedly during my early meetings throughout the Pentagon. A number of talented career civilians left their jobs to pursue other opportunities. The Pentagon bureaucracy certainly needed to adapt, but I often wondered about the impacts on communication flowing uphill. We were getting answers to the questions we were asking . . . but were we asking the right questions? What were we missing by adopting a heavy, top-down approach?

We also faced a more challenging issue: the long-held principle of civilian control of the military, and how that control should be exercised.

Under most administrations, the Pentagon chief of staff would handle a significant portion of the day-to-day operations and coordination. The same would be true with civilian leadership placed throughout the Pentagon. But we were largely a military staff, not a civilian one, and Sweeney was a retired one-star admiral. This had implications.

In the Navy, the commanding officer of a unit is responsible for being "up and out," communicating with senior leaders in other organizations. The second in command, the executive officer, is typically responsible for running the day-to-day administration.

Sweeney brought this division of labor into the Pentagon, staying tied to his desk and managing the interaction with other departments and agencies. His "second in command," Rear Admiral Faller, assumed responsibility for daily operations, a break from the department's civilian-led tradition. This is where my concerns grew.

Historically, the senior military assistant is the secretary's interconnect between the Joint Chiefs of Staff and combatant commanders. In reality, of course, the role becomes whatever the secretary desires to accomplish the mission. Since Sweeney delegated a large portion of staff management to Faller, this resulted in an active-duty admiral issuing directives to senior senate-confirmed Trump appointees.

This "uniform-first" approach propagated to lower levels. Faller led a department-wide coordination meeting every morning in the secretary's conference room. Most attendees from each of the Pentagon's agencies were uniformed personnel, serving as military assistants to far more senior civilians, placing them in the awkward position of returning to tell their bosses what to do. Since the majority of us on Mattis's personal staff were also wearing a uniform, we were routinely placed in a similar position when asked to go and "square away" a senior civilian leader. We referred to the situation as playing "monkey in the middle," since we couldn't compel the results Sweeney or Faller wanted to see. Over time we learned how to positively influence while remaining mindful of our rank and status.

Pentagon leaders expressed frustration about military officers directing civilians to act but were met with a "tough—deal with it" response from our front office. This hardly eased Pentagon tensions and the grumbling never really went away.

There was no malicious intent. It's just the way things were.

Employees in the Pentagon joked we were now "US Central Command—North," America's newest military-led command, and an extension of Mattis's previous job. Another favorite jab was to simply refer to the Pentagon as the "PENTACOM," short for Pentagon Command.

Despite some initial tensions, the early days on Mattis's staff offered opportunities for levity as well. Though we kept a fast pace in the office, Mattis maintained a good-natured attitude and a quick wit.

His positive energy was felt throughout the building. I noticed that Mattis usually made time to chat with the Pentagon workforce. When we entered or exited the building, he walked over to the security guards to talk for a few minutes. When leaving in the evening, Mattis would also chat with the cleaning crew before heading home. A person's station in life wasn't important to Mattis: he was just as happy to talk with blue-collar workers as he was with kings.

He also had a sense of humor. We were closing out a particularly busy week when Mattis presided over former secretary of defense Chuck Hagel's portrait unveiling at the Pentagon. Toward the end of the event Hagel commented, "You know, one day your portrait will be hanging here too." Mattis chuckled, a mischievous glint creeping into his eyes.

He dashed back into his office with me in tow. Snatching a clean piece of paper out of the printer on his desk, he freehanded a sketch of himself as a sailor, wearing bell-bottoms and all. Returning to the party in the hallway, he taped his freehand drawing right next to Hagel's portrait. "Here it is!" he exclaimed. "What do you think of my portrait?"

One of my favorite early events with Mattis was his commencement speech for West Point's graduation ceremony. This soon into his tenure, his speech offered a rare public opportunity to define the ideals and values he cared about as defense secretary. The speech needed to be perfect.

For inspiration we turned to General Douglas MacArthur, President Franklin Roosevelt, and other WWII–era leaders who had produced speeches that still resonate today, decades after they were first delivered. We chewed through dozens of drafts of his remarks in the weeks preceding the event.

After weeks of effort, Mattis was ready. On Saturday, May 27, he boarded a small jet at Andrews Air Force Base and headed to New York. I'd been away from home for several weeks, so I took the weekend to visit the family in Norfolk. We hooked our computer up to the television, and our children joined us in watching "Mister Mattis" deliver his live-streamed speech.

Mattis entered to a prolonged standing ovation. "I would never have imagined, ladies and gentlemen," he said, "when I joined the military at age eighteen that I'd be standing here, nor can you graduates anticipate where you'll be many years from now." Amen. If you'd told me nineteen years before, when I graduated from Annapolis, that I'd be sitting on my couch while the secretary of defense delivered a speech that I'd helped write, I would have said you were crazy.

He expressed his admiration for the path they had chosen in life. Every single one of the graduates could have opted out, but they chose to serve selflessly in the armed forces. "Colleges across this land," Mattis claimed, "would have moved heaven and earth to recruit you for schools that would never make such demands on you as West Point." After four years at West Point, these cadets "understood what it means to live up to an oath . . . the commitment that comes with signing a blank check to the American people, payable with your life." Mattis was delivering his remarks masterfully.

As Mattis moved through the speech, I waited for my favorite part. Mikolay and I had structured the speech around the refrain "hold the line," playing on the theme that all graduates are members of West Point's "long gray line," and a nod to General Douglas MacArthur's 1962 farewell address to the cadets at West Point.

Mattis's voice turned commanding. "For those privileged to wear the cloth of our nation, to serve in the United States Army, you stand the ramparts, unapologetic, apolitical, defending our experiment in self-governance. And you hold the line.

"You hold the line, faithful to duty, confronting our nation's foes with implacable will . . . You hold the line, true to honor, living by a moral code regardless of who is watching . . . and you hold the line, loyal to country and defending the Constitution, defending our fundamental freedoms."

Mattis then paused, looking out into a sea of gray uniforms as he closed. "For duty . . . for honor . . . for country . . . you hold the line. Congratulations, class of 2017, and may God Bless America."

I looked over at Sarah as the crowd broke into cheers and applause. She had a huge grin on her face. Not normally given to profanity, she made me laugh when she said, "Wow, he's a badass. I can't believe you're working for him."

In some ways, neither could I.

FIVE

LOYALTY

I have always believed that many of our later
difficulties have stemmed from our insensitive
conduct toward our allies . . .

—HENRY KISSINGER, WRITING ABOUT OUR
FOREIGN POLICY IN THE 1950s

"We have much great news to share with the American people today," said Trump. "We continue to deliver on our promises. Due to a record-long delay in confirmation and the confirmation process by the Senate Democrats, which I call the obstructionists . . ."

It was June 12, and I was watching President Trump's first full cabinet meeting from a television in my office. White House staff had squeezed extra seats around an already cramped conference table in the White House Cabinet Room to accommodate additional senior administration officials. An entire back row of chairs had been placed against the wall for National Security Adviser H. R. McMaster, White House Chief Strategist Steve Bannon, Senior Adviser Jared Kushner, and a collection of White House staff members to attend. It looked uncomfortable.

Trump welcomed his newest cabinet members, recounted early administration successes, and highlighted his desire to impose steel and aluminum tariffs on trading partners. The members of his cabinet looked wary, shifting in their seats as they shot glances around the room. Was it their new surroundings, or their concern over what he was saying?

Trump then asked each member at the table to introduce themselves and say a few words.

"Most of you know most of the people around the room but I'm gonna start with our vice president. Where's our vice president?" Trump looked down both sides of the table, not finding Vice President Pence, before realizing that he was sitting directly across from him. "There he is! Maybe start with Mike and we'll just go around and just you name your position and then we'll ask these folks to go back and have a good day and we'll discuss our various reports."

Pence was obviously primed and ready to go.

"Thank you, Mr. President. It's the greatest privilege of my life to serve as vice president to a president who is keeping his word to the American people, assembling a team that's bringing real change, real prosperity, and real strength back to our nation." It was a pretty egregious piece of pandering. All Trump had asked was for each person to introduce themselves and their position. I couldn't tell if they had planned this, or if Pence was merely playing to his boss's ego.

And so around the table it went, each member of the cabinet thanking the president for the opportunity to serve in his cabinet. Reince Priebus, the White House chief of staff, chimed in. "On behalf of the entire senior staff around you, Mr. President, we thank you for the opportunity and the blessing that you have given us to serve your agenda and the American people."

Sweeney had asked us to prepare some notes on the current campaign to defeat ISIS to send over with Mattis for this meeting. No one had told us that Mattis would be asked to say a few words on camera, so he'd walked in without any prepared talking points. Like the other cabinet officials, he'd been blindsided by what had turned into an on-air loyalty pledge. Following on the heels of FBI director James Comey's firing a month before, and the subsequent revelation that Trump had demanded Comey's personal loyalty, the scene unfolding live at the White House seemed surreal. I found myself wondering what Mattis would say when it was his turn. Would he simply fall in line with the others?

No way. Mattis was having none of it.

"Mr. President," began Mattis, "it's an honor to represent the men and women of the Department of Defense. We are grateful for the sacrifices our people are making in order to strengthen our militaries so our diplomats always negotiate from a position of strength. Thank you."

In that moment, I was proud that he was my boss. Short and to the point, he managed to recognize the men and women of the Department of Defense while also highlighting the role the military should play in supporting the state department's diplomatic efforts. The consensus among our team was positive. Mattis made clear he was remaining above the fray and refusing to be obsequious. He had set himself apart on principle.

———

Despite taking a different approach during the cabinet meeting, Mattis was taking pains to ensure he stayed aligned with President Trump. He was in high demand at the White House, meeting frequently with the president, McMaster, and members of the National Security Council. He routinely briefed the military's plan to defeat ISIS, updates to the strategy for the campaign in Afghanistan, and the rationale for keeping large numbers of military troops in countries around the world.

Mattis held a great deal of influence with the president. When Trump or the White House made a sudden, public change to America's long-standing priorities, such as working to implement tariffs or withdrawing forces from their overseas locations, Mattis would intervene and the topic would once again be relegated to the back burner.

This isn't to say that Mattis was working to co-opt the president. Far from it. Mattis was playing the role of a loyal secretary of defense. From conversations held in our office, I knew that Mattis, Tillerson, and others were merely counseling an untested president lacking government or military experience. In business, Trump obviously liked to move fast, but with international diplomacy, a steady, consistent, and well-coordinated whole-of-government approach usually carries more weight. Despite their influence, Trump continually questioned the importance of allies and partners.

The US can lay claim to many strengths. We reside on an

island of stability in North America, with oceans buffering us from threats to our east and west. Our economy has proven itself to be resilient, flexible, and innovative. We have a thriving agricultural industry and plentiful oil and natural gas reserves.

But no single strength outweighs the advantages we gain from our diverse and long-standing web of alliances. There's a reason that Russia is constantly seeking to fracture NATO and that China seeks to deal with nations on a bilateral basis. Strong alliances provide strength and stability for their member nations, a fact that continues to underpin America's success today.

Allies also temper external challenges and global instability. I watched as significant threats continued to mount during our first few months. North Korea was pursuing nuclear weapons development. ISIS, an Islamist terrorist group, was carrying out attacks throughout Europe and the Middle East. China was exerting increasing pressure on other nations in the Pacific. Russia was rattling its saber and, at this point, it was widely established that they had interfered in the 2016 presidential election.

Alarm bells were ringing in Washington, DC.

Unfortunately, America's allies were every bit as concerned by Trump's poorly explained "America First" rhetoric as they were with the mounting threats. Trump believed that America had been ripped off for decades by our allies and partners—and he wasn't afraid to share that opinion openly and often.

During campaign stops, then-candidate Trump highlighted the bad deal the US had made through its long-standing defense treaties with Japan and South Korea. NATO was "obsolete" and "costing us a fortune." When CNN anchor Wolf Blitzer asked Trump if the US needed to rethink the NATO alliance, he responded, "Yes, because it's costing us too much money . . . frankly, it's a different world than it was when we originally conceived of the idea." He asserted that the US was wasting billions to station troops overseas and receiving nothing of value in return.

At a stop in Iowa, he said, "You know we have a treaty with Japan, where if Japan is attacked, we have to use the full force and might of the United States. . . . If we're attacked, Japan doesn't have to do anything. They can sit home and watch Sony television, okay?" He followed up by saying that Japan might just have to defend itself against North Korea. He made similar pronouncements regarding South Korea. I was stationed in Japan at the time of his remarks, and I knew that to our allies' ears he sounded like he wanted to abandon them to the wolves.

Campaign rhetoric is one thing. But on his third day in office, Trump formally withdrew the US from Trans-Pacific Partnership negotiations, a twelve-nation trade agreement designed to lower trade barriers and increase protections for US companies. Several years in the making, the agreement was designed to strengthen America's ties overseas while serving as an alternative to China's aggressive—even predatory—trade practices. Trump's withdrawal caused the partnership to collapse, and allies were alarmed all over again. I felt this decision was shortsighted, another step toward abdicating US regional leadership to the Chinese, or at least making it seem that way. I wasn't sure which was worse.

We began to hear allies increasingly inquire of Mattis: Was President Trump truly abandoning America's long-standing commitments? Was America withdrawing from its global relationships?

To reassure allies, within two weeks of entering office Mattis had traveled to Japan and South Korea to counter concerns about eroding US resolve. Aiding his mission was a web of preexisting relationships and experiences accumulated during his forty-three years spent in uniform. He either knew personally many of the leaders or, barring a personal relationship, had worked on issues of importance to their governments. These connections gave him instant credibility.

Mattis arrived in Asia with a message of America's "ironclad commitment" to South Korean and Japanese leadership, ensuring "there [was] no misunderstanding during this transition in Washington. We stand firmly, 100 percent, shoulder to shoulder with you." A week later, he brought a similar message to European leaders in Brussels during his first NATO meeting.

Mattis defended the president's "America First" policy by sharing with me a story about a flight he had taken from the West Coast to Washington, DC. During his trip, the plane had hit turbulence and oxygen masks fell. It reminded him of what flight attendants advise passengers before every flight: put your own mask on first before assisting those around you.

It was clear: America had to get its own fiscal house in order before it could effectively help other nations. As Mattis put it, "America first doesn't mean America alone," a message that Tillerson was also amplifying during his own phone calls and travels abroad.

In general, allies overseas seemed receptive to Tillerson's and Mattis's reassuring message. The thinking went like this: Trump might be sowing uncertainty back in the US due to rapid changes in policy direction or spur-of-the-moment tweets, but those were largely to appeal to his base. Tillerson and Mattis were seen as steady hands fighting to maintain the current alliance structure and forge new partnerships. *Don't worry about the chaos you see on TV,* we were saying. *Mattis and Tillerson are working in concert to keep things on track.*

During a trip to Europe in May, Trump once again called into question America's willingness to stand by our allies.

Standing outside the new NATO headquarters in Brussels, with NATO Secretary General Jens Stoltenberg standing to his right side and a memorial to the World Trade Center towers off to his left, Trump launched into an alarming speech. He lashed into the other heads of state for their failure to meet their defense spending pledge from 2014, in which each nation pledged to increase defense spending to 2 percent of GDP by 2024. The other heads of state were incredulous that Trump was lambasting them in a public forum.

As NATO leaders looked on with disbelief, Trump said, "I have been very, very direct with Secretary Stoltenberg and members of the Alliance in saying that NATO members must finally contribute their fair share and meet their financial obligations, for twenty-three of the twenty-eight member nations are *still* not paying what they should be paying and what they're supposed to be paying for their defense."

President Emmanuel Macron of France and other leaders were huddled together off to Trump's right side but they were still in the camera frame. They started to laugh. This just wasn't how international diplomacy was conducted. But it's how Trump was conducting it.

"This is not fair to the people and taxpayers of the United

States," Trump continued. "Many of these nations owe massive amounts of money from past years and not paying in those past years. Over the last eight years, the United States spent more on defense than all other NATO countries combined." I knew this was wrong: member nations contribute forces to the alliance, but nations did not owe money to the alliance beyond what they mutually agreed to. NATO spending was a reflection of each nation's own domestic military budget.

It was apparent Trump had caught everyone off guard. In an unintended slight, the president failed to reassure the assembled leaders of America's continued resolve to support the NATO alliance, specifically article five's mutual defense agreement. Despite being in existence for seventy years, article five has been invoked only one time: in the aftermath of the 9/11 terrorist attacks in New York City when NATO allies rallied to support us.

Trump's failure to reaffirm a dedication to mutual defense while standing in the shadow of NATO's 9/11 memorial was a misstep. To the gathered leaders, his speech was perceived as all stick and no carrot. The press had a field day.

But the president wasn't just grumbling publicly about the high cost to America for alliances and troops overseas. He continued to challenge their value in private to Tillerson, Mattis, and McMaster, asking whether we could withdraw forces from overseas locations like Japan, South Korea, and Germany.

The solution became a briefing for the president at the Pentagon in mid-July. Surely if they explained the geopolitical situation to Trump, he would then finally understand the value allies provide to America.

We spent weeks preparing. I was responsible for coordinating the event, communicating with McMaster's and Cohn's teams at the White House and Tillerson's team at State to ensure the remarks and slides were aligned. I then set out to make Mattis's talking points and create his briefing slides. Interestingly, Mattis emphasized that I needed to keep his remarks unclassified. Since this was a larger meeting, he didn't want any classified information to be disclosed by someone in attendance. We usually took the same approach when briefing Congress.

As we organized for the event, Mattis asked me to his office to discuss some of the main points that should influence his presentation. They boiled down to the following:

1. Trump likes to build things.
2. Trump likes power.
3. Trump likes to be seen as bullying the bullies.
4. Trump likes to be the best or have the best.

Mattis felt that appealing to Trump's core beliefs would make the briefing more palatable to the president. If the president likes these things, then surely we could convince him that the cost of stationing troops overseas and America's alliance structure were worth the investment for the commensurate amount of power they afforded him in return.

As we discussed the event, more themes began to take shape.

First among them was to demonstrate that America was getting a good deal. As Mattis had stated during a speech in Singapore, "Security is the foundation of prosperity, enabling the free flow of commerce." Mattis wanted to help the president see that "trade follows the flag."

Placing US armed forces overseas preserves stability and enables the "free and unfettered flow of commerce," of which the US is a primary benefactor. Failure to maintain this presence meant that other nations could affect shipping or energy shipments, which could in turn harm American industries or taxpayers.

Mattis told me that he could best appeal to Trump's business side by showing that our allies and partners contributed far more troops in various hot spots around the world than we did. We shaped this concept into America's "return on invested capital," a business term for how well a company is using its money to generate returns.

I appreciated Mattis's enthusiasm on this point, but I wasn't sure it would be as compelling as he hoped. I had not yet met the president, but what I knew about him indicated that he didn't care for sitting through long lectures.

Small, worrying distractors and crossed signals kept popping up from the White House. During a July 6 visit to Poland, Trump met with President Andrzej Duda, saying, "NATO remains critical to deterring conflict and ensuring that war between great powers never again ravages Europe . . . America is committed to maintaining peace and security in Central and Eastern Europe." Now we weren't sure where the president stood on NATO. Did he support the alliance? Was he against it?

Plus, we had a request from the White House to explore moving troops currently stationed in Germany to Poland. Evidently, President Duda had suggested creation of a "Fort Trump" in Poland, and the Pentagon was tasked with determining how expensive the move would be.

To help provide a unified front, a few days before we were

scheduled to brief Trump we journeyed over to the state department for a "pregame" session with Tillerson and his team. Chairman of the Joint Chiefs General Joe Dunford, Donnelly, and I joined Mattis for the meeting at the state department's headquarters located in Foggy Bottom, one of the earliest neighborhoods of Washington, DC. Luckily my counterpart, an army strategist assigned to State, also joined us. We'd ultimately be the ones who took the notes from the meeting and turned them into the products Mattis and Tillerson would use.

Tillerson was on the phone and running a few minutes late, so our team stood clustered in small groups and made idle conversation in his dining room. Soon enough the doors leading to Tillerson's office area opened and he walked through. I was struck by how personable Tillerson was, making it a point to walk over to introduce himself to each of us, shaking hands as he did so. It sounds like a simple gesture, but most senior leaders in the administration tended to ignore staffers. Not Tillerson.

We took our seats, Tillerson's team on one side of the dining room table and ours on the other. I glanced over at my counterpart. He raised his eyebrows sharply as we made eye contact. We were clearly thinking the same thing. *How in the world did we wind up here?* It wasn't lost on us that we were far and away the most junior staffers in the room.

Mattis, always formal, continually referred to Tillerson as "Mr. Secretary." It was a measure of his respect for Tillerson, and a tangible reminder that Mattis viewed the military's role as subordinate to State's diplomatic one.

Tillerson started off the meeting, asking, "How do we convey information in a way that resonates with the president?"

Mattis laid out his plan to focus on the economic security afforded by America's overseas presence, an approach Tillerson agreed with in principle. Tillerson also noted that Trump had created a list of twelve measures of economic effectiveness by which he could judge the US's relationship with other nations, and "South Korea was the worst" in the eyes of the president.

And so it went, as Mattis, Tillerson, and Dunford discussed key points that should be made for President Trump. Mattis was particularly animated about the need for American presence abroad. "We don't want to defend on the one-yard line," he said, a reference to the importance of combating threats away from the US homeland. "We've already seen what happens when we withdraw from the world," Mattis added, referencing Obama's pullout from Iraq and the subsequent rise of ISIS. "It was like clutching defeat from the jaws of victory."

Tillerson agreed wholeheartedly, noting how the US's relationships with allies provided many positive effects. "The Defeat-ISIS Coalition," a global coalition of nations and international organizations formed in 2014 to combat terrorism, "could stand up quickly because they are already our friends and allies . . . and they trust us. It would have been impossible otherwise."

Tillerson was right. Our alliance structure meant we could build a coalition to combat a global issue in minimal time, an important ability since terrorism had metastasized to become a global problem without defined geographic boundaries. He also pointed out that nations that rally to our flag demonstrate a shared sacrifice through similar values. Tillerson, Mattis, and Dunford were aligned for the meeting with Trump.

We left Foggy Bottom and headed back to the Pentagon.

With Trump increasingly skeptical of the costs of America's engagement overseas, Mattis emphasized to me that his talking points needed to be well crafted. "Boil it down, Bus," he said. "Remember, I'm looking for all meat and no broth on this one."

We needed to demonstrate for the president the staggering importance of a strong web of alliances and partners throughout the world. Mattis felt that loyalty to our allies and partners could coexist with loyalty to the president's vision for the nation. Trump's upcoming Pentagon briefing was the perfect opportunity. With today's prep session at the state department, we thought we were prepared and ready for a successful briefing.

We couldn't have been more wrong.

SIX

TRUMPED

There can be no security anywhere in the free
world if there is not fiscal and economic
stability within the United States.

—RONALD REAGAN

As the seconds ticked down, Mattis's nervous energy was palpable. Unusually so. Normally stoic and deliberate with his movements, this morning he was electrified. He was pacing in his office, moving from a standing desk that faced the Potomac to the small circular table and back again. He shuffled his notes, putting them into a nondescript dark blue folder, pausing for a few seconds in hesitation before pulling them out again to rearrange their order. Things needed to be perfect.

I understood why. We all did. It was July 20, 2017, and President Trump was on his way to the Pentagon for the meeting we had prepared for with Tillerson and other administration leaders. Today Mattis, joined with Tillerson and others, would offer the president his first Pentagon briefing on America's military and diplomatic "laydown," a term of art used to describe all the locations around the world where US forces and embassies are located. At any time this would be a big deal for the department, regardless of the president. But in Trump's case, the briefing had a heightened importance.

Just a few weeks earlier, Trump had declared America's unilateral withdrawal from the Paris Agreement. Signed by 195 members of the United Nations, the Paris Agreement set out a series of ambitious goals to minimize the effect of climate change. President Trump's withdrawal fulfilled a campaign pledge to abandon a pact he saw as too restrictive to America's manufacturing and economic health, surrendering too much of America's independence to the global community.

It was viewed by staff members in Mattis's office primarily as a way to dismantle yet another piece of President Obama's legacy.

Tillerson and Mattis were alarmed. Trump's decision was evidence of the administration's abandonment of America's longstanding commitment to the world order it had helped to create in the aftermath of World War II. Trump was also threatening to dismantle the nuclear deal with Iran, withdraw from NATO, pull US forces back from South Korea, Germany, and Japan, give Russia a pass on its electoral interference in the 2016 election, and, in his spare time, start a war with North Korea. Mattis was fielding phone call after phone call from nervous allies, each one seeking reassurance that America would stand by its obligations to preserve the global status quo.

Tillerson and Mattis feared these various actions signaled America's diminished authority as a world leader and, worse, was emboldening China, Russia, and Iran to fill the vacuum. Both men felt incredible pressure to educate the president. If only Trump could be made to recognize the value America derives from a strong relationship with allies and the stability afforded by the forward presence of our troops, they thought, surely he'd reconsider and alter course. Having this briefing at the Pentagon, we hoped, would give the presentation extra weight. At this point, only six months into his presidency, Trump very much enjoyed talking about "his generals" and was clearly impressed by the uniforms, protocols, and pageantry the military offered.

If anyone could change the president's mind at this stage of the administration, it was Mattis. He had managed to maintain a close relationship with Trump, as he would be called over to the White House two or three times a week for meetings, lunch, and sometimes dinner with the president. Trump lacked government and national security experience when taking office, and it was obvious to us that he valued Mattis's opinion and simply liked having him around to bounce ideas off.

I suspect he also liked the fact that as far as cabinet members go, Mattis was about as low-key as a senior official could get and he didn't create headaches. Mattis clearly understood the perils of being seen to overshadow Trump, so he minimized his interaction with the press to avoid saying something that would contradict the president's own rapidly changing message. As Mattis saw it, the press were looking for any reason whatsoever to drive wedges into the administration, leading him to remark, "If I say six and the president says a half dozen, I guarantee you the article the next day is going to be 'the secretary of defense and the president disagree on the fundamentals.'" Mattis knew that when it came to the president, it was better to keep his head down than seek the spotlight.

For days prior, Mattis had all of us working on various aspects of the briefing in excruciating detail. The staff was forced to obsess for more than a week over the exact number of US service members at each location around the world, with Mattis requesting updates on our progress on a near-hourly basis.

It sounds like a simple task: just phone up each location and ask how many troops were there. But with personnel constantly on the move the numbers were changing daily. It didn't matter if the amount was 10,000 or 10,005 troops, the number had to be exact, and we exhausted more time chasing rounding errors than we did with the content of the brief. Everything had to be flawless, including the run of show.

The plan was for Mattis to speak first, walking President Trump through details on every US deployment abroad in an attempt to demonstrate America's return on its investment. Tillerson would follow with slides to walk through the location of every US embassy and mission abroad. Cohn would speak last to highlight the importance of global trade flows. I would be in an adjoining room, able to control the slide show, listen to the conversation, and watch the room from multiple angles using several computer monitors.

As lead organizer for the briefing, I arrived hours early to check the computer monitors, provide printed copies of the slides for each of the seats around the conference table, and ensure everything was ready before setting up shop in the control room. Lieutenant Colonel Brian Griese, a US Army officer currently detailed to Tillerson's team, joined me in the control room just prior to President Trump's arrival. The president, however, was running a few minutes behind, which only added to the tension.

Outside, Trump's motorcade pulled up to the River Entrance, the Pentagon's ceremonial entrance facing toward the Potomac River. Mattis greeted the president at his armored limo, known as "The Beast," and they both proceeded to the top of the steps to pose for a quick photo. Reporters shouted questions, to which the president simply replied, "We're doing very well against ISIS. ISIS is falling fast," before Mattis whisked him into the entryway and to the conference room.

We shut the door to the control room just as the president entered. We were senior military officers and trained to keep a professional distance. Still, we were admittedly enthusiastic to be a part of such a unique moment.

The list of attendees was impressive. President Trump stood at the head of the table facing three large television screens. He was joined by Vice President Mike Pence, Secretary of State Rex Tillerson, Chief of Staff Reince Priebus, and Senior Adviser Jared Kushner. Seated to his left were Mattis, Chairman of the Joint Chiefs of Staff General Joe Dunford, and Chief Economic Adviser Gary Cohn. Notably absent was National Security Adviser H. R. McMaster. This meeting also included "back benchers," or senior officials who typically would sit in chairs along the walls of the room. Mattis's team included Sweeney, Faller, and Donnelly. They sat next to White House Chief Strategist Steve Bannon.

We watched as Trump took his place at the head of the table, offering few opening comments to anyone and a frown fixed on his face. His body language was not encouraging. It communicated that he knew he'd have to suffer through multiple presentations. To us it seemed that his mind was already made up. He appeared to see this entire briefing as pointless—but perhaps I was reading too much into all of this. At least I hoped so.

As planned, the methodical, disciplined Mattis kicked off the meeting with remarks we had rehearsed in his office a number of times. Mattis tends to turn professorial during important meetings, providing the audience with excessive detail rather than tailoring his approach to the group he's speaking with. This instinct worsens when he is anxious about an event. Mattis will spend an inordinate amount of time on tactical details that have little bearing on strategic outcomes in order to bolster his confidence level. Unfortunately, to the room his opening sounded too much like a lecture.

"Good morning, Mr. President," he began. "Today I'd like to show you our global laydown of forces, a forward presence created by the greatest generation from the ashes of World War II. These men returned home and said, 'What a crummy world, but we're a part of it,' before rolling up their sleeves and getting to work. From World War II, we learned the hard way that we had to be forward deployed . . . that we can't defend effectively from America's one-yard line. Our presence abroad also supports millions of American jobs at home by ensuring the free and unfettered flow of global trade, and that our economy is the real engine of our national defense."

President Trump crossed his arms and scowled.

Mattis worked through his first meticulously produced slide. He explained the nature of "chokepoints," extremely narrow, landlocked corridors between larger bodies of water. Chokepoints are frequently traveled by ships full of fuel and products destined for overseas markets, such as the Suez and Panama canals. He then shared his philosophical view about America's two fundamental powers of intimidation and inspiration, telling the president a story I'd heard many times.

Years before, a terrorist had attempted to kill then-two-star general Mattis with an improvised explosive device. Marines found the terrorist trying to place the device on the road he had traveled down, using two 155-millimeter mortar rounds, a car battery, and a detonator. Not the terrorist's finest day. As Mattis told me, "The terrorist realized as he stared down the rifle barrels pointed at him that he was in danger of losing his 401(k)."

Mattis decided to speak with the terrorist after he was apprehended. Once in a holding room, Mattis slid a cup of coffee across the table to help break the ice as he sat down. Ultimately, the terrorist wanted to know: "Do you think if I'm really good at Guantanamo, will they let me move to America after I'm released?" As Mattis told it, the story represents two fundamental powers: we can intimidate others through our military superiority, but America's power to inspire is every bit as—and perhaps even more—powerful.

Mattis continued with his briefing, walking through in exacting detail the force ratios in each major geographic location. He sought to convince President Trump that our allies and partners put forward far more troops in support of stability abroad than

America does. In short, America gets a good deal from an overseas military presence.

The president frowned, fiddling with the papers in front of him while glancing around the room.

Mattis's third slide triggered a stronger response from Trump. A visual depiction of our Pacific posture, this slide zoomed in on the US forces located in Japan and South Korea—forces that had kept the peace in both countries for more than six decades. It detailed the numbers of troops in each country, the cost to American taxpayers, and the costs borne by our allies to support forces in their country. Mattis made the point that America had been willing to accept unfair terms following World War II in order to get both countries back on their feet, but that now would be an opportune time to update our trade agreements should Trump desire to do so.

Mattis loved this slide because it outlined the significant contributions both nations were making, with Japan footing the bill to shift US Marines from Okinawa to Guam, and South Korea paying to move Army soldiers to a new base. He emphasized to the president the importance of Japan paying to offset the costs for a new base, saying it was the first time in history they'd done so.

"Who is paying the rest of the bill for the move to Guam?" the president demanded. He looked irate.

There was silence. But only briefly.

"Our trade agreements are criminal," Trump thundered. "Japan and South Korea are taking advantage of the United States." This was decidedly not the message Mattis's slide intended to convey.

Out of nowhere, the president added, "And the USS *Ford*

[the navy's newest aircraft carrier] is completely out of control with cost overruns!"

Mattis struggled to regain control. In one sense he got what he'd wanted. The president was definitely engaged, but not in the way Mattis had hoped. His next slide underscored the importance of America's broad network of worldwide alliances, emphasizing the positive influence this had on relationships and economic development. The way to reach Trump, it had been reasoned, was to focus on the positive economics of having troops abroad. The president wasn't impressed.

As Mattis pressed on, Trump reacted viscerally to the mere mention of Iran—"in complete violation of the nuclear agreement!" he snapped—and to a recent incident where Iranian boats had harassed a US warship in the Persian Gulf. "If surrounded by Iran again," Trump said to a room full of military and civilian leaders, "the captain oughta blow them out of the water!"

Twenty-five minutes later, it was Tillerson's turn to run the gauntlet. Tillerson was by nature a slow talker. I could tell at once that was not an endearing quality to Trump. The president again quickly lost interest, though the tempo eventually picked up as Tillerson moved into a discussion of China's approach to a regional economic partnership structure they called "One Belt, One Road." In all, Tillerson spoke for twenty minutes. To this day I regret not having recorded Tillerson's voice. His deep baritone and measured pace would have made a terrific recording to help those who suffer from insomnia. When it was over, Trump looked like a kid who had been told it was time for recess.

Cohn's brief was easily the best of the three. It consisted of only three slides. Sensing the president's mood, Cohn was in and out in under five minutes. All eyes shifted to the president.

"A very good study, thank you," said Trump. "This is one big monster created over a number of years. Japan . . . Germany . . . South Korea . . . our allies are costing more than anyone else at the table!" Again, not the message any of us had intended.

Then the president paused. His eyes seemed animated by a thought.

"I just returned from France," he said. "Did you see President Macron's handshake?" he asked no one in particular. "He wouldn't let go. He just kept holding on. I spent two hours at Bastille Day. Very impressive."

Another pause.

"I want a 'Victory Day.' Just like Veterans Day. The Fourth of July is too hot. I want vehicles and tanks on Main Street. On Pennsylvania Avenue, from the Capitol to the White House. We need spirit! We should blow everybody away with this parade. The French had an amazing parade on Bastille Day with tanks and everything. Why can't we do that?"

We shifted uncomfortably in the control room, shooting glances at each other. Where was this going? We'd opened the control room door thirty minutes before to improve air flow. A Secret Service agent poked his head in, apparently uncomfortable with the conversation and the light it cast on the president. "Hey," he asked, "do you guys need to still be in here?"

Yes. Yes, we did. Just try to get us to leave.

Mattis and his team were adamantly opposed to a military parade down Pennsylvania Avenue, concerned that a parade like what Trump wanted would harken back to Soviet Union–like displays of authoritarian power. Mattis was adamant that precious taxpayer dollars would be better spent elsewhere, and that the optics of such a display of power would boomerang, causing more harm to America's international prestige than any domestic benefit could outweigh. Mattis was also concerned that a parade would risk eroding the military's long-standing apolitical reputation.

It didn't matter—Trump was serious. Mattis deflected and played for more time by saying, "We'll take a look at some options and get back to you, Mr. President."

Trump shifted again. "South Korea has been a major abuser. China, South Korea . . . they both rip us off left and right." Trump gestured toward the slides that Mattis and our team had so carefully put together to show the importance of global relationships. "I look at these slides and think, 'Wow, that costs us a lot of money.'" I could almost feel people's hearts sink from the other room. Then, almost as if he wanted to jab everyone further, the president added, "I'm ready for a trade war with China."

On it went, with Tillerson and Mattis taking turns with the president, each jumping in to try to keep the discussion focused on the importance of America's alliance structure, of the critical nature of our global footprint and the economic benefit the US derives from ensuring global stability and order. "Mr. President," said Tillerson, "We gain a lot of value by having embassies and troops stationed overseas. We gain influence with our allies, and in many cases, it helps us avoid conflicts before they reach a critical point."

"It doesn't matter, Rex," replied Trump. "We've spent over a trillion dollars . . . a *trillion* . . . in Iraq and Afghanistan. We need to get out of there. We're paying too much money and getting nothing in return! And for what?" Referring to an Iraqi city just liberated from ISIS, he added, "And now we'll have to rebuild Mosul before we can leave?"

Along the way Cohn interjected some, as did Priebus, trying to find some areas of common agreement that would satisfy the president. Even Bannon jumped in, surprising us with the clarity of his argument. "The president is right," said Bannon. "The status quo is simply unsustainable here. We're expending too much money maintaining a continual presence overseas."

His remark was a point of rigorous debate within military circles. Global stability was important, but at what cost? Many were concerned that Afghanistan had turned into a long-term conflict without an acceptable conclusion, one that was costing billions of dollars and thousands of lives. All that the three of us had known about Bannon prior to this meeting was that the media portrayed him as a looney fear monger who was pulling Trump's strings behind the scenes. Today, Bannon didn't appear to hold much sway in the room despite the clarity of his argument.

Pence and Kushner sat stone-faced, not uttering a single word throughout the entire meeting. Maybe they were the smart ones.

Over time Mattis began to shut down, sitting back in his chair with a distant, defeated look on his face. He had cared so much about this meeting, had poured his heart and soul into it, and had believed firmly in his ability to bring Trump around to his way of thinking. None of his attempts were working. From our vantage point, Mattis was playing a game of chess against a president fixated on "Rock, Paper, Scissors."

Mattis did not think Trump was a raving lunatic, as some were trying to portray the president. In fact, Mattis made a point of noting to us that America elected Trump for a reason. That the president had tremendous political skills, a sharp intuition, and a formidable business career. Those qualities deserved respect. But still Trump could tax Mattis's patience, and the president's view of the world was both simplistic and troublesome. That was clear today.

Across the table from Mattis, Tillerson also became increasingly frustrated, jousting verbally with the president before becoming so exasperated that he stopped talking completely for the last half hour of the meeting. Tillerson sat back in his chair with his arms crossed, an incredulous scowl on his face as he shot pointed looks over to Mattis.

Many times during Secretary Tillerson's tenure, reporters would claim that he thought his boss was an idiot—and each time Tillerson would deny it publicly. But there was no doubt among most observers in the room that day that Tillerson was thinking exactly that. Both men—Mattis and Tillerson—were despondent. We had just witnessed a meeting with Trump, up close and personal.

Now we knew why access was controlled so tightly.

For the remainder of the meeting, President Trump veered from topic to topic like a squirrel caught in traffic, dashing one way and then another. There had been an unfavorable story about him reported in the *Washington Post,* prompting the president to rail for about ten minutes on leaks and "how the reporter should be sued."

Syria? "Claim victory and get out."

Mexico? "Mexico is not our friend."

He argued with Cohn about the trade imbalance with Canada, before swinging back to deficits and the "need to bring our boys home." President Trump looked back at the maps. "It's a monster," he said, remarking on our expansive overseas presence. "It's a monster."

The issues were complicated, yet all of the president's answers were simplistic and ad hoc. He was shooting from the hip on issues of global importance.

With that, the meeting ended.

I closed down the presentation from the control room, exiting after the president had walked from the conference room. I trailed behind the entourage before making my return to Mattis's office, dejected and shaken to my core by what I had just witnessed. Several friends commented about how pale I looked. What happened at the meeting? "No time," I said, "I can share a bit more after we get back from the Capitol." Already wearing my formal service dress blue uniform, I grabbed my cover (the Navy's term for a hat you wear while in uniform) and sprinted toward the door.

I found press reporting on the president's short attention span to be entirely accurate. This isn't to say he lacks intelligence. To the contrary, my experience is that President Trump thinks quickly on his feet and can ask piercing questions if the subject matter catches his notice. But he has to be captivated by the subject. You have to grab his attention.

I learned an important lesson that would pay off when President Trump returned for a briefing the following January: only use slides with pictures . . . no words.

SEVEN

POLICY BY TWEET

Consistency is the true foundation of trust.

—POLITICIAN ROY T. BENNETT

Mattis followed Trump down to Norfolk, Virginia, the weekend following his Pentagon briefing to commission the Navy's newest nuclear-powered aircraft carrier, the USS *Gerald R. Ford*. A completely redesigned ship, America's newest carrier sported the latest technological advancements. Mattis, the sixth speaker, would give a five-minute speech before introducing the president.

Halfway through the second speaker my attention began to drift. *Who came up with this plan? Why is every guest speaker talking for six to eight minutes apiece? Don't they know that the president of the*

United States is waiting? It was rough. The first five speakers prattled on for over thirty minutes.

When his turn finally arrived, Mattis made his way over to the lectern. Abandoning his prepared remarks, Mattis wisely chose to speak extemporaneously for only thirty seconds, wrapping up with, "Enough words have been spoken. Let me say what you've all been waiting to hear. Ladies and gentlemen, our commander in chief, President Donald Trump. Thank you." The crowd loved it, rising to their feet to welcome Trump.

We'd spent weeks working on his speech, but Mattis understood that discretion was the better part of valor. Trump stood on board America's newest warship, an incredible backdrop for any president dedicated to rebuilding the military. Mattis wisely demurred to the president and kept his powder dry, especially after Thursday's Pentagon session. He'd likely win points for not keeping the president waiting another five minutes, a great way to generate goodwill.

Or so I thought—until Trump sandbagged us with his trio of transgender policy tweets a few days later. I was standing in the secretary's action group office as each tweet appeared on our screens.

Will Bushman was the first to see the tweets. "You've got to be kidding me!" he said, shaking his head in disbelief. "POTUS [President of the United States] just tweeted out that he's banning transgender members from serving in the military."

I walked over to look at his computer monitor. Sure enough, two tweets were already out. The third followed a few minutes later.

We were less than a week after the meeting in the Pentagon, and President Trump had just U-turned a major defense department policy. Via Twitter. We hadn't even received the courtesy of a heads-up from the White House.

Trump's combined tweetstorm read, "After consultation with my Generals and military experts, please be advised that the United States Government will not accept or allow Transgender individuals to serve in any capacity in the US Military. Our military must be focused on decisive and overwhelming victory and cannot be burdened with the tremendous medical costs and disruption that transgender in the military would entail. Thank you."

Why in the world is he tweeting about this? Like Bushman, I shook my head, incredulous. "This is ridiculous. The boss had a strategy, and the president knew it," I said.

"Yeah, I know," Bushman agreed, "our best-laid plans undone in an instant by an impulsive tweet."

It was no secret that President Trump was unwinding many of Obama's policy initiatives, including the ability for transgender individuals to serve openly in the US military. Trump had spoken with Mattis about it, but the secretary was much more circumspect on the issue.

Mattis knew that any decision he or the president made on such a highly charged political topic would be scrutinized, no matter the outcome. The best way for the department to render a defensible decision was to study the issue in depth, a process Mattis had initiated the month before. He decided on a six-month study period to postpone implementation.

To explain the delay, Mattis sent a memo to the force. "Since

becoming the Secretary of Defense," he wrote, "I have emphasized that the Department of Defense must measure each policy
decision against one critical standard: Will the decision affect the
readiness and lethality of the force? Put another way, how will
the decision affect the ability of America's military to defend the
nation? It is against this standard that I provide the following
guidance on the way forward in accessing transgender individuals into the military Services." His guidance mandated a review
that included "all relevant considerations," one that "in no way
presupposes the outcome."

For Mattis, a decision of this magnitude hinged on lethality
and readiness. Would it strengthen America's military? If the
factors—in time, money, and unit cohesion—supported retaining transgender individuals, then they should be allowed to serve.
If costs were too high, then they shouldn't.

Trump's tweets created chaos in the Pentagon. Top brass
asked, "Does a tweet constitute a viable policy shift?" Compounding their confusion was Mattis's absence. He was back in
his hometown of Richland, Washington, enjoying some rare and
well-deserved time off. The uncertainty continued until the next
day, when General Dunford released guidance to the department
saying that the transgender policy would not change until officially directed by the White House, and only after Mattis had
issued policy guidance.

But the policy damage was already done. It was a terrific example of how an ill-informed, and ill-considered, tweet from
1600 Pennsylvania Avenue could result in a strategic defeat.

Mattis described the lack of a cohesive White House strategy in more colorful terms. Back from Washington State, he labeled the situation as one where the administration was holding itself hostage. He formed his right hand into a make-believe pistol and pointed it toward his temple, saying, "No one move or the hostage gets it!"

Mattis needed to salvage the careful study on the issue he'd already begun. He coordinated with the White House to delay implementation of the ban until formal completion of his previously announced study. We knew the offending tweets could only undercut the president's desired policy position, providing advocacy groups with ammunition to challenge the president's policy. An orderly, informed process was necessary to withstand the challenges we anticipated having to face in the courts.

Assisting Mattis's effort was Trump's newly installed chief of staff and Mattis's longtime friend, General John Kelly.

Kelly had served as secretary of Homeland Security for nearly seven months. Then, the day after tweeting about transgender service members, another surprise Trump tweet announced the departure of Reince Priebus, his chief of staff, unceremoniously dumping him following a flight from New York.

Unaware, Priebus got off Air Force One and jumped into the presidential motorcade with two other senior White House staffers. As word of Priebus's sacking rapidly circulated, they fled from Priebus's car and into a different van in the motorcade. Priebus, left abandoned, was unceremoniously driven away after the motorcade departed for the White House.

Trump's newest bombshell tweet read, "I am pleased to inform you that I have just named General/Secretary John F Kelly as White House Chief of Staff. He is a Great American and a

Great Leader. John has also done a spectacular job at Homeland Security. He has been a true star of my Administration."

Cementing his status with Trump, Kelly, as Homeland Security chief, had fully supported the administration's stance on illegal immigration. When Priebus's star fell, Kelly was a natural to replace him. As Kelly had restricted access at the border, he would now restrict access to the Oval Office. Where previously chaos reigned and former reality show stars like Omarosa Manigault could just waltz into the Oval Office, Kelly would crack down. One of his first acts was to fire newly appointed White House Communications Director Anthony Scaramucci. He followed that up by jettisoning White House Chief Strategist Steve Bannon and then Deputy Assistant to the President Sebastian Gorka.

Kelly helped Mattis with the transgender issue, coordinating a presidential memo that authorized Mattis and Kirstjen Nielsen, Kelly's successor as secretary of Homeland Security, to conduct a study before offering the president recommendations on a long-term policy.

After a few weeks, the transgender topic finally died down. We'd been caught off guard previously, such as with the announced US withdrawal from the Trans-Pacific Partnership trade negotiation, but this was on an entirely different level. In the interim, Mattis advised us to restore a "steady as she goes" mindset in the department, keeping our heads down and focusing on our long-term strategy and day-to-day operations.

Spontaneous tweets emanating from the White House complicated our ability to carry out the president's goals, though Mattis's "steady as she goes" guidance was becoming easier to implement now that the Pentagon was finally getting some long-delayed senior personnel confirmed. Pat Shanahan, the deputy secretary of defense and Mattis's second in command, now came on board. Shanahan's arrival could never heal our lack of coordination with the White House, but it would enable Mattis to hand off much of the Pentagon's day-to-day operations to a capable deputy.

A thirty-one-year employee of Boeing, a large commercial and military aerospace firm, Shanahan won confirmation only after an extremely contentious hearing. Senator John McCain, chairman of the Senate Armed Services Committee, had dressed down Shanahan over his hesitation in providing Ukraine with defensive weapons needed to defend against Russian aggression.

Shanahan explained that he lacked the security clearance required to fully understand the issue. McCain not only brushed aside his response, he expressed concern that Shanahan worked for one of the five largest defense contractors, a situation McCain warned was like "letting a fox loose in the henhouse." Shanahan, however, remained calm under pressure, recovered, and was now setting up shop in the Pentagon.

Tony DeMartino, the deputy chief of staff who had interviewed me, also guided Shanahan through his confirmation process and would now serve as his chief of staff. DeMartino was a great fit for the deputy's office. I caught him in the hallway as he moved boxes to his new office. "Hey, Tony, are you glad to be changing jobs?" I asked.

"Look, Bus, I helped select a large number of the political appointees in the department," said DeMartino. "I also know where a lot of the bodies are buried around here. I'll have Shanahan up and running in no time." DeMartino also enjoyed a background in strategic planning, a great resource for a new deputy secretary who lacked military and government experience.

Shanahan had big shoes to fill. His predecessor, Bob Work, a former Marine, performed well as deputy secretary, advancing the military's use of cutting-edge technologies through the department's "third offset strategy." Shanahan needed to keep the momentum going on innovation.

Designed to provide America's military with an asymmetric advantage over an adversary, the military's first offset centered on America's development of nuclear weapons to counter the large number of Cold War Soviet forces. The second offset involved the rise of precision-guided weapons—bombs and missiles delivered using laser or GPS guidance—that enabled US forces to attack targets with pinpoint precision. The third offset strategy, defined but not yet enacted, would bring artificial intelligence, high-speed hypersonic weapons, advanced manufacturing, and other technological advances to bear against modern-day threats. With his decades of manufacturing experience, Shanahan was a natural fit to help the department leap forward.

Beyond all the positive changes, however, the department had become trapped by its own inertia and wedded to the status quo. The equipment we bought cost a fortune—we paid more and got less for most everything, including ships, aircraft, and ground vehicles. Members of the "status quo" camp claimed that less, but more powerful, equipment was better for the military. But at some point, fewer ships—or other equipment—just means a reduced capacity to influence world events or successfully wage war in time of conflict. Just as troubling, our "tooth to tail" ratio was out of balance. We had far more people dedicated to support roles than to actual warfighting.

Even the department's claimed victories in fixing these issues were turning out to be a bit of a sham. Take the F–35 Joint Strike Fighter, America's newest and stealthiest fighter plane. It's the largest single defense program in history, estimated to cost more than $1 trillion. To score political points, Trump belatedly inserted himself into ongoing discussions with its manufacturer, defense contractor Lockheed Martin, to try to lower the cost for each aircraft.

He accomplished nothing but subsequently boasted that he'd saved the program $700 million for the next round of aircraft purchases. The only problem? Those savings had been already planned for years in advance—costs decreased as the rate of production increased and more orders rolled in. Lockheed officials, sensitive to the president's ego, said that his involvement sped up negotiations. "This was a thing that was out of control and now it's great," Trump said. No, not at all, but it was important to pick our battles. Having Deputy Shanahan now on board would give us some more leverage to actually fix the big, systemic problems within the Pentagon.

Sally Donnelly pulled me into her office shortly after Shanahan's arrival. "Hey, Bus," she asked, "What do you think Mattis's legacy will be?" I didn't miss a beat. "That's easy," I said. "The department's three lines of effort. But of the three, the one that'll really matter a decade from now is if Shanahan is truly able to 'reform the department for performance and affordability.'" Improving how the department buys equipment, manages talent and encourages retention, and incentivizes risk-tasking could positively alter the very fabric of our military.

The division of labor between Mattis and Shanahan was clear. As secretary of defense, Mattis looked "up and out" from the department, focusing his efforts on the military's lethality and building strong international alliances. Shanahan looked inward, taking responsibility for tackling business reforms within the department. As a business executive, Trump felt the most affinity for the third priority, a reality that put Shanahan in a relatively good long-term position.

Tony and I had talked at length about the right way to "staff" Shanahan. It was well within bounds to create another speech team to cover the deputy's needs, but I demurred. I felt it would be better to handle both Mattis and Shanahan with a single, unified speech team. We already had enough disconnect in this administration. Writing for both Mattis and Shanahan would ensure a consistent message between leaders. But that decision meant that I was now chief speechwriter for Mattis and Shanahan. This led to a significantly increased workload for a smaller-than-normal speech team already punching above its weight.

To be honest, a big part of me just wanted to work with someone from a completely different background than my own. I was looking forward to learning how to operate the Pentagon more like a business than a government behemoth. As Shanahan told me, "Businesses strive to get the best value for every dollar spent. Government is used to spending every last penny appropriated to it so that it can get the same—or more—the next year." As a military, we needed to learn how to extract the most value from every taxpayer dollar spent on America's defense.

Of course, having the right team in place was only one part of the equation when it came to enacting the president's agenda. A deep knowledge of history and broad connections were also important, and might serve to negate the need for tweets to drive policy.

Mattis's personal web of external connections ran deep, a fact highlighted during a special, undercover trip in August. While Mattis was out touring West Coast technology companies, I was on a train speeding toward New York City to accept a highly sensitive personal package for the boss.

Henry Kissinger had been trying to get some of his personal notes to Mattis for the better part of two weeks. The former secretary of state for presidents Nixon and Ford, Kissinger had mentored Mattis for many years, and he wanted to pass along some of his personal material. The kicker was that he considered his notes so sensitive that he didn't want to mail them—he only wanted them hand-carried. This was extraordinary. The US government routinely mails classified material to other offices as long as it is properly handled, wrapped, and tracked during shipment. What could be so important that it required a courier to hand-carry it?

The task was originally assigned to another of Mattis's special assistants, a Marine infantry officer. Like most people in the front office, he had previously served with the secretary. In his case, he'd served as aide de camp when Mattis was a three-star general in charge of US Marine Forces Central Command. But he was joining Bushman and Mikolay on the trip to the West Coast and wasn't available for the Kissinger mission. I was asked to fill in.

I had finished reading Walter Isaacson's biography *Kissinger* a few months before, and his subject made for a fascinating historical figure. Kissinger had climbed to the top of international diplomacy in the 1970s, then managed to exploit that position for continued influence—and financial gain—in the decades since. What information would he share with Mattis?

I worked with Kissinger's staff to arrange a time to come by, coordinated with our travel office, and then took a 6:00 a.m. train from Washington to New York's Penn Station. I hiked the mile and a half over to Kissinger Associates, located in a nondescript Park Avenue skyscraper. A member of Kissinger's staff popped out upon my arrival, handed me a sealed 11×14 manila envelope, asked me to sign for it, and that was it. I hurried back to the train.

I dutifully dropped the package off on Faller's desk along with a quick note signifying "mission complete." The only hint as to the contents was the table of contents that Kissinger's point of contact had handed to me. Listed were multiple transcripts of conversations Kissinger conducted with world leaders and foreign interlocutors, no doubt to influence Mattis's view of current world events.

About a week later, Sally Donnelly came by and dropped the manila package off at my desk. "Hey, Bus, here you go. Take a look if you want."

Inside were twelve transcripts of conversations between Kissinger and world leaders he had interacted with. The transcripts included conversations between Kissinger and Russian President Vladimir Putin and Foreign Minister Sergey Lavrov, Chinese President Xi Jinping, and several other Chinese and Indian functionaries. Every transcript reflected an attempt to strengthen relationships with the United States. Lavrov, for example, lamented Congress's desire to find any pretense to make Trump's life miserable, but said that Russia was ready to move forward with an improved US-Russia relationship as fast and as deep as Trump's administration felt comfortable.

Evidently, Kissinger was still sought after as a go-between with other nations, someone who can carry messages back and forth under the radar, what is referred to as "track two," or back-channel, diplomacy. What struck me the most was that Kissinger only provided Mattis with a transcript of what other leaders discussed—everything Kissinger had said was redacted. *What had Kissinger told them?* Was Kissinger being an honest broker, or merely feeding Mattis selective information to influence decisions?

It appeared the shadowy Oracle of Park Avenue didn't want anyone to know, not even his protégé, Mattis. If only the White House could have remained so tight-lipped about major policy decisions. Or at least informed us before announcing them.

The trip to New York City caused me to reflect. I retrieved my copy of *Kissinger* and reviewed the notes I had scribbled in each chapter. What stood out was that even in the Nixon White House, much of the administration's diplomacy had been carefully crafted and coordinated. While not perfect—it never is—the actions they took across departments had aligned to achieve strategic results. I felt we were losing a step in the Trump administration by not carefully coordinating significant policy announcements across every branch of the government, or at a minimum, the departments directly affected by the announcements.

While the transgender tweets weren't the last surprise we would endure from the White House, fortunately we did manage to coordinate a better rollout for our next major announcement.

EIGHT

WAG THE DOG

Integrity is doing the right thing when you don't
have to—when no one else is looking or will ever
know—when there will be no congratulations
or recognition for having done so.

—CHARLES MARSHALL

"Sir, can I get you anything else before we land?"

I looked up from my laptop and noticed a member of our flight crew standing in the doorway. "No, but thanks for asking, Alex. I'm all set. Appreciate all the support this flight."

"No worries, sir," she replied. "Have a good time in Amman."

We were about fifteen minutes out from landing in Jordan, the first stop of our overseas trip. It was August 20, and this was my first international trip with Secretary Mattis and his team. We'd also make stops in Turkey, Iraq, and Ukraine before heading back to Washington.

I stretched my arms to get the blood flowing again after an eleven-hour flight. We'd pulled a "Mattis Special," which is to say that despite taking off at 9:00 p.m., we'd worked during the entire flight. Internationally, we always flew on the E-4B "Night-watch" plane, one of only four in existence. Whenever we were airborne, it assumed the title of "National Airborne Operations Center." Although utilitarian—it had none of the creature comforts of Air Force One—it was enjoyable to fly on board, reminding me of the mission-oriented focus on board an aircraft carrier on patrol.

At the very front of the aircraft is the secretary's private cabin, complete with a desk, personal restroom, couch, and a bed for long flights (though Mattis rarely, if ever, slept on flights). Directly behind his cabin is the galley for food preparation as well as the main entrance where the secretary enters and exits the plane. Behind the galley is a fully self-contained conference room, used by the true insiders on the secretary's personal staff. Every person had both their unclassified and secret laptops ready and waiting for them as each flight began. The Pentagon employs different computer systems for different levels of classification, and we needed to stay connected and up to speed on the latest events, especially during weeklong trips.

The conference room's back wall had a large television and clocks that displayed the current time in Washington, the time in our destination city, and the travel time remaining for each leg of the trip.

Behind us was the cabin reserved for the traveling press pool. We could carry members of the press, but Mattis decided early on to limit the number to between eight and ten. He didn't like landing in a foreign country and having a million people spill out of the aircraft—he preferred to travel relatively light. It also meant that Dana White, our head of Public Affairs, could use those eight seats as carrots for the media. White had plenty of experience in DC: a previous job in the Pentagon working on policy, followed by stints as a Senate staffer in Congress and private-sector communications roles. Her unspoken rule for members of the press was "Behave and you might be invited on the next trip. Write an article that the secretary doesn't like and, well . . ."

Next was the largest area of the plane, a cabin filled with the airborne equivalent of workstations for other members of the secretary's staff and the country experts we'd take with us during overseas travel, as well as our communications specialists and security agents. On this trip we were first heading to the Middle East, so members of the "Policy" shop that worked that region of the world were on board. As we shifted over to Ukraine, those members would fly commercial back to the US. Meanwhile, the European team would fly out to meet us and then fly back to the US with us. Overall, the system worked very well. We benefited from having the experts with us, and they gained valuable experience to further hone their craft.

The last segment of the plane consisted of extra seats and a sleeping area with about ten beds, most of which were stacked three high. These were a precious commodity. Being assigned a bed meant you'd made the big leagues, even if you didn't get the chance to use it. Seasoned professionals, like the Navy captain in charge of travel operations, just slept on the floor of the aircraft, a jacket thrown over their faces to shut out the light.

On many of the flights, however, we'd just stay awake and work all the way through to support the boss.

I completed a final scan of my inbox as the wheels touched down, then closed the lids to both laptops so the communications team could quickly collect them for transport to our workspace in the hotel communications room. Those of us in the conference room stood and started to make our way over to the front door. That's when Rear Admiral Faller caught my attention.

"Hey, Bus, I want you to take the lead on the rollout plan for the president's South Asia strategy."

I was caught off guard. I had written the final version of the strategy for Afghanistan and the cover letters addressed to congressional leadership but hadn't participated in any rollout or strategy planning meetings.

The strategy document itself had been a mess. The Policy shop had sent their draft to our front office, where it ran into the brick wall known as Kevin Sweeney. He immediately declared it "crap" and ordered me to rewrite the entire strategy . . . in one day. I'd managed to pull it off to his—and the secretary's— satisfaction in time for it to be transmitted to the White House for President Trump's review. The downside was that we cut the Policy team completely out during the rewrite, making the front office a single point of failure, a tendency we would repeat often in the coming months.

Faller was waiting for my answer. "Sir, happy to help but I'm not tracking on the rollout plan."

"I don't care, Bus. We're going to be extremely busy on this trip and I need you on point for this one. This is the administration's first major rollout. We can't afford to screw it up."

So I did what all military officers are trained to do—salute smartly and figure it out later. "Yes, sir. I'm on it."

A Marine lieutenant colonel sat next to Faller. A member of our front office team, he was with us on this trip to coordinate information arriving for the secretary, so I expected he'd know more than I did on this one.

"Colonel, can we chat in a bit? I'd love to see where we are for the rollout." The lieutenant colonel looked up at me, his expression conveying frustration mixed with complete disinterest. "Naw, I think you're good, Bus. It looks like you've got everything you need."

This was odd. He was plugged in tight with Faller and the Pentagon staff, so if anyone knew what was going on, it'd be him. Despite the repeated last-minute scrambles from the White House, there was absolutely no way that we hadn't come up with some semblance of a plan for the rollout, even a basic one.

I pushed it aside. "No problem. Let's catch up when we get to the hotel and figure out a way forward."

The aircraft doors swung open, and we spilled out. We snaked our way to the waiting caravan of cars and jumped inside.

Travel with the secretary is a well-oiled machine. The travel team works hard to ensure everyone has everything they need to stay focused on the task at hand. Envelopes awaited us as we climbed into our assigned van. Inside were room keys, a list of room assignments, and even coupons for the hotel's morning breakfast. Mattis finished shaking hands on the tarmac, climbed into his sedan, and sped off. Our vans followed close behind.

A dozen police cars escorted us into Amman. Streets were shut down in anticipation of our motorcade. Police and military waved us through each turn. Twenty-five minutes later we arrived at the hotel in downtown Amman.

The secretary's personal staff proceeded to our rooms on the main floor. We always dedicated several rooms on our floor for communication gear and workspace for our computers. The comms team headed straight to those rooms, installing our laptops and printers so that we could operate as seamlessly as if back in the Pentagon. Although operating on a much more senior level, it reminded me of my time as a TOPGUN instructor: no messing around—all business, with everyone pitching in for team success.

I caught the lieutenant colonel inside the hotel. "Hey, what do you have for me on this rollout plan?" He just shrugged. "I think you're all set, Bus." He seemed upset, but I couldn't pin down why that would be. I headed off to the secretary's comms room to read email, start a rollout plan from scratch, and check in with Stephen Miller, my counterpart in the White House.

Miller was a fascinating character. A far-right ideologue who had worked for Senator Jeff Sessions (R-AL), he had a reputation for being a provocateur and difficult to work with. He was also regarded as the mastermind behind Trump's hardline immigration stance.

He occupied two positions for Trump: senior policy adviser and de facto chief speechwriter. Despite his television persona, I found Miller relatively easy to work with when it came to coordinating speeches for Trump, Mattis, and other senior administration officials.

Miller emailed me the latest draft of the president's upcoming speech to announce his Afghanistan strategy, though we had

taken to calling it a "South Asia" strategy to reflect that its importance extended far beyond any single country. Flipping through
the speech, I knew Mattis was going to be disappointed. The
draft Miller shared was an "America First, America Only" ora-
tion from start to finish, implying that our allies and partners
took no part in attempting to bring the Taliban to the negotiating table. As written, the speech would inflict lasting damage on
America's relationships, further isolating us from our overseas
allies.

Sure enough, Mattis was not pleased. He summoned Faller,
Dana, Sam—our embedded intelligence officer—and me.

"How bad is it?" asked Mattis.

"Well, sir, it's focused solely on America without any mention of our allies and partners in the region." I paused. "Bottom
line, it doesn't include any of the language we need to recognize
our allies. I want to go back to Miller and add language to help
us take our own side in this fight. Then we can point back to this
speech as a foundation for the next year or two."

Mattis pondered this. "Do it. America first doesn't mean America alone." He continued to flip through the president's draft,
obviously frustrated. "You're right, it doesn't mention a single
one of the thirty-eight nations assisting us with this fight. We
don't do things *to* our allies. . . . We have to work by, with, and
through our partners. No nation can do this alone." We continued for the next few minutes before he motioned me off to get
to work. Another key point: Mattis wanted Trump's speech to
make it clear that we waged war on terrorism, not the nation of
Afghanistan like the current draft suggested.

This is one of the areas where my job proved to be powerful.

After five months, I knew what Mattis stood for as well as the points that the Department of Defense needed to make to enable us to piggyback off the president's speech for the next couple of years. This was also a military-centric speech, so Miller needed my help with that. It was simply (if such matters are simple) a matter of cutting about two pages of the president's speech and inserting everything we needed to hear the president say. If my material survived, we'd always be able to fall back on this major policy speech with, "as President Trump said on August 21 . . ." to bolster our position.

So that's exactly what I did. The final speech included language emphasizing that our allies were in this fight every bit as much as we were. The new strategy was a conditions-based, not time-based approach. We were implementing *all* elements of American power, not just military. Allies play a significant role in the strategy: NATO is a key part of this fight, as are the people of Afghanistan. I wrote it exactly like I knew Mattis would want to say it if he was giving the speech.

Miller accepted my changes, passing them along to the president in the next draft. It represented a significant achievement for Mattis, the department, and our allies. Most importantly, it was the right thing to do. The new language was reflective of international teamwork versus an America-only approach. Better yet, it represented what we could achieve when we worked together as a coordinated, well-planned administration team.

The only sticking point was the location for the speech. Mattis was troubled that the president was planning to use Fort Myer, adjacent to Arlington National Cemetery. That location would once again inject the military into a political position. Worse,

Trump wanted the room filled with military members in uniform to serve as his backdrop. Mattis was adamant that no military members should take part, but to no avail. The president wanted troops as a backdrop, so that's what he ultimately got.

I returned to the painful process of starting a rollout plan from scratch. All I knew was that Mattis and other cabinet officials would need to make calls to senior members of Congress and our international allies and partners in advance of the major policy speech. Where to start?

The lieutenant colonel had returned to our comms room, so I asked for a third time, "Isn't there something conjured up somewhere? Has the NSS [National Security Staff] given us anything?"

He gave me the same soft soap as before. "I think you're on the right track, Bus. I'll be sure to let you know if I hear anything."

Later that night, Faller pulled the lieutenant colonel, Sam, and me into his hotel room. "Bus, where do we stand on that rollout plan?"

"Sir, I'm going to need some more time. It's 4:00 a.m. back in the US and I can't get ahold of anyone to confirm who the boss should call, let alone get phone numbers for the members of Congress. I put together an Excel spreadsheet with placeholders but it's not ready yet."

"That's B.S., Bus!" Faller was unmistakably upset now, and we were all tired. "This rollout is happening in less than thirty-six hours and you don't have a plan yet?" *Oh, boy,* I thought. *You just handed this to me with zero notice about five hours ago, and I've spent most of that time working to rewrite parts of a presidential speech. How in the world would I have this ready to go by now?*

The lieutenant colonel had been standing to my left, but now he stepped forward and slightly in front of me. "Hey, sir, we can't blame Bus—this is his first trip. I've got some stuff on my computer. Give me a few minutes and I can take care of it."

The lieutenant colonel dashed off to our comms room. Now I was upset. This was the first time I'd been deliberately torpedoed by a coworker. Perhaps I had been lucky throughout my nineteen-year career. More likely, it was a reflection on my profession as an F/A-18E Super Hornet pilot, a community where trust is paramount. We had to be able to look at the young sailors who had prepared the aircraft and trust that when they said, "Sir, your plane is ready," that in fact it was. Each time, every time.

The lieutenant colonel returned to the room and handed some materials to Faller, who departed to transmit them to Mattis. I rarely curse, but I was tired and angry. "What the f—k was that?" I asked the lieutenant colonel. He looked at me. "What do you mean?"

"You know exactly what I mean. I asked you three times for support and you told me you had nothing. You set me up for failure and then swooped in to save the day at my expense. That's B.S."

He softened slightly. "Look man, I've been working on that rollout for over a month. Then Faller assigns it to you at the last minute, right before we get off the plane? That's not cool."

Ultimately, we both talked ourselves down out of the rafters. It had been my first real taste of "politics in DC." I never would have expected something like this from our own team, let alone another military officer. *Semper Fidelis?* Not this time. I was reminded of a Mattisism that applied to this situation: "Use initiative and aggressiveness to go after what needs to be done, but retain a spirit of collaboration with the members your team assembled around the table." That hadn't happened here.

The rollout was pulled together at the last minute, and Mattis was able to call the individuals that the NSC had assigned to him. I woke up at 3:00 a.m. on Tuesday morning in Amman to watch President Trump's speech live from our communications room. Mattis joined me a few minutes later, as did Faller, Stoddard, and a few other teammates. The president performed admirably, and all of our language had survived into his delivered version. Faller, sitting next to me, thumped my leg about halfway through. I looked over, and he shot me an emphatic thumbs-up.

Trump wrapped it up after twenty-six minutes. Mattis had been leaning forward in his chair, watching the television intently the entire time. He stood up and looked my way. "Nice work, Bus."

Everything worked out in the end, but it would have been a lot easier without the "friendly fire" from the lieutenant colonel. It was a strong lesson—we had a good team, but it was still necessary to watch your own back.

NINE

GOOD COP, BAD COP

Most of us spend too much time on what is urgent
and not enough time on what is important.

—STEPHEN R. COVEY

"Hey Bus, here you go. I made some minor alterations throughout. Overall, they look good. Can you go ahead and make the
changes now?" Mattis handed back the draft remarks for the day's
bilateral meeting with his counterpart, the newly appointed Indian Minister of Defense Nirmala Sitharaman.

It was the end of September, and we were in New Delhi, the
first stop of a weeklong trip that would take us to Afghanistan
and Qatar. The focus of our India stop was to build on goodwill
generated by Trump's June White House meeting with Indian
Prime Minister Narendra Modi. We saw India, the world's largest

democracy, as a natural strategic partner in the region. Last month's South Asia strategy rollout had been well received internationally, so our trip presented an opportunity to build support in the region. The best way to do this was through Mattis's speaking engagements.

"Yes sir. On it." I took the speech and made my way over to my laptop. I glanced down at my watch. Ouch—less than ten minutes until Mattis was scheduled to depart the hotel. This was going to be close. I caught movement out of the corner of my eye and noticed him still standing in the doorway, waiting for my changes.

I was about halfway through when he piped up again. "How we looking, Bus?" I didn't even glance up, so as not to waste precious time. He could obviously see I was typing furiously on the keyboard.

"I need another few minutes, sir." His shuffling in the doorway made me look over, catching him temporarily dour before he resumed his normally impassive demeanor. "No sweat, Bus. Go ahead. Take your time." He stepped back into the hallway to talk with Faller while I finished up. It was going to be one of *those* days. Because we moved so fast, Mattis could be both meticulous and impatient. It was easy to draw his ire if a single word was misspelled or punctuation was found out of place. Still, he always wanted everything *right now*. It was a delicate balancing act and difficult to get right, even on a good day. This wasn't unusual. My time as a TOPGUN instructor and previously as a speechwriter had been similar: move with "a sense of urgency" while ensuring accuracy at the same time.

I finished typing up my changes and sent the updated document to the printer. A minute later I was out in the hallway with copies—for Mattis, Faller, and Mattis's aide de camp, Ryan Stoddard. "Okay, Bus, are all the changes in here?" Mattis flipped through the new pages. I nodded. "Yes, sir, I went through and double-checked." He slipped the remarks into his folder, saying, "Alright then. So let it be written, so let it be done." With that, he walked briskly back down the hallway to his room to grab his bag before joining the motorcade.

After a long night, it was great to have a little downtime while Mattis attended meetings. North Korea was back to its normal tricks, launching three short-range ballistic missiles in its latest test. Mattis and Faller had shuttled in and out of the comms room all night to check on the status of the launches. As was the norm on overseas trips, a member of the action group and I arose at 5:15 a.m. to check every overnight email and message that had come in. The department has global responsibilities, so emails arrived not only from the Pentagon but from our outlying combatant commands, each responsible for a distinct world region. Updates we deemed important would be printed, highlighted, then stacked on Faller's laptop so he could review them when he arrived around 5:30 a.m. It was critically important to be out in front of Mattis, who typically arrived by 6:00 a.m.

My stock had continued to rise during the first five months on the team. I was now a permanent fixture on the secretary's traveling team. Justin Mikolay, my original boss, who held the title of director of strategic communications, had left the team earlier in the month to pursue opportunities in the private sector. With his departure, I became the director of communications in addition to my current responsibilities as chief speechwriter for both Secretary Mattis and Deputy Secretary Shanahan. I was now responsible for coordinating and aligning our public/private message within the administration, at the Pentagon, and with our allies and partners. As a Navy commander, I was in uncharted territory. My team of two speechwriters was now handling the duties that had historically required eight. We were swamped with little relief in sight, but they continued to perform marvelously.

Having completed our meetings in India, we boarded the plane for Mattis's next stop: Afghanistan. He traveled to Afghanistan several times a year, a chance to reinforce America's commitment to both the region and the counterterrorism campaign being waged there. The primary event was a tricky one, a joint press conference in Afghanistan. I needed to coordinate and align three sets of remarks: the first for our host, President Ashraf Ghani of Afghanistan; the second for NATO Secretary General Jens Stoltenberg; and the third for Mattis. Stoltenberg was there with Mattis to reinforce a message of the NATO coalition's unity in fighting the war on terrorism in Afghanistan.

Stoltenberg summed up Trump's recently announced South Asia strategy succinctly, saying that it was "about making sure that Afghanistan doesn't once again become a safe haven for international terrorists." For Mattis, the visit was an opportunity to reinforce America's unity with international partners. He highlighted the determination of all thirty-nine partner nations involved with NATO's Resolute Support Mission and reinforced the message that the Afghan people—not foreigners—were taking the lead in securing their own country.

The trip was also Mattis's opportunity to counterbalance Trump's ever-changing proclamations.

The week before, Trump had addressed 192 countries at the UN General Assembly in New York. The president began positively enough, saying, "This institution was founded in the aftermath of two world wars to help shape this better future. It was based on the vision that diverse nations could cooperate to protect their sovereignty, preserve their security, and promote their prosperity."

This was language we had passed off to the president's speechwriters. The first part of his speech extolled how such international organizations provided invaluable "pillars of peace." But then his speech turned aggressive. Trump's language became alarming. Referencing North Korea, Trump blustered, "The United States has great strength and patience. But if it is forced to defend itself or its allies, we will have no choice but to *totally destroy* North Korea. Rocket Man is on a suicide mission for himself and for his regime." The camera panned to show Secretary Tillerson and UN Ambassador Nikki Haley, the former governor of South Carolina, looking on, both stone-faced.

Trump characterized Iran as "an economically depleted rogue state whose chief exports are violence, bloodshed, and chaos." He continued, "Frankly, that deal [the Iran nuclear agreement made under President Obama] is an embarrassment to the United States, and I don't think you've heard the last of it, believe me.

"As president of the United States, I will always put America first, just like you as the leaders of your countries will always and should always put your countries first," Trump said. "The United States will forever be a great friend to the world and especially to its allies," he continued, "but we can no longer be taken advantage of or enter into a one-sided deal where the United States gets nothing in return."

Once again, President Trump's words were counter to the reassurances Tillerson and Mattis had provided to their international counterparts. This doubtlessly left our allies wondering, *Who speaks the truth for the United States? Is there a coordinated strategy here?*

Unfortunately, the answer was no. It felt like poor "good cop, bad cop" playacting. And it was a far cry from Trump's July speech in Warsaw, where he had vowed, "The transatlantic bond between the United States and Europe is as strong as ever and maybe, in many ways, even stronger." Frankly, I found *that* speech uplifting and well delivered. Mattis expressed frustration with the situation. Like the transgender tweets, it seemed like the president wasn't carrying out a well-thought-out plan but rather reacting uniquely to each moment in time.

Our disjointed approach and conflicting announcements made it difficult for allies, partners, and even Americans to understand where the administration actually stood on issues of long-standing significance.

At the Pentagon we were, once again, caught off guard. The White House had provided me with the president's latest draft UN speech, but the alarmist language he actually delivered hadn't been included, so there was no opportunity to flag any concerns. The draft I saw held Iran, North Korea, and others accountable for their actions using language the various relevant arms of the administration had collectively agreed to. The speech was significantly transformed to include this more inflammatory language only at the last minute.

Once again, we weren't coordinated on the world stage. Moreover, differences in personalities and priorities, even within the "adults in the room," impeded efforts to improve the outcome.

In Qatar, at the end of the trip, we boarded our E-4B for the flight back to Washington. It was going to be brutal—fifteen long hours. The E-4B crew was qualified to conduct aerial refueling, so we never once stopped, no matter how long the flight was. Instead, fully loaded tanker aircraft met us at various points along our route to deliver more fuel while we were airborne. Scheduled to land back at Andrews AFB just before midnight, we'd be working the entire flight home. In total, we'd have been awake for over thirty hours as we landed.

We were airborne for a few hours when we got word that National Security Adviser H. R. McMaster wanted to speak to Mattis on the phone.

The communications team connected the White House Situation Room with Mattis's phone on the plane, routing the conversation into the conference room so that several of us could listen in (as was standard practice). Stoddard made his way back to Mattis's cabin. "Sir, we have General McMaster on the line."

Mattis glanced up. "Okay, thanks, Ryan." He picked up the headset. "Hello, H.R., you there?"

"Good evening, Mr. Secretary."

The first few minutes went well, but McMaster was obviously amped up, almost like he'd inhaled one too many energy drinks. When Mattis pressed him for help with the president, McMaster chimed right in with an exasperated tone, "Mr. Secretary, you don't know *how it is* over here. I'm doing everything I can. It doesn't work the way you think."

McMaster had a point. His proximity to the Oval Office meant that he was much closer to the action than we were. Mc-Master was also being denied the one resource he needed most from Tillerson and Mattis: empathy. Despite their differences, Mattis owed McMaster an opportunity to build harmony across the administration. As Mattis had said many times, "leaders must be willing to listen to others . . . to be persuaded." But he wasn't giving McMaster that chance, weakening McMaster's standing within the White House and the administration. Mattis's failure to strengthen McMaster's position diminished one of his most important allies in the White House—and we needed all the friends we could get.

Compared to McMasters's case of jitters, Mattis sounded professorial by comparison, answering with a steady, measured tone, "Well, now, H.R. . . ."

When he got this excited, McMaster would interrupt Mattis mid-sentence, which Mattis hated. Their conversation grew heated, and the boss just stopped talking altogether.

"Mr. Secretary, are you there?" In the background, I could hear him telling someone that he thought that the call had disconnected. We could hear him loud and clear, but Mattis was simply icing him out. He waited another five seconds before saying, "H.R., you there? I think I lost you for a second."

Overall, it went like this with most of Mattis's calls with Mc-Master. There were few people in the administration who could get as firmly under the secretary's skin as the national security adviser.

Mattis wasn't alone in his frustration. Tillerson complained to him on a weekly basis about McMaster and his running of the "interagency process," a term describing the coordination between the White House and each of the executive branch departments.

Tillerson and Mattis were frustrated by McMaster's attempts to consolidate power. They felt he was using the National Security Staff to direct policy from the West Wing rather than as an honest broker coordinating and aligning interagency efforts.

Tillerson simply chose to ignore most of McMaster's directives. True, he might align with McMaster in general. But Tillerson would periodically freeze him out, ignoring memos or requests from McMaster he didn't agree with. Mattis occasionally did the same.

After the call, Mattis returned to the conference room. Shifting gears, he looked ahead to the next week's events. Catching Faller's attention, he announced, "Craig, I want to make sure everyone is taking a day off tomorrow. It's been a long week." Faller replied smartly, "Yes, sir, I was just looking at that plan now." That meant Faller would start planning as soon as Mattis left the room.

Mattis looked across the table at me. "Bus, I'll need you with me tomorrow for a one-on-one meeting I'm having with Senator McCain," he said. Mattis paused before saying, "Oh, never mind. You'll need to take tomorrow off because of the trip."

The meeting was an opportunity to align my writing of Mattis's South Asia strategy congressional testimony, scheduled for delivery the following week. It was paramount to include what he and McCain would discuss during their meeting, ensuring his testimony was aligned with McCain's expectations. "Sir, no, I'm good. I'm writing your remarks for the Senate hearing, so it makes sense for me to accompany you."

Mattis thought about this. "No . . . no . . . you've been work-ing hard. How about I take your new speechwriter, Nicole [Magney], with me?" I was grateful for the offer of time off, but I knew it would make more work for me in the long run. Mag-ney was a brand-new addition to the team and hadn't yet learned the boss's voice. "Sir, she just joined the team. If she goes with you, she'll have to turn right back around and repeat all her notes back to me so I can write your opening remarks. We'll be play-ing a game of telephone. We won't have much time between your meeting and the testimony." But he didn't budge from his position and left the conference room to head back to the desk in his cabin.

Faller looked over and said, "Forget it, Bus. He never changes his mind once it's made up."

"Yeah," I said, "but it's a bad decision. Doing it this way will make things far more difficult than they need to be. Writing his remarks will take twice as much work," before heading out of the conference room to follow the secretary.

I knocked on his door, which was already open. "Sir, do you have a second?" He looked up, surprised. "Sure, Bus, come on in."

The plane is loud, so I walked over and took a knee beside him at his desk. "Sir, I appreciate what you're trying to do for my family. It'd actually mean a lot more if I could have next Wednes-day off so I can take my wife to lunch. If you're willing to do that for us, then I can go with you tomorrow to ensure I get all of McCain's needs to write your testimony."

Mattis smiled. "Okay, Bus, only if it'll help you out. Don't come in too early tomorrow. Let's plan to meet up around 8:30

a.m. to head over." That worked for me—a chance to see the children off to school for a change. "Yes, sir, it's a deal."

Faller was floored when he learned Mattis had changed his mind. "That's the first time I've seen that. Nice job, Bus." I suspect Mattis felt inclined to give in as a way of saying, *Well done. You felt a strong conviction and stuck to your guns.* It was a tremendous confidence boost.

There was a downside, however. The person most appropriate to join Mattis, our assistant secretary of defense for legislative affairs, Rob Hood, was cut out of the loop.

Hood's career included a wealth of experience in Congress and President Bush's (43) White House. Hood's stock, however, was down in Sweeney's and Faller's eyes. The legislative affairs team was taking arrows for missing the mark on products and planning for the secretary. Rather than provide Hood with guidance to help course correct, Sweeney and Faller consistently trashed him behind the scenes to Mattis.

Trusting his lieutenants, Mattis soured on Hood for a period of time. This kept Hood out of the loop on important engagements or planning processes like this one. It was a lost opportunity. Hood's team wasn't making mistakes on purpose— they just weren't aware of the way Mattis liked to be prepared for congressional events. Hood was not alone—this cycle repeated at various times between Faller, Sweeney, and other senior leaders. A few of us in the secretary's front office assisted Hood and his team behind the scenes, working constructively to improve communication flow and the quality of their products.

The next morning, Mattis and I climbed into the back of his

Suburban, just the two of us, for the meeting with McCain. Mattis made idle small talk as we drove across the Potomac and toward the Capitol. A member of the Capitol Hill police met us at the drop-off point, walking us through the twisting underground passageways and into a conference center private room to meet with McCain.

McCain had Chris Brose, the staff director of the Armed Services Committee, with him. Mattis always required military members to be in uniform, so I wore my service dress blue uniform. McCain, himself a former naval aviator and a legend to members of the military, had just been diagnosed with glioblastoma—a rare brain tumor. He nonetheless made it a point to come over, shake my hand, and chat for a few minutes.

Despite the initial pleasantries, what followed was one of the most uncomfortable meetings during my time in Mattis's office.

Mattis started off. "Senator, I'm here today to listen to you and I've prepared accordingly," he said, motioning to the materials on the table. The secretary had packed a bag chock full of binders and folders, unsure of where their conversation might go.

McCain cut straight to the chase. "Mr. Secretary, I have an appreciation for you and your leadership team at the Pentagon. I admit I'm no fan of President Trump but think he's done okay during his first six months. I remain dedicated to your leadership. However, during your confirmation you said we'd be in communication with each other, but this is only the third time in *nine months* that I've seen you."

Uh—oh. This was a bad start. McCain was obviously agitated.

McCain continued, "There's a whole lot going on around the world but no one is coming over to inform us. There's been no hearing to make us aware of what's happening. You know, I can *subpoena* you if I have to." There was no mistaking McCain's frustration. "I've served on this committee for thirty-one years, and I have not seen an environment with less information in that time."

"Senator, frankly I'm shocked," replied Mattis. "I'm working twenty hours a day at the Pentagon, and I just got off the plane from Qatar at midnight. I thought this [communication with Congress] was one part that was going well."

McCain jumped right back in. "The requirement for a South Asia strategy is written into *law*. Are we ever going to hear about it?" He grew more animated. "Right now, I can't do my job unless you share what's going on. It's one thing to brief the full Senate . . . quite another to brief the committee responsible for exercising oversight authority on the military." McCain was referencing closed-door briefings, first for the House and then for the Senate, that Mattis, accompanied by Tillerson and General Dunford, had conducted three weeks before to unveil our strategy.

Mattis tried to change gears, bringing up a request to confirm department nominees that had stalled with McCain's committee. "Senator, if I could only get our nominees through. We're quite shorthanded . . ."

McCain grew more heated. "I have sympathy for your request but there is an *obligation* for you to brief us."

Mattis still hadn't fully recognized how upset McCain was. "Sir, there just aren't enough hours in the—"

McCain cut him off, visibly fuming. "Mr. Secretary, you have a *constitutional responsibility* to appear before my committee."

The lightbulb went on.

Mattis turned to Chris Brose and said, "Chris, give me a list of topics you want briefed. I will, within forty-eight hours, name a briefer and get them right back over to you."

Having elicited the desired response from Mattis, McCain's demeanor suddenly calmed. He said, "We will get into your department's personnel needs in good time. I continue to have an issue, however, with the 'Big Five' [defense contractors] and what appears to be a revolving door with industry."

Before Mattis could respond, McCain pivoted again to talk about his children. He spoke of them with a great deal of affection, specifically mentioning Jimmy, Jack, and Meghan by name. The meeting concluded, we all shook hands before Mattis and I returned to his vehicle.

It was a very quiet car ride back to the Pentagon.

Mattis had told me several times before that there are only three jobs that he, as secretary of defense, could do: advise the president on military affairs, communicate with his international counterparts, and oversee active, ongoing military operations.

We needed to add a fourth: routine consultations with senior congressional leaders, especially the chairs of defense-specific committees.

For months, Hood had been warning our front office that Congress was grumbling: Mattis wasn't paying them the attention they felt they were due, nor was his stock as high on Capitol Hill as we believed it was. And Hood was right. Congress isn't a military unit—a commander can't issue orders and expect to see them carried out. As a cabinet secretary, Mattis was expected to build relationships and goodwill, and that took time and presence. Not investing in these relationships created unwelcome tension. In the words of former chairman of the Joint Chiefs Admiral Mike Mullen, "Virtual presence is actual absence." If Sweeney and Faller hadn't soured Mattis's relationship with Hood, we might have sidestepped this setback altogether.

The meeting with McCain served as a stark reminder. First, we had to maintain focus on our strategic relationships. It was yet another task among the hundreds that Mattis already had on his plate, but a lesson we couldn't afford to forget. Second, we couldn't afford to marginalize senior leaders within the Pentagon, especially out of petty spite.

Too much was at stake.

TEN

SECRETARY OF REASSURANCE

Yet, for the United States of America, there will
be no forgetting September the 11th.

—GEORGE W. BUSH

Despite the previous week's contentious meeting with McCain,
I appreciated that the senator vented his frustrations to Mattis in
private. Having fired his salvos, I thought McCain would let bygones be bygones during today's hearing.

I was wrong.

In his opening remarks, McCain made it clear that the Senate
Armed Services Committee had been kept in the dark regarding
details of the administration's new strategy. The Trump administration, he insisted, owed him more. Much more. President
Trump had announced the South Asia strategy six weeks before.

It was now October 3. McCain expected a regular flow of detailed information about the war in Afghanistan.

Sixteen years before, our forces had begun combat operations in Afghanistan to eliminate Al Qaeda. The terrorist group, led by Osama bin Laden, had been responsible for carrying out the September 11 attacks. US military forces were widely believed to have achieved their primary mission: prevent Afghanistan from becoming a safe haven for terrorists to attack America or its allies and partners. "But that success has come at a tremendous price," McCain said. "More than two thousand Americans gave their lives in this war." I knew that another twenty thousand had been wounded. The prolonged war on terrorism was exacting a heavy price, in both lives and funds.

After sixteen years of fighting, McCain wondered, did the administration's renewed strategy offer anything original? What innovation would finally jumpstart America to victory in Afghanistan, where so many others, including the British and, more recently, the Soviets, had failed? McCain noted that few leaders in 2001 would have predicted that sixteen years later we would still be fighting in America's longest war. Why was this plan any different?

Mattis shared in private that he felt the war in Afghanistan was fundamentally a winnable proposition. His thinking was underpinned by two core beliefs: First, driving the Taliban to the negotiating table would further reduce safe havens for global terrorists. Second, he felt strongly about the coalition the US had helped to construct in Afghanistan. As he'd shared with the president during the Pentagon meeting, stepping away from another international commitment—one the US led—could be viewed as a further erosion of America's global influence. It also risked weakening our ability to work with allies and partners in the future.

But McCain was right to have a questioning attitude. I was now helping Mattis write the nation's strategy, but even I didn't have a clear answer for when this war would terminate and we could transition to peace in Afghanistan. As a nation we had allowed the fight against terrorism to overtake many of our national priorities. This was allowing other countries—such as Iran, North Korea, Russia, and China—to take advantage of our diverted attention. Without a clear path to victory, we could find ourselves still in Afghanistan ten years later.

I watched as Mattis shuffled his remarks. It was now his turn to respond.

This new strategy was designed from the start to be a combined effort. Mattis emphasized that the war in Afghanistan was not America's alone. The Trump administration's strategy, developed in coordination with thirty-eight allied and partner nations, provided much-needed certainty for the region.

Mattis launched into an explanation of the main points of the strategy using an awkward acronym: "R4+S." It was the administration's attempt to take an incredibly complex subject and turn it into an understandable, somewhat catchy phrase. It'd be hard to convince taxpayers that the new strategy was a game changer if they couldn't understand it.

In a nutshell, the strategy's "R4+S" stands for regionalize, realign, reinforce, reconcile, and sustain.

In the past, Mattis explained, previous American leaders focused exclusively on Afghanistan. This time, the administration would "regionalize" their strategy, ensuring that India, Pakistan, Iran, Russia, and China were considered from the start to help generate support from Afghanistan's neighbors. We would now seek participation, not dictate rigid terms to other sovereign nations.

The administration was also shifting the main effort to "realign" military advisers to provide support to the Afghan army's lower levels where it was more effective. Afghan soldiers were carrying out most of the fighting, but our advisers would accompany tactical units into the field to coordinate airborne fire support when needed. At the time, America provided approximately 11,000 troops to serve alongside 6,800 from NATO and coalition partners. Afghanistan supplied 320,000 national security forces.

Mattis wanted to add an additional 3,000 US troops to extend the advisory effort to Afghan troops—the "reinforce" part of the strategy.

"Reconciliation," said Mattis, "is the desired outcome from our military operations." Convincing our foes that the coalition is committed to a conditions-based outcome, Mattis wanted to force the Taliban, considered to be the current terrorist threat, into reconciling with the Afghan national government. As he said numerous times, "The Taliban have turned to the use of bombs because they know that they cannot win at the ballot box."

Mattis also recognized that any new strategy had to be "sustainable," so it would be carried out with "our Afghan partners and within the coalition framework, ensuring this campaign is politically, fiscally, and militarily sustainable."

I agreed with this latter point—it made no sense to produce

a strategy that was unsustainable. But despite the behind-closed-doors debate raging within military circles about whether we should stay in Afghanistan or not, I wasn't aware of any senior leaders in the Pentagon advocating a withdrawal option. The only path forward—no matter the cost—was to win.

McCain had departed to attend to other matters, leaving Senator Jack Reed (D-RI) to close out the hearing. While plenty of good questions were asked, it wasn't clear if Mattis swayed anyone's opinion. After sixteen years of conflict in Afghanistan, opinions were entrenched.

———

Although the hearing focused on the new South Asia strategy, the overarching topic of the day was terrorism. Despite the administration's multilayered dysfunction—crossed wires, leaks, firings, spurious decisions, and spur-of-the moment tweets—the global fight against terrorism was a case where President Trump and his administration could justifiably claim resounding success. I was surprised we hadn't taken more advantage of that fact.

Trump, having secured the Republican nomination, used terrorism as one of his main talking points to differentiate himself from former secretary of state Hillary Clinton during the run-up to the November 2016 election.

During a campaign stop in Sunrise, Florida, Trump had said, "ISIS [the Islamic State of Iraq and Syria] is honoring President Obama. He is the founder of ISIS . . . He founded ISIS. And, I would say the cofounder would be crooked Hillary Clinton." When asked how he would eradicate the terrorist group, however, he deemed the plan too sensitive to share with the American people. "If I win," he said, "I don't want to broadcast to the enemy exactly what my plan is." It sounded a lot like Richard Nixon's much-derided "secret plan" to win in Vietnam. Trump, however, later course corrected, saying that if elected he would ask his generals to provide him a plan within thirty days.

Trump followed through. By the time I had joined the team in April, the campaign to defeat ISIS was already kicked into high gear. Mattis was holding a meeting with General Joseph Votel, the commander of US Central Command, and other senior military leaders every week. The meeting's frequency was an indicator of the importance Mattis placed on defeating ISIS.

What made ISIS distinctive was their 2014 proclamation that they were a worldwide Islamic caliphate, claiming dominion over all Muslims worldwide. At the time, they controlled territory in the Middle East the size of Colorado. Eight million people were under their control. They were bringing in billions of dollars per year in revenue and plotting major terrorist operations, not only against the United States but actually carrying them out in cities like Brussels, Paris, and Istanbul.

The Obama administration initiated the campaign to defeat ISIS. By the time the Trump administration started in early 2017, fifty percent of the territory had been retaken. On his first day in office, President Trump told Mattis and Brett McGurk, the president's special envoy to the global defeat-ISIS coalition, that he wanted to accelerate the campaign and utterly defeat the physical caliphate.

To accomplish this task, Mattis asked for and received greater delegated authority for military commanders in the field. Trump obliged. President Obama had taken the opposite approach. He had required the military to seek approval from the White House for many of the raids and airstrikes during his tenure, a restriction Trump loosened to enable commanders on the ground to use their best judgment. "No longer will we have slowed decision cycles because Washington has to authorize tactical movements on the ground," said Mattis. "I have absolute confidence as does the president, our commander in chief, in the commanders on the ground."

With some initial successes in hand, Trump wanted Mattis to publicly acknowledge his role in taking the renewed fight to ISIS. He wanted to demonstrate results to set himself apart from Obama.

This resulted in a May Pentagon press conference where Mattis, General Dunford, and McGurk publicly announced the shift in the fight against ISIS. It was my responsibility to craft Mattis's remarks and coordinate the speaking roles between Dunford's and McGurk's staffs to ensure alignment. I kept the remarks apolitical, but Sweeney wisely intervened in the draft, providing Trump with ample credit for unleashing a more aggressive campaign. He knew the president planned to watch the press conference live.

We met in the Pentagon Briefing Room, a venue offering iconic shots of senior department officials. Traditionally, the secretary and other speakers would wait in a nearby green room before taking the stage at the appointed time.

Not Mattis.

He arrived fifteen minutes ahead of schedule and went straight in to speak with similarly early members of the press. Word spread quickly. CNN's longtime Pentagon correspondent,

Barbara Starr, nearly knocked me over as she hustled in to catch Mattis before he began his speech. Arriving early was a savvy move by the secretary, making him seem much more approachable and accessible.

At the appointed time, Mattis took the stage. Dunford and McGurk took up positions to Mattis's left and right. It was a powerful optic—a secretary at war, flanked by the nation's anti-terrorism czar and top general.

Mattis adopted a matter-of-fact demeanor, channeling decades of experience as a senior Marine general. Looking straight at the reporters, he outlined recent Middle East trips that he, Dunford, and McGurk had completed.

"President Trump directed the Department of Defense to lead all departments in a comprehensive review of the campaign," Mattis explained, "He then ordered accelerated operations against ISIS." The most substantial change in the way we'd now approach counterterrorism was a shift from an attrition fight— trying to pick off the enemy—to surrounding ISIS strongholds and *annihilating* them.

This might sound unrestrained, but it was sound strategy that would save lives in the long run. As a broad-based strategy, Mattis wanted to send a clear message: joining with ISIS was a losing proposition. Surrounding terrorists would prevent them from fleeing the combat zone. The last thing we wanted was for them to return to their home country and wreak havoc there.

Although Trump had for months questioned the importance of our allies and partners, Mattis remained steadfast regarding America's alliance structure. He knew defeating ISIS was a global fight requiring global support. Mattis made sure to recognize the state department's "Coalition to Defeat ISIS," a group then comprising sixty-eight members "fully committed at the political and military levels to the destruction of ISIS."

Before yielding the podium to Dunford, Mattis summarized this shift in tactics by promising that it would "crush ISIS's claim of invincibility, deny ISIS a geographic haven from which to hatch murder, eliminate ISIS's ability to operate externally, and eradicate their ability to recruit and finance terrorist operations." The change in tactics was proving effective: not one inch of territory seized from ISIS had been retaken by the terrorists. We were holding on to our gains.

Dunford described the military-specific aspects of the campaign. More important, though, was the role played by McGurk, representing the renewed campaign's diplomatic element. As hostilities concluded, McGurk would coordinate the stabilization efforts needed to restore electricity, running water, and basic services. Failure to do so would only serve to speed ISIS's return. McGurk advocated for a continued US presence to provide stability to newly liberated areas of Iraq and Syria.

Trump's decision to provide the military with greater autonomy led to the defeat of ISIS's physical caliphate with stunning speed. At the time of the press conference, the coalition had retaken over 55 percent of the territory once held by ISIS at the height of their power. By the time Mattis testified to Congress in October, less than six months later, the last stronghold in Raqqa, Syria, the so-called capital of ISIS's physical caliphate, was retaken.

Fighting in the Middle East would begin to slow considerably in the coming year as ISIS's territory continued to shrink. With no safe haven available to flee to, the terrorists dug in for a pro-tracted fight, prolonging the conflict.

The Coalition to Defeat ISIS would expand its membership, soon encompassing seventy-nine nations and international orga-nizations. The fight continued, spanning military, intelligence, economic, and diplomatic lines of effort. Defeating ISIS would remain a top priority, but there were other concerns involving the Middle East.

Mattis and the administration were also concerned about state-sponsored terrorism. We all zeroed in on the country widely considered to be the largest source of funding and training for external terrorism: Iran.

One of the hot-button topics during Mattis's October 2017 testimony was the Obama administration's 2015 agreement with Iran to limit its nuclear weapons capability. Under the terms of the agreement, known as the Joint Comprehensive Plan of Ac-tion, or "JCPOA," Iran committed to forgo the pursuit of nu-clear weapons. As long as Iran fulfilled the terms of the deal, the United States and other countries would lift economic sanctions. It was a polarizing decision. Defense hawks didn't trust the Ira-nian regime. Doves, those opposed to conflict, saw the agree-ment as a bridge to the Iranian people.

The international community was worried about the future of the Iran agreement. After all, it was not just between the US and Iran. Britain, China, France, Germany, and Russia were also signatories. Trump had railed against the Iran agreement while seeking the Republican Party's nomination, saying on the campaign trail that "My number-one priority is to dismantle the disastrous deal with Iran."

Mattis also harbored a long-standing distrust of Iran, and of one man in particular: a powerful Iranian operative, Major General Qasem Soleimani.

Actually, "distrust" doesn't adequately convey Mattis's view of Soleimani—I knew Mattis *hated* him. Normally stoic, Mattis's demeanor visibly soured when discussing his longtime nemesis. The leader of Iran's elite Quds Force, a military unit that handles clandestine operations, Soleimani was viewed as the principal military strategist responsible for countering US efforts in the Middle East.

Another reason for Mattis's hatred may have been that Soleimani was Iran's version of "Mad Dog" Mattis—a widely respected military leader well known for his meticulous planning, a concern for those he leads, and his willingness to visit front-line Iranian troops. Perhaps Mattis saw too much of himself in Soleimani and realized the threat that he posed to American interests. I suspected Soleimani harbored the same feelings about Mattis.

Regardless of the administration's disdain for Iran, after watching the dominos fall on the Paris climate agreement and Trans-Pacific Partnership, allies were left to wonder: Would the US soon be backing out of yet another international agreement? The question was fair game.

The agreement required periodic reviews by the administration to certify Iran's compliance—or lack thereof. Fissures within the administration grew wider when Secretary Tillerson issued the state department's finding that, yes, Iran was complying with the agreement as written.

In a letter to House Speaker Paul Ryan, Tillerson wrote, "This letter certifies that the conditions . . . are met as of April 18, 2017." Translation? Iran hadn't done anything to materially breach the agreement. If the US found otherwise, it would have had options for reimposing or possibly renegotiating sanctions that had been lifted. But there were no violations. Tillerson re-certified Iran's compliance on July 17.

The senators at Mattis's October hearing knew Mattis was a globalist who cared deeply about preserving the rules-based international order, so they sought to highlight this difference with Trump's "America First" policy. Independent senator from Maine, Angus King, went straight for the jugular, pointedly asking, "Do you believe it is in our national security interest at the present time to remain in the JCPOA?"

Mattis paused, weighing the consequence of his words. He stuck to his beliefs despite knowing they would signal a break from the president's vow to scrap the deal.

"Yes, senator, I do." When Senator Mike Rounds, a Republican from South Dakota, followed up on King's question, Mattis stated, "If we can confirm that Iran is living by the agreement, if we can determine that this is in our best interest, then clearly we should stay with it." Mattis had confided to me before the hearing that he worried about leaving the agreement under false pretenses. When America gives her word, she should keep it.

It's a dangerous precedent for Trump to scrap many of his predecessor's international agreements. What will prevent Trump's successor from immediately doing the same to him? Either way, walking away from the agreement would weaken America's standing with our allies and partners.

Tillerson also agreed with Mattis's testimony. While Tillerson felt Iran was taking advantage of the agreement, both he and Mattis understood the importance of America maintaining its international promises. The US should honor its obligations, even if those extended into a prior administration. Both were concerned that continuing to abrogate our global responsibilities could weaken America's standing as the leader of choice. Diminishing that standing could create a vacuum that China, Russia, and others would be more than willing to fill.

As for the Iranian nuclear deal, Tillerson had said, "We'll have a recommendation for the president. We're going to give him a couple of options of how to move forward to advance the important policy toward Iran."

All this sensationalism didn't matter. On October 13, President Trump took to a lectern in the White House to declare that he would not certify that Iran was following the "spirit" of the agreement.

Claiming that "the Iran Deal was one of the worst and most one-sided transactions the United States has ever entered into," Trump proclaimed that he was unwilling to make the certification. "We will not continue down a path whose predictable conclusion is more violence, more terror and the very real threat of Iran's nuclear breakout."

The US was storming away from yet another international agreement.

The administration's fissures were now splitting wide open. A few days before Mattis's testimony, Trump had made headlines for undercutting Tillerson's efforts to apply pressure on North Korea, tweeting, "I told Rex Tillerson, our wonderful Secretary of State, that he is wasting his time trying to negotiate with Little Rocket Man. Save your energy Rex, we'll do what has to be done!"

Mattis's closest friend and confidant in the administration was now under public attack.

The other shoe dropped the day after Mattis's testimony, when NBC reported that Tillerson had called the president a "moron" during Trump's July Pentagon visit. Every major news network shouted the same message: "Tillerson calls Trump a moron." This caught my attention. I'd been at the July meeting and hadn't heard Tillerson utter any such thing. That didn't mean that it hadn't happened, but the timing of this bombshell seemed peculiar, coming months after the meeting.

The situation grew perilous enough to force Tillerson into holding a press conference to dispute the rumors . . . sort of. He never actually disagreed with the reporting.

Asked by a reporter, "Could you address the main headline of the story, that you called the president a moron?" Tillerson replied, "I'm just—I'm not going to deal with petty stuff like that." A man of deep conviction, he expounded. "I mean, this is what I don't understand about Washington. Again, I'm not from this place, but the places I come from, we don't deal with that kind of petty nonsense. And it is intended to do nothing but divide people. And I'm just not going to be part of this effort to divide this administration." Tillerson's nondenial spoke volumes.

Tillerson did, however, take the time to expound on his close relationship with Mattis. "General Mattis and I communicate virtually every day, and we agree that there must be the highest level of coordination between our diplomatic efforts and our military efforts. You can't have a stronger partner than a secretary of defense who embraces diplomacy, and I hope he feels he has the partner he needs at the state department." It was a gracious show of his support for Mattis.

When *Forbes* magazine asked the president about the moron remark, Trump replied, "I think it's fake news but if he did that, I guess we'll have to compare IQ tests. And I can tell you who is going to win . . ." *Yeah,* I thought when I saw the quote, *Tillerson.*

The damage from Tillerson's alleged comment—and the widespread reporting of it—never healed.

Mattis grasped what level of pure venom was playing out in the public space. He addressed the situation on October 6, two days after the press covered Tillerson's comment, at a long-scheduled Senior Leaders Conference at the Pentagon. Originally intending to discuss the forthcoming National Defense Strategy and our strategy for increasing overall military lethality, Mattis felt the climate was so toxic that he dedicated a majority of his opening remarks to recent events.

Mattis advised America's thirty most senior civilian and military leaders that they "represented the civilian-military cohesive team effort that has to hold together. We need you to hold the line." I watched as the mood in the room grew somber.

He continued, saying, "We live in a time where we must recognize what is going on in this town, but we cannot allow ourselves to be distracted. I need each of you to stay the course and 'keep your eyes in the boat,'" a naval caution to ignore what's going on around you and remain focused on the task at hand.

"We operate in a town with a mendacious press, who are looking for any opportunity to cause division."

The leaders arrayed around the table knew that Mattis held a dim view of the media. Mattis concluded, "You all heard Secretary Tillerson recently. It's far too easy to see yourself caught up in a maelstrom, so just focus on your jobs and on cooperation with each other. It's our jobs to be thinking five to seven years down the road . . ." He was right on that point: we can't control the outcome, but we can control our output. It was far better to stay focused on our mission. It was the one thing we felt we could control.

ELEVEN

WINTER OF DISCONTENT

The mark of a great shiphandler is never getting into
situations that require great shiphandling.

—FLEET ADMIRAL ERNEST J. KING

The whole team was exhausted as November finally rolled around. The thin veneer of civility that usually held us together had worn away, leaving behind a group of people who simply wanted to survive from one day to the next.

We were all dragging, Mattis included. We had officially entered the challenging period of winter that my classmates at the Naval Academy had called the Dark Ages. At the Academy, that time of year was constantly cold, with the sky and buildings turning gray and morale trending downward. Now at the Pentagon it was much the same—dark outside when we arrived at work, and dark when we left to go home at night.

Compounding that problem was Mattis's habit of jamming his schedule full of events.

I read with envy the biographies of secretaries from decades past who arrived at the Pentagon around 8:00 a.m., safeguarded time on their agenda to discuss issues or simply think, and then departed for home around 5:00 or 6:00 p.m. Not us. Mattis was always in before six in the morning and usually kept a steady, if not frenetic, pace until after six in the evening. This regularly translated into a thirteen- or fourteen-hour workday for the rest of us. But it was hard to complain, as our access ensured us a graduate-level education in statecraft.

The packed schedule was reflective of Mattis's desire to make the most of the time he had available to him.

It was no secret that the clock was ticking on his tenure, regardless of his relationship with the president. Mattis had pulled me into his office months earlier to discuss some upcoming events. We were sitting at his small round table when he suddenly looked up at me. Fixing me with a steady gaze, he said, "Bus, never forget that we all have an expiration date. Every day that passes brings you one day closer to the end of your tenure." He paused for a few seconds, reflecting. "Especially in a political job. You never know when the end will come, so make the most of the time you have." I liked his sentiment, as it echoed one of my leadership axioms as a commanding officer in Japan: "Never wait to make a difference."

Mattis's desire to wring every last opportunity out of the time available justified our breakneck pace. We had returned from Asia just in time to sprint our way through a week of congressional testimony on the use of military force overseas and on the requirement for a full budget for the military.

The dust had hardly settled from our last DC event before we went wheels up from Maryland's Andrews Air Force Base to begin our next weeklong overseas trip, this time to Europe. Our desire to overload Mattis's schedule catapulted everything into automatic crisis status, especially throughout these incredibly busy periods of time. During our flight, Mattis felt on edge—like he was behind on everything. This caused Faller, his senior military assistant, to lash out at everyone within earshot on board the plane.

There were really only two kinds of senior leaders around Mattis: attenuators and amplifiers. Attenuators were the best. They were the ones who, having emerged from Mattis's office after suffering his tongue-lashing, addressed you in an ever so calm and collected manner. They rarely raised their voice or treated people poorly. They merely identified the areas that needed to be fixed and then worked with the team at fixing them, all while keeping a positive, supporting attitude. Like an electrical attenuator, these leaders simply absorbed the stress on behalf of their subordinates.

Unfortunately, we didn't have many of those in Mattis's front office, though Sally Donnelly, the secretary's senior adviser, was certainly one. Instead, the two leaders closest to Mattis—Craig Faller and Kevin Sweeney—were unbridled amplifiers. You never had to guess the secretary's mood, because if it was good, they were happy. If he was the least bit sour, they would berate the people around them, complaining that the work produced by various components in the Pentagon was . . . "not up to standards" (to put it mildly). Yet, while this made life difficult and exhausting at times, it provided a clear window into Mattis's state of mind.

The stress on this trip wasn't solely attributable to working hard and a full schedule. Much of it was magnified by the increasing sense that Mattis had become something of a shadow secretary of state.

Mattis never once sought to undercut Tillerson, who would remain secretary of state for a few more months. Quite the opposite—Tillerson was Mattis's closest administration confidant besides Chief of Staff John Kelly at the White House, and Mattis always carefully selected his words and actions to reinforce Tillerson's state department.

Yet last month's press coverage had wounded Tillerson. Members of the press began to speculate on what they felt was Tillerson's imminent departure. Despite this conjecture, Tillerson's dedication to his tasks never wavered when I monitored phone calls between him and Mattis. Despite his resolve, though, foreign leaders began to imply during meetings or phone calls that Mattis's was the only voice they felt they could rely on in the administration. It became clear that Tillerson's days were numbered.

One by one, the other "adults" began to come under fire too.

On October 12, after months of negative comments about White House Chief of Staff John Kelly playing out in the press, Kelly made an extraordinary appearance during a White House press briefing to dispel rumors of bedlam in the West Wing. "Unless things change, I'm not quitting, I'm not getting fired, and I don't think I'll fire anyone tomorrow," Kelly told the assembled reporters. "I don't think I'm being fired today, and I'm not so frustrated in this job that I'm thinking of leaving."

It was an incredible admission—you don't hold a press conference to tell everyone that things are going okay. But that wasn't the end of it.

The next month, Kelly caught blowback after giving an impromptu speech at the White House. Having taken the podium to defend the president's conversation with the widow of a soldier slain in an attack in Niger, Kelly found himself ensnared in another difficult-to-defend political situation. Representative Frederica Wilson (D-FL) had been with the soldier's widow when the president called and claimed that his remarks were insensitive. To combat this narrative, Kelly delivered a powerful speech regarding the sacrifices—sometimes the ultimate sacrifice—made by those who serve. He even shared a moving recollection of what it was like to lose his own son to combat.

But he tripped while attempting to clean up the mess his boss had made, making a false accusation about a speech Wilson had previously given. The press, and Wilson, pounced on Kelly and the situation turned ugly. When Mattis read about the brouhaha in the next morning's papers, he said, "You're assumed to be innocent in this country until appointed to high office." Sure enough, as if on cue, we were already starting to hear about a new round of White House acrimony: Trump and Kelly were at dagger points with each other.

Rumors swirled that National Security Adviser McMaster's relationship with Trump had become untenable. The "adults" in the administration were taking fire at the same time.

All of these issues placed additional stress on Mattis to get it right. So it was no secret that we were all worn out when we arrived in Helsinki for Northern Group meetings, a defense collective that includes the UK and Baltic and Nordic countries. Mattis would deliver sixteen sets of remarks over a six-day stretch, an exhausting pace especially when every word had to be perfect. I was up until 2 a.m. the next morning, laying the pages of an upcoming speech out on the floor so that I could get a better feel for the logical flow of his remarks. Needless to say, as a team we were working hard.

Events in Finland went well. We were soon wheels up again and on our way to Brussels for the latest NATO ministerial. Unfortunately, Mattis was himself behind on his preparation. Our schedule hadn't afforded him time to sufficiently review his remarks in advance. His apprehension put everyone on edge.

Mattis has a few "tells" that betray his level of preparation. He's a voracious reader who normally devours all the material he's given, annotating in detail in the margins of his papers. He underlines sentences that hold particular interest and writes follow-up questions for the staff. When he's done, he'll flip back to the front page and write an "M" in the top right corner with the month and day that he read it.

As we prepared for this trip, Mattis had walked into our Pentagon conference room with his binder. Setting it on the table in front of him, he declared, "Thanks for the hard work, everyone. I took it home last night and read every word." "I read every word" was the operative phrase, which usually translated into, "I was exhausted and didn't get a chance to look at it, but I don't want you to think you wasted your time in preparing these materials . . . or that I wasn't prepared for this meeting."

His claim that he had "read every word" sometimes occurred with the speeches and other papers he handed back to me. My interpretation was verified when I flipped the binder open and every page was completely clean. No notes? Not read.

Sometimes when this happened with a speech being handed back to me, I suspected I was seeing a Henry Kissinger move. Kissinger was known for handing something back to its author while saying something to the effect of, "Are you sure this is your best work?" The author would dutifully spend more time trying to improve it before bringing it back to Kissinger. He would take the paper, skim it, and say, "Yes, this is much stronger." The kicker? Kissinger had never even read it in the first place. He just knew that the author could always make things better.

Mattis would periodically return speeches in the same manner—no notes, just a few spoken comments for me to consider. If I felt strongly about the speech, I'd hold it for a day, leave it alone, then return it to him the following day. I smiled on the inside when Mattis would say, "Ah, yes, this looks much better." It was a reminder that timing and his mood mattered.

And his mood in Brussels wasn't good. He hadn't read his materials for NATO in advance, and he suddenly had a crisis of confidence with each of his speeches for the upcoming three days. They were to be delivered in what were called "interventions," the term used for his speaking role during meetings with all of NATO's defense ministers present. If he doubted his material this late in the game, when he was already tired, it was like pouring gasoline on an already smoldering fire.

Conferences like the ones held quarterly at NATO are highly

choreographed events. Weeks of pre-meetings occur, with increasingly senior representatives from member nations coordinating each defense secretary's ultimate comments. Mattis's remarks had circulated around the Pentagon, and they were cleared through the state department, reviewed by NATO Ambassador Kay Bailey Hutchison, and shared with US Army General Mike Scaparotti and his team at European Command. They were also aligned with what Mattis had previously said at NATO. Put simply, Mattis's remarks were fully vetted and coordinated.

But he wasn't happy, and he let me know about it, pulling me into his hotel room along with Katie Wheelbarger, the Pentagon's principal deputy assistant for international security affairs.

"These remarks aren't going to cut it," he said, tossing them on the table in front of where I was sitting. "I need to quote the president while he was in Seoul [South Korea]. We need to talk about Kim Jong Un's outlaw provocations . . . and remind them that even here in Brussels we sit closer to North Korea than in Washington, DC." He paused, chewing on his lower lip. "Also, make sure you mention that it is my role to ensure America's diplomats speak from a position of strength." On and on he went for another thirty minutes, while I filled pages in my notebook.

Wheelbarger and I exchanged glances when I took a pause to shake my cramping hand. She had edited the draft and knew what I did: most of what he was telling us was already in there. The only new line he gave us, which was admittedly very good, was, "In doing everything possible to prevent the unmistakable trajectory of North Korea's nuclear path, silence as a result of timidity will not wish this problem away." That definitely had to go in.

Mattis finally dismissed us to start work. I glanced down at my watch and sighed. 11:34 p.m. It was going to be another late night. Katie just patted me on the shoulder, saying, "Let me know if you'd like me to take another look."

Mattis was always the good soldier, reminding me in private that his remarks had to align with the president's and with Tillerson's, routinely instructing me to "go exactly along the lines of what POTUS announced." That was why it was so important to influence and mold the draft versions of White House speeches— they were like Christmas trees that we could hang ornaments on, enabling us to craft our speeches using language issued from the White House. I made all of the changes to Mattis's speech, turning in for the night at 3:30 a.m.

I was awoken at 5:45 a.m. with Mattis's aide de camp, Ryan Stoddard, standing in my hotel room. I had been so deep asleep— and so exhausted from the past few days—that I hadn't answered when he'd repeatedly rung the doorbell, forcing him to go get a spare room key to let himself in. Stoddard was apologetic. "Hey, Bus, sorry to wake you but the boss needs to see you. He has some changes to his speeches."

I dutifully updated Mattis's remarks, and we were soon off to NATO headquarters.

One of our first events of the day was to meet with Ambassador Hutchison and General Scaparotti. I soon learned that Hutchison, my former US senator from Texas, was notorious for being a "table dropper." No matter how much coordination we conducted with her and her team in advance of NATO meetings, she always held back one or two pieces of critical information that she provided only after we'd arrived.

In person, it seemed like she wanted to demonstrate her value

Here I am in 2016, airborne off the east coast of Japan with a Japanese F-4 Phantom on my left wing. Finally, back in the Navy after leaving my first Pentagon job, I was living my dream—one that first took hold in middle school. I had wanted to become a fighter pilot ever since watching jets fly by during Boy Scout fundraisers at Carswell Air Force Base in North Texas.

My wife, Sarah, and I with our two boys on the VFA-102 Diamondbacks flight line in Japan in 2010. My career in the Navy required frequent travel. When Secretary Mattis's office called in 2017, we'd already moved nine times.

I first heard General Mattis speak while I was attending the US Naval War College in Newport, Rhode Island. I listened to a wide variety of accomplished leaders during my studies, but Mattis stood out for his depth of knowledge, love of history, and ability to inspire the audience.

President Trump swore in James Mattis as the twenty-sixth secretary of defense on January 27, 2017. Here, Trump, Mattis, and Vice President Mike Pence walk up the stairs at the Pentagon's "River Entrance" in Washington, DC, before the ceremony.

Despite his differences with the president, Mattis held the line overseas. In February 2017, he took his first trip to the Indo-Pacific to offer reassurance amid rising tensions with North Korea, China, and Russia. Here, he shakes hands with the Japanese prime minister Shinzo Abe at the prime minister's office in Tokyo, Japan.

In July 2017, President Trump attended his first briefing at the Pentagon. The briefing was nothing like we expected. Trump was irritable, and Mattis realized that their approaches to national security were radically different. Strengthening US relationships with key allies would prove to be an uphill battle.

In August 2017, President Trump gave a speech to the nation announcing the South Asia strategy, which we anxiously anticipated in the days beforehand. The first drafts of the speech had a clear "America alone" message, but I was able to intervene and rewrite part of the speech to include support for America's allies. Mattis was also concerned that Trump was using uniformed military members as a backdrop for what he regarded as a political speech.

While Trump emphasized America's role in fighting North Korea, Mattis met with our key allies in Asia. During the height of the "maximum pressure campaign" against North Korea in October 2017, Secretary Mattis and South Korean minister of defense Song Young-moo visited the Demilitarized Zone between North and South Korea.

When Secretary Mattis traveled to Cairo to meet with Egypt's minister of defense General Sedky Sobhy in December 2017, Mattis was more "Warrior Monk" than "Mad Dog."

Secretary Mattis announced the National Defense Strategy at Johns Hopkins University in Washington, DC, on January 19, 2018. Frustrated with traffic, Mattis left the motorcade, walking the remainder of the way to the college to avoid being late.

Mattis understood the importance of getting to know John Bolton, the national security adviser brought in to replace H. R. McMaster. When first he met Bolton at the Pentagon in April 2018, Mattis joked, "I've heard you're actually the devil incarnate, and I wanted to meet you."

Despite the incredible demands on his schedule—and increasing political pressures now that Secretary of State Rex Tillerson and National Security Adviser H. R. McMaster were gone—Mattis still made time to host my family on April 30, 2018, my last day in a Navy uniform. Here, my daughter, Natalie, is showing off her two stuffed "pocket huskies" to Mattis.

It was an incredible honor when Mattis presented me with the Defense Superior Service Medal. At this point in my tenure, I'd been with the secretary in the Pentagon for just over a year.

Although we're smiling in this photo, June of 2018 proved to be a difficult month for Mattis's front office staffers. With most of President Trump's original staff having been replaced, Mattis was out of alignment with the White House, which only elevated our stress levels. Chief of Staff Kevin Sweeney is directly behind the secretary, with then–Vice Admiral Craig Faller to Sweeney's right.

The June 2018 NATO Summit in Brussels, Belgium, proved a challenging visit for Mattis. Here, he's pictured with NATO Secretary General Jens Stoltenberg, who was surprised and angered by Trump's position regarding the NATO alliance.

Reporters grilled Secretary Mattis as we started our multistop trip to China in June 2018. Mattis routinely met with the press in his cabin onboard the E-4B "Nightwatch" aircraft while traveling overseas. Here, he speaks to reporters during our first leg, a flight from Andrews Air Force Base, Maryland, to Alaska.

Secretary of Defense James N. Mattis meets with President Xi Jinping of China at Diaoyutai State Guest House in June 2018 in Beijing, China. Despite Mattis's high hopes for the trip, Xi used the visit as an opportunity to reiterate that their "stance is steadfast and clear-cut when it comes to China's sovereignty and territorial integrity....We cannot lose one inch of territory passed down by our ancestors."

Easily my favorite photo of my tenure with Secretary Mattis. I had to cancel Christmas plans to author the unclassified 2018 National Defense Strategy in time for its January 19, 2018, release. Here, my children are "helping" me determine the right order for each of the pages in an early draft. Writing the unclassified version of the strategy was one of the highlights of my career.

Pat Shanahan unveiled Mattis's official portrait as one of his last official acts before leaving the Pentagon as the acting secretary of defense. Hanging in the secretary of defense's corridor, this finished painting is a tad different than the hand-sketched version Mattis drew of himself in bell-bottoms the year before.

to Secretary Mattis by sharing some late-breaking updates. All it ever did was frustrate Mattis, as it meant he felt compelled to update his remarks yet again. Her actions were made more damning because we always shared Mattis's draft speeches with her before we arrived in town. It was one of those small points of friction that our busy schedule only magnified. Mattis wanted everything aligned and coordinated well in advance.

Despite these concerns, the NATO talks went off without a hitch. We were soon airborne en route to our last stop, and Mattis began to visibly relax. Entering his plane's conference room during the flight to London, the final destination of our week-long trip, he asked, "You all know what the acronym NATO stands for, right?" He paused for half a beat, a slight smile tugging at the corners of his lips. "No Action, Talk Only!" We all appreciated the much-needed levity.

After landing in London, we made our way to our hotel located near Buckingham Palace. We put our luggage away and checked the latest on email, then a few of us headed out with Mattis to find some dinner and a beer. Although we seldom left the hotel during travel, every few trips we'd make it a point to peel away for a dinner with four to six members of the core team. These moments presented opportunities to shake off the stress and simply enjoy one another's company.

Tonight we headed to the Rose and Crown, a quintessential British pub located nearby. The talk turned to books. Stoddard recommended a satirical one, *Flashman,* the first of a twelve-book series. We were unsurprised to learn that Mattis had already read it—one of the many thousands he'd devoured over the years.

It wasn't long before uniformed members of the British Army made their way into the pub for a "dining out"—a formal dinner as a regiment—they were having. A few recognized Mattis and asked to take a picture with him. He obliged.

———

London had served as a refreshing stop on an otherwise hectic weeklong trip, a welcome respite after weeks of sprinting ahead, but the challenges weren't over. November was quite easily the most difficult month of my naval career, the month that permanently altered my career path and forever affected my relationship with Mattis.

Since joining the team, my stock with Mattis had risen to stratospheric levels, which translated into a lot of extra duties outside my job description. I genuinely enjoyed the challenge, though it meant I was rarely at home.

Two days before we departed for Europe, Faller called me in the evening. "Congrats, Bus!" he said. "You've been selected for nuke power!"—an expression that meant I'd been selected for the pathway that would ultimately lead to command of a nuclear-powered aircraft carrier. I was incredibly honored to be one of only seven officers in the US Navy offered the opportunity that year.

But it was also the one career path that I'd repeatedly said I couldn't accept because of my family's desire to finally have a husband and a father at home. Accepting the aircraft carrier path would mean two years away from the family as a "geographic bachelor" for mandatory nuclear-power education. After training, I'd be assigned to three consecutive tours at sea: first as an executive officer (the number two) for an aircraft carrier, then two years as the commanding officer of an amphibious assault ship, and finally culminating as the commanding officer of an aircraft carrier for three years. The aircraft carrier "career pipeline" would take somewhere between eight and ten years to complete.

I'd been largely absent the previous decade, which is why we'd been positioned for command of an air wing—a chance for the family to recharge. I'd made that point clear when I was asked to join Mattis's team back in April. Apparently, it had fallen on deaf ears. The Navy selection board, not aware of my particular situation, had selected me for carriers instead of an air wing.

If I turned it down, things would get dicey.

Mattis has an uncompromising view on military service. He had committed his entire adult life to the Marine Corps and military service. He believed to his very core in putting service before self and expected others to internalize the same values. There were no shades of gray around Mattis—you were either all in . . . or you were all the way out. This worldview had caused Mattis to adopt a life of solitude, making it difficult for him to understand how having a family holds sway over a person's decision-making.

I'd been physically absent from my family for a significant majority of the past ten years. Sarah was tired of being a single parent and the kids were starting to perform poorly in school, a difficult reality I'd observed with others who had accepted the aircraft carrier career path. I was struck by the fact that it's easy to follow your dreams when someone else foots the bill. Sarah had been paying that bill for fourteen years. Accepting a job that required me to be away even more than I already was seemed infeasible.

If I said no, Mattis wouldn't understand. What made this prospect even more difficult to stomach was that I'd been on a sustainable path upward while we lived in Norfolk. Life as an air wing commander would have allowed us to recharge our batteries as a family for the next four to five years—a path I had willingly sacrificed to join Mattis's team as lead speechwriter.

I was hesitant to advocate for my position. Officers are trained from the start on the importance of humility and having a humble attitude. I'd asked Sweeney and Faller to champion my case, but that's not how "the system" works. They made clear that senior leaders are expected to go where the Navy tells them, regardless of circumstance. In some ways, I was lucky to be seeing this reality before committing to another ten years.

Rather, they said that not accepting the path toward an aircraft carrier would result in lasting damage to my relationship with Mattis. I was now being cut adrift—there would be no support. This office mentality would be the reason that Mattis's aide de camp, Ryan Stoddard, felt compelled to remain in uniform and take another job following his time with Mattis, even though he had already decided to retire—he wanted to remain in Mattis's good graces. In either case, I would like to have seen Sweeney and Faller take better care of their people. As a leader, I believe loyalty down the chain of command is every bit as important as loyalty up.

Throughout my career, I had watched as rising leaders took the most difficult jobs, their bosses squeezing every last drop of effort from them. In the end, though, those same leaders understood the importance of taking care of those they led. It was the same way I'd run my command in Japan—I asked a lot of my sailors, but I also ensured they were positioned to move onward and upward. I had been naïve to expect the same consideration from Sweeney and Faller.

Passing on this opportunity was the toughest decision of my career, and I had to make it during what turned out to be one of my most challenging months with the team. Ultimately, I chose my family over the path being offered. The repeated warnings that my relationship with Mattis would suffer drove Faller and Sweeney to do what they apparently felt was the most logical thing: they hid my decision from him.

This seemed childish to me. I could see how my decision would disappoint Mattis but I thought I would be okay, as he'd witnessed my dedication for months. Not wanting to take any chances, I decided to prove Faller and Sweeney wrong about my devotion. I recommitted to working twice as hard and renewed my commitment to the team. I'd show Mattis that I was a team player through and through. That's just part of the military ethos—no matter what comes your way, you deal with it to the best of your ability. You always stay in the fight.

These beliefs would be tested in the coming months, but my renewed resolve came at just the right time. My personal path may have been derailed, but we had a critically important document—a strategy to direct the nation's defense path—to write.

TWELVE

LEGACY

Of the four wars in my lifetime, none came about
because the United States was too strong.

—RONALD REAGAN

"C'mon in, everyone. Please take a seat. I'll be right over." Mattis was standing by his desk, thumbing through the pages of his binder. We took our cue and made our way to the conference table.

Today's session was among the most crucial of Mattis's tenure. We were now well into December and needed to finalize the National Defense Strategy, the one document responsible for informing the US military, the American public, and other nations—friend and foe alike—about our defense priorities for the next three to five years.

Soon Mattis joined us. Rather than sitting at our table's head, he elected to pull out a chair in the middle. That was a good sign. He was feeling relaxed.

"Okay everyone, thanks for taking time out of your busy days to meet up." He rocked back in his chair a bit, another good omen. "I want to ensure we get the widest dissemination on our strategy so that we can reach the largest possible audience. That includes the public. The defense of this country should be important to *all* Americans."

This reinforced my opinion that the publicly available version of the strategy should be clearly written and comprehensible. Anyone should be able to pick it up, find it engaging, and understand where America's military is heading.

Still rocked back in his chair, he considered his next thought. "One thing we need to be very careful about is discussing the tradeoffs we need to make with our military. On one hand, the strategy should describe in stark terms the absolute mess we're in from sixteen years of constant war, reduced budgets, and continuing resolutions. The military is worn out and worn thin."

Mattis made plain what we all knew, and what I had personally experienced. Equipment was wearing out faster than planned because of a decade and a half of fighting the "war on terror." The Obama administration and Congress had greatly reduced the military's budget at the same time that military commanders were demanding more operations, a situation that had squeezed all branches of the military.

Aviation units were experiencing more mishaps, training was significantly curtailed, and retaining quality people had become a significant issue. The situation was painfully illustrated by two incredibly harrowing—and easily avoidable—ship collisions the Navy suffered in the Indo-Pacific. Seventeen sailors died. The tragedy was largely attributed to the immense stress placed on deploying units. Senior leaders demanded ships be put to sea without providing the necessary equipment or training needed for safe operations. The lack of resources in the face of unlimited demands was a tinderbox just waiting for someone to strike a match.

Mattis continued, "We need to inform Congress in compelling terms so they can provide the budget we need. On the other hand, we don't want to overstate reality so as to embolden our adversaries. As Kissinger put it, "you never tell your adversaries what you're *not* going to do."

Despite our shortfalls, the American military was quite capable of taking on any challenge, but we needed restored funding to rebuild our forces while also preparing to shift to where any future conflicts might take us . . . and not remain solely focused on the present day's conflicts in the Middle East.

The front lines of competition were shifting eastward.

Mattis looked out the window, gazing toward the Potomac. "I believe this administration inherited a strategy-free situation, a dangerous place to be. Any nation requires a strategy to allocate resources, prioritize efforts, and adapt."

He looked back at the table and reached out, picking up a wayward paper clip. "We need to find a way to expand the competitive space," a term reflecting the importance of America using all elements of national power—not just the military—to deter adversaries or win conflict. Mattis began to fiddle with the paper clip. "All strategies are ultimately adaptive. We steer by the stars, but if a rock shows up in front of your ship, you'd best ma-neuver to avoid it. Perhaps we should consider updating the strat-egy every six months to prevent it from becoming static or brittle." It was a statement, not a question.

Updating the strategy once every two years might be possi-ble: a chance to pause, evaluate the new situation, and then ad-just our aim point. Updating every six months was too aggressive for an organization as large and diverse as the Department of Defense. Plus, rolling out a nationwide strategy takes time. Se-nior leaders needed a chance to read the new strategy, under-stand it, and then enact it.

Mattis was still thinking out loud. "It's no secret that we live in an unsettled time. America is being faced with a choice, and I believe we must choose to stand and fight. We're a nation that remains capable of tough things . . . great things. America is a guidepost for the world, so the public strategy needs to be inspi-rational and not hollow political rhetoric."

He scowled, changing topics. "I learned this morning that early draft copies of our strategy were leaked to the press."

Nothing, absolutely nothing, made the boss angrier than leaks to the press.

"I'm willing to release the strategy as soon as we're ready. We need to accelerate to get out in front. Tell McMaster we won't wait until after [next month's] State of the Union address to get it on the street." Mattis's drive for speed only intensified the ad-ditional pressure on Bridge Colby, the senior executive leading the strategy team, and on me. Colby's team wrote the full, clas-sified version of the strategy. I took responsibility for writing the unclassified version that would be made widely available.

We'd originally planned for the president to give his State of the Union address without the distraction of competing strategies out in the public space. Accelerating the strategy—as Mattis now demanded—meant I'd have to move at the speed of light to get my version done. Colby would then need to drive the language I crafted in Mattis's "voice" back into the classified strategy, ensuring both documents sounded the same.

We finally landed on a date for Mattis to unveil his strategy: January 19, eleven days before the president's State of the Union address. The next order of business was to determine where we would do the rollout.

Sally Donnelly, Mattis's senior adviser, wanted a nonstandard location. "How about a public university? Everyone always heads over to Johns Hopkins for events like these. You'd get a lot of attention if you went someplace different. Maybe even Howard or American University?"

We'd look into it, but Mattis wanted a central location where it would be easier to ensure a positive outcome. Unsurprisingly, we finally settled on Johns Hopkins. Howard was deemed too distant from Capitol Hill to attract congressional staffers, and American University had previously witnessed protests over a political speech. The last thing Mattis needed was the optic of students protesting the military. It was unlikely, but it was not only a risk but an unnecessary one at that. We found there were very good reasons people used Johns Hopkins—convenience and a guaranteed friendly environment.

The final topic involved ways to win the public messaging battle well in advance of the actual release.

We tackled the problem from several angles. Frank Hoffman,

a friend of Mattis's and a well-respected member in the think tank community, and Donnelly would float the draft to influential leaders so they could read it before it was released. We also chose a prominent Republican, Eliot Cohen, and a top Democrat, Susan Rice, to review the strategy and provide feedback. We would thus inoculate ourselves against at least some of the slings and arrows guaranteed to come our way. Better to build support early on than fight to regain it if we stumbled out of the gate. It was a careful, well-thought-out approach.

Those factors having been decided, Mattis turned to me. "Okay, Bus, let's get to it. We'll get it out for review just as soon as you can get it to us."

———

Twenty years in the military had taught me that strategies were typically convoluted, academic, and often incomprehensible. I needed to break that mold, so when Mattis had asked me a couple weeks earlier about the Colby team's current draft, I had dared to share my true feelings: it was far too academic as currently drafted.

The first page started with the following quote: "Per National Defense Authorization Act for Fiscal Year 2017, Section 941 titled National Defense Strategy . . . in January every four years . . ." and so on.

That was the problem. A lot of great information was included within this long draft, but the overall feel reminded me of strategies that I'd tried, and failed, to engage with as a young officer. The department needed something different. Mattis wasn't impressed either. Based on his notes on the copy he'd handed me, he never even made it past the first page of the draft.

So I passed the draft back to Mattis with a summary of my take. I volunteered to produce a five-to-seven-page executive summary incorporating Mattis's enduring themes, his three lines of effort for the department, and other core messages—all to translate the unclassified version into something capable of resonating with the American public, Congress, and our allies and partners.

I got Mattis's response when he caught me in the hallway on a Sunday. "Here you go, Bus. I agree—put this into my voice. You know what I'm trying to do here. Remember, make every word count . . ." That was all he had to say. I'd been with the team for eight months at this point and knew instinctively what he was trying to achieve and how to deliver it to him.

This was exciting—a chance to write *the* foundational document for the Department of Defense. The only downside was that Mattis had handed it to me on Sunday, *December 24*. Christmas Eve, and a scant three weeks before we were scheduled to roll out a finished, polished product. The situation reminded me of what I'd heard the acronym "NAVY" stood for: Never Again Volunteer Yourself. But I was excited by the opportunity. It was time to cancel holiday plans and get to work.

A week earlier, President Trump had announced the release of his keystone strategy document, called the National Security Strategy. This made my job my easier, as I needed to ensure our strategy married with the president's direction. Our department's strategy needed to "nest" inside the nation's.

The department's strategy would inform the military's goals for the next few years and provide justification for what would rapidly become a $700 billion budget. The president's strategy, on the other hand, would set the goals for an entire nation and influence a 1.1 *trillion* dollar budget.

Stephen Miller allowed me a sneak peek at what the White House team had assembled for the president's announcement. It was well-written and, frankly, *presidential*.

Trump caught a lot of flak for his use of Twitter and his wayward remarks during press conferences, but his release of the national security strategy was Trump at his best. His content was clear, direct, and appropriate to the task at hand. If I could offer one suggestion for the president moving forward, it would be to stick closely to his prepared remarks and to ad lib less—he gives a focused, powerful speech that way.

Although Trump's speech lasted a full thirty minutes, the parts I needed to hear resonated loud and clear. Trump talked about "America's security, prosperity, and standing in the world." He reinforced his view that previous presidents had "failed to insist that our often very wealthy allies pay for their fair share for defense, putting a massive and unfair burden on the US taxpayer and our great US military." The president emphasized three major threats: a nuclear menace in North Korea, a bad deal with Iran, and terrorist threats such as ISIS.

The most important—the crucial—part of his speech was an acknowledgment that the nation was now engaged in an era of renewed global competition. We faced rogue regimes, terrorist organizations, as well as a hostile Russia and China—rival powers seeking to challenge American influence, values, and wealth.

He also hit on an element that I knew to be critically important to Tillerson, McMaster, and Mattis, explaining, "To succeed we must integrate every dimension of our national strength, and we must compete with every instrument of our national power." This was great language, aligned with what Mattis meant when he said that "the role of the military is to ensure that the president and America's diplomats speak from a position of strength." American success requires steady, administration-wide coordination of diplomatic, military, and economic resources, especially in the face of communist nations like China that can simply dictate aggressive national economic policies.

The president's speech delivered all the clues I needed to fully align Mattis's defense strategy with Trump's national strategy. Nadia Schadlow, one of McMaster's deputy national security advisers and the principal architect of the president's national security strategy, visited the Pentagon to help ensure we were on the right path. Schadlow's visit also highlighted for me how Mattis meticulously crafted his public persona.

Mattis was usually all business with his personal staff, but this changed if you sat in with a guest he was hosting. Then, for the public audience, he'd make a show of asking if you wanted any refreshments. "Bus," he asked, "can I get you a cup of coffee?" or "Here, Bus, have a chocolate chip cookie." This was the second time this had happened. Those of us on staff chuckled about it—this was not his style, and the switch betrayed a vulnerability, a desire to bolster his reputation with those from the outside world.

We soon wrapped up our discussion. Time to get to work. What followed was a week of nonstop writing during the Christmas break. I commandeered the family dining room, laying out three dozen pages of unclassified material that I'd draw from. I always liked to lay an article or a speech out so I could grasp its entirety, enabling me to more easily spot inconsistencies or faulty logic. My three young children even got into the act, walking around the table while offering helpful suggestions. "This page looks fun, Daddy. Maybe put it over there?" One of my favorite photos from my time on Mattis's staff is one where my kids are standing around to help Dad write America's defense strategy. Sarah was there too, encouraging me to take breaks now and again to share a meal with the family.

There was a lot of pressure to perform. The unclassified strategy and a good rollout were critical to ensuring Congress would agree to restore full funding to the military. The more compelling the strategy and accompanying speech, the more likely we were to succeed in that mission. I appreciated that Mattis had put so much faith in me. Actually, the absence of work distractions during the holidays undoubtedly helped. I was cranking out thousands of words per day, and the unclassified strategy zoomed from concept to a near-final version in just over a week.

With a solid draft in hand, we arranged for the review copies to go out to Eliot Cohen and Susan Rice. It was tricky business that required a certain level of concealment, what with Cohen being a "Never Trumper" and Rice having worked as a senior official in the Obama administration. I suspected that the White House wouldn't agree with our approach had they ever discovered it.

At the end of the day, we received excellent critiques from all parties. I collated their inputs, provided a revised copy of the strategy to Mattis, and incorporated the points that I felt needed to be stitched into the final copy.

Mattis was pleased, making only minor changes before we "went smooth" and started producing professionally printed copies. I even created the electronic version, an Adobe PDF file, on my computer. Attention to detail was important, so in case anyone decided to check, I put "Jim Mattis" as the author (and my name for the writer) as an Easter egg in the file's preferences. Bridge Colby's strategy team then worked the language back into the much longer, classified version. Overall, I felt this exercise served as a great example of real teamwork when crafting a document of national—even international—importance.

The opportunity to produce a strategy with such lasting significance easily ranks as one of my most meaningful professional experiences.

Now all we had to do was get President Trump to sign off on it.

THIRTEEN

LEADING UP

A bluff taken seriously is more useful than
a serious threat interpreted as a bluff.

—HENRY KISSINGER

It was Friday, January 18, 2018. I was in the conference room to run the media presentation for our second briefing to President Trump.

And running behind.

Deputy Secretary Pat Shanahan had asked me for some last-minute tweaks to a slide on the F-35 Joint Strike Fighter. I had to change the slide and then rebuild the entire slide show. It's a healthy challenge when you become the single point of failure for an event. My predicament became a race against the clock to ensure the latest and greatest slides were loaded and ready to go before Mattis escorted the president and vice president into the room.

Today's presentation was of paramount importance, as tomorrow we were set to unveil the 2018 National Defense Strategy at Johns Hopkins University—the first strategy of its kind in a decade. Mattis had kept Trump, Pence, and McMaster apprised of our progress as we developed the strategy to avoid any surprises. But you never knew what to expect with Trump, and any decision other than a "go" from the president would not only derail the event but supremely embarrass Mattis.

It was game day.

In the six months since our first briefing of President Trump at the Pentagon, I'd pondered the hard lessons we'd taken away from that session. We had spent too much time (and capital) trying to lecture the president, loading up the slides with too much information. Friends at the White House backed up my suspicions—Trump hated being lectured.

I now steered Mattis away from complicated, data-congested slides and campaigned for a more straightforward approach: just pictures. I'd seen this approach used with great success in other venues—choose photos to capture the president's attention while Mattis and Shanahan provide the voiceover.

There was less fanfare today than during his first visit, and the room was largely empty except for the department's most senior uniformed leaders. They milled about, chatting with one another in anticipation of the president's arrival. Every member of the Joint Chiefs of Staff—senior leaders from the Army, Navy, Air Force, Coast Guard, and Marines—were represented, as was the National Guard.

I was joined in the control room by two other staff members. We stood at attention in the doorway as President Trump, Vice President Pence, and Secretary Mattis turned into the conference room. As soon as they passed, we ducked back inside, took our seats, and closed the door. The control room speakers were loud, and we didn't want to disturb the brief in the next room.

Trump took his place at the head of the conference table. Seated along his right side were Pence, General Dunford, and half of the Joint Chiefs. To his left were Mattis, Shanahan, and the remainder of the Joint Chiefs. Trump leaned forward and crossed his arms on the table in front of him. Unlike the first brief, this time he looked rested and attentive.

Mattis kicked off. "Mr. President, welcome back to the Pentagon." He glanced over at the blank screen. "Can you bring up the first slide?" I dutifully brought his first slide up, a series of four boxes demonstrating how the collection of national strategies would work together.

The outermost box represented the National Security Strategy that Trump had unveiled at the White House exactly one month before. The second box, nested inside the first, represented the primary purpose for today's briefing: the National Defense Strategy, the document that would drive the military's focus and investments for the next three to seven years.

The final two boxes, the smallest on the chart, represented Nuclear Posture Review (NPR) and Missile Defense Review. The NPR, set to be announced shortly after the defense strategy, was likely to garner significant interest. It detailed the challenges posed by America's adversaries and our intention to compete with their expanded portfolio of refreshed nuclear capabilities.

The Missile Defense Review, on the other hand, was a hot mess and was indefinitely delayed.

Mattis cleared his throat and launched into his brief. "Mr. President, you inherited a military that has languished for a long time. After years of reduced defense budgets and continuing resolutions, you can now ask for more money from Congress as it fits within your strategy. To be clear: you'll have no strategy if [Congress] shuts down the government in the coming months. Trying to implement a strategy without a fully enacted budget is a hallucination, nothing more. This is the situation you inherited . . ."

Trump fretted, shaking his head and saying, "Just terrible . . . terrible situation . . . ," as Mattis continued to talk.

Mattis didn't miss a beat. "I appreciate your words from last month when you highlighted the preservation of peace through strength. As you said then, our strength is magnified by allies who share our principles . . ."

Trump didn't let him finish. "Europe has to address this, general . . . it's a real mess is what you're telling me . . . do you realize we're *$21 trillion in debt?* Other countries have to pay us for protection. You want us to protect you? You have to *pay* us. We get *nothing,* which is why we have a depleted military . . . though I don't mind protecting people if it's right."

Mattis jumped right back in, attempting to placate the president. "[NATO] Secretary General Stoltenberg understands, and we're seeing the increases needed for nations to meet the 2 percent spending goal . . ." True, but I knew the increases had been agreed to back in 2014 under President Obama, a fine point Mattis wisely avoided.

Trump continued, "Look, NATO has been a lot better for Europe than it has been for us . . . we're *owed money* from the last thirty years." This was a fundamental misunderstanding of how NATO works. The agreement for each nation to spend 2 percent of gross domestic product on their militaries was a target, not a requirement. The US was drastically outspending other nations because of our global engagement and, frankly, global ambitions—though Trump made a good point. Other nations, seeing the US paying so much for defense, merely coasted along on America's bandwagon.

Trump continued, speaking about himself in the third person, saying, "Stoltenberg is *by far* the biggest fan of Trump." He then jumped to an entirely new topic. "Aircraft carriers cost us $18 billion and it takes *years* to build them. They're an old ship before they ever sail the seas!" It was a similar point to what the president had made during the first meeting. He was nothing if not consistent.

Mattis struggled to get back on script, but Trump had commandeered the briefing. "You know, I blame everything on the Democrats." He paused for a few seconds, then looked over at Mattis. "What about Afghanistan? How are we doing there?"

Mattis reengaged. "I'd be the first one in your office to say we need to leave if it wasn't worth it—"

He didn't get a chance to finish his thought, as Trump jumped back in. "We're really not helping ourselves . . . we're helping everyone *else* out there. You know, Kazakhstan is a very rich country. On my last visit they kept saying, 'Oh thank you, thank you.' Well, why aren't they *paying* us? Why aren't *they* fighting?" The president glanced back up at the slide with each of the strategies listed. "Fine. We've done this crazy strategy . . . so, let's see if it works."

Mattis moved into one of his favorite talking points, as it gave him a chance to praise the virtues of working with partner nations. "When it comes to your South Asia strategy, we now have the United Arab Emirates and Qatar in Resolute Support Mission, bringing us from thirty-nine up to forty-one partner nations."

"Resolute Support Mission" was a NATO-led endeavor to provide training and assistance to Afghanistan forces so that they could stabilize their own country against extremist organizations like the Taliban. The United States provides approximately 8,500 of its 17,000 troops.

Trump was not impressed. His arms remained crossed, a scowl on his face. He said, "Seriously, who gives a shit about Afghanistan? So far we're in for $7 trillion, fellas . . . *$7 trillion* including Iraq. Worst decision ever and we're stuck with it. We could get out of 90 percent of our commitments and countries, and just bring it all home."

Despite being an active-duty officer working for Secretary Mattis, a part of me agreed with the president. Military officers were prone to debating where we were headed in the Middle East and South Asia, as both regions had begun to feel like "forever wars." Most concerning to me was the sheer volume of American treasure we were expending in terms of people, money, and equipment.

During the Cold War, the US and its allies had pursued a long-term competitive economic strategy against the Soviet Union. This strategy forced the Soviets to spend progressively higher sums of money to compete with the West. While there are numerous factors that coalesced to cause the Soviet Union's demise, runaway defense spending was certainly one of them.

Against this backdrop, several of us on Mattis's staff feared we were now similarly strangling a nation—except this time it was ourselves. It wasn't lost on us that rivals like Russia, Iran, and China were likely thrilled to see America both distracted and increasingly ensnared in endless conflicts.

Friends at the White House told me that Trump wanted to know what we were getting for our investment. If we continued committing forces to overseas excursions, what was our return? No, Mattis's answer of "blanket security" would not suffice. Trump wanted to know specifically what America gained each time a soldier died or we spent another trillion dollars to fight a war that, at best, produced a stalemate.

Trump continued, "It's a losing deal! If [South Korea] paid us $60 billion a year to keep our troops overseas, *then* it's an okay deal." He paused to reflect. "You know, trade people have been so stupid. We must be doing something right. The stock market is waaay up, have you seen?" He shifted back to the topic at hand. "We should follow China's policy—just go into Afghanistan and take out all that wealth." He was referring to Afghanistan's ample mineral reserves.

Mattis didn't like where this was going. He tried a new angle. "Well, Mr. President, [China] is comprised of state-run agencies, but we're taking your guidance and putting it into reality." That comment didn't resonate at all with the president.

Chairman Dunford spoke up for the first time, taking a swing at convincing Trump. "Mr. President, you could have given Secretary

General Stoltenberg's speech . . . It mirrored your themes on burden sharing, the importance of our allies paying their fair share . . ."

Trump waved him away. "This is ridiculous! Just *pay* us!"

Dunford tried a different tack. "Mr. President, I've been in this job for two and a half years. The change in attitude I'm seeing in NATO is significant."

Trump glanced at Dunford, sitting to his right. "No, General, we are getting ripped off by NATO."

The energy in the room was turning dark. Mattis and Dunford were both at a loss for how to get the brief back on track. The meeting seemed doomed to follow in the awkward footsteps of our first one.

Mattis interjected, seeking to recapture a positive tone. "Mr. President, the [NATO] nations that are meeting the 2 percent pledge need a public pat on the back."

Trump just looked straight ahead, this portion of the meeting apparently finished. "Okay, let's do that."

Mattis spoke to the room's microphone. "Let's switch over to the nuclear posture review now . . ."

In the control room, I advanced the next slide, filled with full-color photos of the key elements of America's nuclear deterrence. Known as the "triad," the slide held photos of the B-2 Spirit stealth bomber, Ohio-class ballistic missile submarine, and Minuteman intercontinental ballistic missile.

The US adopted the nuclear triad back in the 1960s during the earliest years of the Cold War as a means to significantly reduce the likelihood of the Soviets destroying our nuclear capability with a first strike. Ground-based silos represent the most responsive leg of the triad, with missiles launched in short order should a counterstrike become necessary. Bombers represent the most flexible element of the triad, able to carry a variety of weapons and to be launched or recalled as the situation warrants. The final leg, ballistic missile submarines, recalls scenes from the iconic movie *The Hunt for Red October*. Submarines represent the most survivable leg of the triad, capable of remaining underwater and undetected for months at a time.

President Trump perked up, interested by the photos displayed on large screens at opposite ends of the room. "Why aren't we building more of those submarines?" he asked.

Mattis didn't miss a beat. "We are." President Trump nodded, "Good, let's do that." He paused for a second, gaining energy. "We should absolutely do this! It's starting to sound like the military is becoming the military again! How refreshing!"

The final slide was Deputy Secretary Shanahan's picture of the F-35 Joint Strike Fighter.

Shanahan enjoyed a good relationship with the president, managing to be both conversational and matter-of-fact with Trump. It did not hurt that his background was solely business-based—just like the president's. He was very astute, able to read the president's mood and tailor his message accordingly.

Produced by Lockheed Martin, the F-35 had, unfortunately, come to symbolize a prototypically bloated defense program—estimated to cost more than 1.1 trillion dollars. One of Shanahan's primary goals was to bring the program back under control.

Shanahan emphasized the bright side. "Well, we'll be buying a lot more Joint Strike Fighters based on our ability to reduce their cost." He discussed a few specifics before sliding into a savvy line. Playing to Trump's desire to strike the best possible deals—"The

Art of the Deal"—for defense equipment, Shanahan looked at him and said, "Well, you *are* the chief procurement officer for the United States."

Trump visibly preened. In the control room, I looked over at the officer to my left and said, "Well played."

The president wanted to chat a bit more about the F-35. "Did you know that the Chinese are copying the F-22 [a stealth fighter flown by the US Air Force]? It's a much better-looking plane than the F-35." No disagreement from me there. Trump then made those of us in the control room chuckle. "I tell you, I would never want to fly a one-engine plane." *Yeah, you and every Navy fighter pilot I know,* I thought.

Navy fighter pilots usually flew off aircraft carriers sailing in the middle of an ocean, well beyond the range of land. At least in the F/A-18 we had two engines, so you had options if one of your engines quit, a fact that had served me well during my own in-flight emergencies. If you lost your only engine in the F-35, you were going to have to put the plane in the ocean.

We were nearing the meeting's end, but Trump wanted to hear firsthand from the assembled Joint Chiefs—all largely silent to this point. Specifically, their concerns were regarding more budgetary uncertainty from Congress.

The Army stated that without a budget the National Training Center would have to stop training and that they would be unable to recruit the correct number of soldiers they needed. The Marine Corps focused on the loss of valuable civilians and the inability to buy new equipment they'd need to remain competitive. The Navy contended that a continuing resolution would wreak havoc on their ability to fix and deploy ships, bringing readiness to a halt. The Air Force highlighted that without a budget their planes would be forced to stop flying, delaying critical pilot flight qualifications for months—if not years.

The Air Force also pointed out that budgetary uncertainty drove talented individuals out of uniform, a point that Chief of Naval Operations John M. Richardson agreed with. "Mr. President, I agree. We're in a war for talent . . . and the harsh reality is that our smartest people are the first ones to go."

That was an incredibly honest—and particularly damning—acknowledgment, but one I'd seen played out many times in the past. The tough reality is that the most talented military leaders I had crossed paths with left the military at their first opportunity. I'd even written a long whitepaper about talent management in 2014. Retaining the best talent is difficult, particularly since military leaders tend to focus their attention elsewhere. It's a system—and a painful reality—that needs to be addressed if the military wants to retain its best and brightest service members. The military can't hire people directly into senior uniformed positions of leadership. Future leaders are merely the best of what's left as people make the decision to seek greener pastures in the private sector.

President Trump had one last item on his agenda to discuss before the meeting broke.

Surveying his audience, Trump said, "You know, Bastille Day in Paris . . . what a sight! It was so impressive to see all those tanks. Let's do that on Pennsylvania Avenue, maybe like a Fourth of July parade."

Mattis had deliberately slow-rolled this idea when President Trump had first brought it up last July, hoping that the parade would be forgotten. Now it was back.

General Dunford correctly read Mattis's expression and dared to push back against the idea. "Well, Mr. President, a parade like the one you're suggesting would come at a very high cost. Not only that, but the optics would look bad. The only nations that do parades like that are Russia . . . North Korea . . . and other authoritarian regimes. It won't send the right signal to Americans."

President Trump nodded but only said, "But . . . think about the spirit!"

General Paul Selva, vice chairman of the Joint Chiefs, jumped in. "The American military is about selfless sacrifice. And we already have three days recognizing the men and women of the military: Memorial Day, Veterans Day, and Armed Forces Day. I'm not sure we need a fourth."

Mattis, who wanted to kill the conversation before it went too far, said simply, "Mr. President, let's put some options together for you." With that, the meeting ended. The officer to my left looked over at me in the control room, saying, "You thought the parade idea was over? Wishful thinking, my friend."

FOURTEEN

GREAT POWERS

The reality is, the United States has global interests.
Our defense budget is about the same as the
defense budgets or military budgets of every
other country in the world put together.

—FORMER SECRETARY OF DEFENSE
ROBERT GATES

The next day I was sitting in the auditorium at Johns Hopkins University for Secretary Mattis's rollout of the National Defense Strategy when it hit me—the president never actually gave us the thumbs-up to release the strategy.

The briefing had careened so far off track that we just packed up and kept going with the rest of our day. It was a good example of how Mattis "managed up," taking the absence of a strong "no" from the president as tacit acknowledgment to press forward with a defense strategy that would drive America's $700 billion–plus in military investments for the next three to four years.

Arriving at the university's auditorium had been an exercise in comedy. I had helped Ryan Stoddard and the boss collect everything he'd need, provided them both with the latest copies of Mattis's speech, and compiled a listing of its most quotable quotes. Mattis always ordered his public affairs lead, Dana White, and me to "write the headlines we wanted to see." I found that the best way to do so was to help the reporters do their job. Who wanted to dig through an entire speech to mine its relatively few real nuggets? Better to offer them up front. To ensure maximum coverage, that morning I'd sent the draft to Colonel Rob Manning, the director of Pentagon press operations. He'd assisted by forwarding an embargoed copy of the remarks to all defense-related reporters.

Ready to roll out the strategy, Mattis, Stoddard, Faller, and I had made our way downstairs for the motorcade to the university. About five minutes later, I received a panicked text from Stoddard, who was riding with the secretary:

Whatever you do, don't give the speech out in advance!

I made a game-time decision to let that one slip by, texting Stoddard,

Thanks for the head's up, got it.

before adding:

Hey, don't offer up the fact that we've already given the speech out.

Better to not bring it up unless Mattis asked one of us directly. Today was not the day to risk letting something minor bother the secretary, and, frankly, providing the speech early allowed the press to tweet updates and write articles in real time. We always embargoed the material so the press couldn't use it until Mattis actually said it. First crisis averted.

We hit gridlock as we crossed into DC. Mattis abhors being late to anything, particularly an event as high-profile as releasing his own strategy. Bogged down in traffic, we hit every red light. I rode in one vehicle, watching as Mattis's head of security, Jim Rivera, became increasingly agitated. At one point, he wanted to use Mattis's vehicle's flashing red-and-blue lights to run through the intersections and push traffic out of the way, but Mattis always vetoed that. If normal Americans could sit stalled in traffic, well, so could he.

Well, maybe up to a point. We were still about five blocks away from the university when Mattis's vehicle door flung open, and he leapt out into congested traffic, determined to hike the rest of the way. We piled out to join him.

About a block down the road, a driver recognized Mattis. He quickly rolled down his window and yelled out "Oorah, General Mattis!" We never broke stride. Ten minutes later, we arrived at the front entrance to the auditorium, a little winded, but on time. Waiting curbside were our vehicles. They'd beat us by several minutes, so we'd walked for nothing. But the exercise raised Mattis's stock yet again, as a photographer captured us walking along the sidewalk with our game faces on. The photo went viral, sending the message, as words never could, of Mattis's can-do dedication.

Things finally went smoothly once we arrived. Mattis was rested, poised, and looked every inch the part of a secretary of defense as he took the podium. He looked out into the audience. ". . . This is a defense strategy, but what it really is, is an American strategy. It belongs to you . . . and we work for you." This was one of the things I enjoyed the most about working for Mattis—he always wanted to put the focus on others before himself. This wasn't his strategy or the administration's strategy. He firmly believed it was a strategy that belonged to all Americans.

In machine-gun fashion, he laid out the primary issues affecting America's military: "rapid technological change, the negative effects on military readiness resulting from the longest continuous stretch of combat in our nation's history, defense spending caps, and operating for nine out of the last ten years under continuing resolutions have created an overstretched and under-resourced military." Mattis was adamant that Congress needed to get its act together, having watched the military languish during the last few years of his time in uniform.

Mattis also pointed out that "our military's role is to keep the peace for one more year . . . one more month . . . one more day . . . to ensure our nation's diplomats who are working to solve problems do so from a position of strength." He noted with pride that "this is our nation's first national defense strategy in ten years." What Mattis really wanted to reinforce was the military's renewed sense of direction, saying, "Today, America's military reclaims an era of strategic purpose." This speech represented an opportunity to not only roll out the new strategy, but to restore confidence in the armed forces—for the public and for members of the military alike.

Catching everyone's attention was his declaration that the return of "great power competition—not terrorism" represented "the primary focus of US national security." This was a tectonic shift in focus after seventeen years of continuous war against terrorism. He further warned his audience to resist the temptation to lower its guard, as "America has no preordained right to victory on the battlefield."

Mattis concluded with a line that I would inject into our budget testimony on Capitol Hill. "For too long we have asked our military to stoically carry a 'success at any cost' attitude. Loyalty must be a two-way street. We must remain faithful to those who voluntarily sign a blank check to the American people, payable with their life." It was a tough reminder to Congress and the public that failure to adequately fund the military poses real risks. The reaction from the audience, the media, and the punditocracy was near-universally positive. They loved Mattis's personal embrace of the strategy. They admired its clarity and brevity, with Brookings Institution saying, "At first glance, what is most notable about the NDS [National Defense Strategy] is its length and its tenor. At eleven pages, the NDS is approximately 80 percent shorter than its most recent predecessor. . . . To their credit, Secretary Mattis and his team largely avoided the 'Christmas tree phenomenon' that plagues so many strategies, wherein every participant puts his or her own ornament—or pet issue— in the document. Remarkably, the NDS manages to be both pithy and blunt."

Releasing the strategy merely set the stage for a much more serious fight: restoring predictable and adequate DOD funding. The military had seen its annual budgets decrease precipitously during the preceding five years due to sequestration. The lack of funding and spare parts meant planes being grounded, ships not put to sea, and troops lacking training. In short, a military charged with fighting a nonstop war against terrorism and providing global presence was denied the very funding it needed to succeed. The military was overused and underfunded, leading to increased accidents and a large number of talented individuals heading to the exits for greener pastures.

Restoring the military's budget was now Mattis's top priority. The defense strategy was largely a means to that end, providing the department the justification it needed to increase congressional support. As Mattis had said, "a strategy without the budget to enact it is just a hallucination." We needed to raise military spending to levels that aligned with our requirement to fight the war on terrorism while also repairing years of decay and preparing for more difficult adversaries.

Mattis wasn't alone in this pursuit. Senator John McCain had recently released a well-received whitepaper entitled "Restoring American Power," a road map for rebuilding the military in order to preserve America's global leadership. Representative Mac Thornberry from Texas echoed McCain, and several Washington-based think tanks rang the alarm about sequestration's toll on the military.

President Trump had also pledged to restore the military during his campaign, saying, "We want to deter, avoid, and prevent conflict through our unquestioned military strength." All the good intentions were in place—now it was time to drive them home.

Mattis had campaigned for restored funding and budgetary certainty throughout his first year, so much of the groundwork was already laid. Congressional Democrats were largely opposed, as they wanted a one-for-one increase to match increased domestic spending with increased military spending. Mick Mulvaney, the director of the Office for Management and Budget, was also seeking to hold the defense department to a lower "top-line" budget, as were other Republicans concerned about ballooning federal deficits and the national debt.

Mattis knew that we had to be relentless about restoring military spending, especially since the latest continuing resolution was expiring in February.

Our first goal was alignment. Everyone had to be on message.

Mattis had previously briefed Trump on his proposed budgets for the department. Despite his reservations, Mulvaney agreed to a significant increase for 2018's budget, lifting defense spending to $700 billion with a smaller increase in 2019 to $716 billion to offset inflation. The military would have the funding and the certainty needed to invest in the big programs required for the renewed threats posed by China, Iran, Russia, or North Korea.

Speaker of the House Paul Ryan spoke at a prominent Washington think tank, the Center for Strategic and International Studies, the day before Mattis unveiled the defense strategy. I worked with Speaker Ryan's staff to help shape his remarks, incorporating into his speech the overall themes and language

Mattis would use to create a "one-two" punch to land renewed funding. Half the battle is just getting everyone on the same sheet of music.

Mattis had also hosted a closed-door briefing for the "Big Eight," the senior defense-related members of Congress, to provide advance notice of his requested funding. Most in the room understood the need, but reactions, nonetheless, fell largely along party lines. Mac Thornberry and his fellow Texas Republican, Representative Kay Granger, encouraged Mattis to "make the consequences clear to the American public." Democrats proved more skeptical and wanted an equal increase in nondefense spending if the military received more funds. Senator Dick Durbin was the most vocal, lamenting that "there is just a continuous call for more and more and more" from the military. No matter what their party, all were aware of the national debt at that point: 21 trillion dollars and counting.

We continued to lobby for congressional support through compelling, fact-based arguments rather than demands. As Mattis said, "Marines are known for our ability to take any hill . . . but the one hill we know better than to charge is Capitol Hill." The lesson? No one wins in an all-out fight with Congress, so we needed to help them get to "yes."

The campaign to win hearts and minds continued for the next two weeks. Mattis joined the Republican retreat of Senate and House members held at the Greenbrier Resort, West Virginia, to speak on the urgency for restoring the military budget now, not years later. As he put it, "I know you'll give me the money at the time of crisis, but by then it's too late. We need the money now to ensure we have the people and equipment required to ensure we can fight and win."

The pursuit of money came to a head the week of February 5, 2018. Mattis testified on Tuesday regarding the budget, including a closed-door session with a bipartisan group from the House Armed Services Committee.

I was struck by how collegial members of Congress tended to be behind closed doors. In front of the cameras, congressional members happily tear into the opposing party, whether during a hearing or when caught by reporters in the hallway. But behind closed doors, with media and cameras excluded, they were friendly and deferential to one another. I found myself wishing that their public personas matched their private ones, bypassing the venom that infuses today's 24/7/365 news cycle. I wasn't sure whether to be reassured that things functioned well in these settings, or dismayed that most posturing for the media was just theater.

Another closed-door session followed, this time with the Senate National Security Working Group to provide more depth on the emerging threats facing America—China, Russia, North Korea, and Iran. Senators Dianne Feinstein and Jack Reed were the first to arrive, followed by more of the "who's who" I'd watched on TV: Ben Sasse, Tammy Duckworth, Roy Blunt, and Heidi Heitkamp, to name a few.

The conversation was sobering, as Mattis outlined the global threats facing America. In his traditional, no-nonsense style, he warned, "I cannot defend America sufficiently without a budget." Senator Feinstein was particularly concerned about North

Korea, as California is closest to the Hermit Kingdom among the continental states.

The next day Mattis returned to the Capitol for a meeting with Representatives Kay Granger and Pete Visclosky from the House Appropriation Subcommittee on Defense. Again, Mattis emphasized that the military exists to give "Secretary Tillerson and our diplomats time to resolve crises through diplomatic channels . . . a confidence [that] can only be underpinned by the assurance that our military will win should diplomacy fail . . . Those who would threaten America's experiment in democracy must know: if you threaten us, it will be your longest and worst day."

Overall, the meeting went well. I was in Mattis's office with Faller and Sweeney to discuss how things had gone on Capitol Hill and what our next steps should be to restore the military's budget. We'd been in the office for maybe two minutes when the phone on Mattis's desk rang. The secretary's scheduler called out from the office next door, "Sir, it's the president."

Mattis put the call on speaker, as he usually did so we all could hear the conversation. "Good morning, Mr. President. What can I do for you?"

The president was in a great mood. "General, how is everything? I think you're doing a great job over there . . . just great. I think we're close to getting what we need for the budget, so close, but we have to get this done . . . it needs to get done. We're doing a press conference at 1:30 and I need you there. You need to tell America what we need. I need you there."

Mattis had hitherto refused any White House–related press appearances. Mattis had also previously told press secretary Sean

Spicer—and then Spicer's replacement, Sarah Sanders—that he wouldn't go on Sunday shows where cabinet officials were expected to make the rounds. But now the president himself was asking. How would Mattis handle this one?

It's fascinating to hear your boss interact with *his* boss, especially in private. I'd participated in two presidential briefings at the Pentagon, but there Mattis had an audience in addition to Trump. On this call, he was essentially alone except for a few of his closest staff members.

I was surprised when Mattis's voice turned very ingratiating. "Mr. President, things are going well. I think we have them where we want them. You know I'm here for you. I'm happy to come over if you think that's what we need."

I'd never seen this side of Mattis before. While I had accompanied Mattis to the White House, I had never been inside an Oval Office meeting with him. This phone call likely reflected what their interactions were like at the White House, how Mattis "manages up."

The president was pleased. "Okay great, General. We'll see you over here in a while."

Now the real scramble began. In an act of supreme confidence that I appreciated, Mattis simply looked over at me and said, "Bus, you know what I want to do. Get me something as fast as you can." I nodded in assent. "Yes, sir—on it."

I sprinted to my desk and put together a short, distilled version of the message Mattis had refined during the previous month. By this point I had written more than two hundred speeches, letters, and memos for the boss. I knew his voice, but this was going to be tough. His remarks had to be pithy, tailored to deliver the soundbites the press would need to rebroadcast across America. Normally I agonize over a speech, cranking out multiple revisions to distill remarks down to the best possible version. Today's urgency wasn't affording me that opportunity.

Sweeney, who rarely ventured all the way to the other side of our office suite, materialized at my desk within ten minutes. "Okay, Bus, what do you have?" I briefly glanced up—he knew I was under the gun. "Almost there, Admiral. I just need a few more minutes to make it sing."

Sweeney's impatience wasn't helping—but it was an accurate reflection of the secretary's state of mind. The remarks had to be written quickly. They also needed to be persuasive and error-free.

I wrapped up the remarks with enough time for Mattis to go through two rounds of revisions.

An hour later, Mattis joined Sarah Sanders in the White House press briefing room. After a brief introduction, Mattis stepped to the lectern, his voice back to its normal stoic, commanding tone.

"I am heartened that Congress recognizes the sobering effect of budgetary uncertainty on America's military, and on the men and women who provide for our nation's defense." For a decade the military had not received the funding needed to accomplish all its missions, but "America can afford survival."

He continued, emphasizing that for too long the military has had to carry on with a "success at any cost" attitude. "The fact that America's volunteer military has performed so well," he said, "is a credit to their dedication and professionalism. We expect the men and women of our military to be faithful in their service, even when going in harm's way. We have a duty to remain faithful to them."

His speech came just in time, providing Congress with all the ammunition they needed. The last significant push came the next day when Rob Hood, his legislative director, and I joined Mattis in his office for calls to members of Congress still on the fence. He made call after call, all with the same message: "We face tough consequences if we don't get the budget."

The message was near-universally the same. Members were now willing to vote for the bill because they could tell constituents that while the spending bill wasn't perfect, Jim Mattis had called them personally for their support. All they asked in return was for Mattis to continue to publicly justify the need for rebuilding the military to provide top cover for their vote.

The Bipartisan Budget Act of 2018 passed both chambers of Congress the next day, February 9. President Trump signed it the same day. This experience reinforced the importance of Mattis's strong reputation as arguably the most respected member of the administration. Coupled with the consistent efforts of the entire Pentagon and administration teams, his last-minute push cemented the sorely needed two-year budget deal that had tortuously maneuvered its way through Congress.

At long last, we had a defense budget. Our work to achieve a budget, however, was about to be replaced by challenges with far more significant consequences.

FIFTEEN

LAST ADULT STANDING

Leadership consists of picking good men and helping
them do their best for you. The attributes of loyalty,
discipline and devotion to duty on the part of
subordinates must be matched by patience, tolerance
and understanding on the part of superiors.

—FLEET ADMIRAL CHESTER NIMITZ

"Hey, take a look. This isn't good."

I swiveled my chair around to check the television screen on
the wall. The Marine lieutenant colonel with whom I shared
space in Mattis's office was watching the news.

We routinely cycled between the cable news channels. He
happened to be watching MSNBC. A chyron splashed on the
bottom of the screen: "McMaster Out, Bolton In as Trump Natl.
Security Advisor."

"Whoa," I said, watching as the screens updated. "Things are
about to get ugly for the boss."

The lieutenant colonel looked over at me. "Yup."

It was March 22, 2018, and President Trump had just fired his second national security adviser in the span of fourteen months.

Their strained relationship had spilled into public view back in February. McMaster, speaking before an international audience at the Munich Security Conference in Germany, had confirmed Russian interference during the 2016 elections, saying, "As you can see with the FBI indictment, the evidence is now really incontrovertible." McMaster had just stumbled over a tripwire—mentioning the allegations that Russia had supported Trump for president, which had triggered former FBI director Robert Mueller's ongoing investigation.

Friends at the White House confided to me that the president was furious. His tweets soon confirmed this.

"General McMaster forgot to say that the results of the 2016 election were not impacted or changed by the Russians and that the only Collusion was between Russia and Crooked H, the DNC and the Dems," Trump tweeted. "Remember the Dirty Dossier, Uranium, Speeches, Emails and the Podesta Company!"

The situation only escalated, and by the end of February, the media buzzed with speculation about McMaster's impending demise. Now, McMaster was being cut loose. But McMaster wasn't the only one suffering Trump's wrath. Tillerson was also out.

On March 13, the week before McMaster's firing, Rex Tillerson took the stage at the state department to confirm that he too had been fired by President Trump. Tillerson was out with such speed that he essentially ceased working on the spot, telling the world that "effective at the end of the day, I'm delegating all responsibilities of the office of the secretary to Deputy Secretary of State [John] Sullivan . . ."

This was yet more turbulence in a national security team that had already endured far more than its fair share, and far more than any other administration in recent memory. It was customary for strong-willed cabinet members, national security advisers, and White House staff to differ. But it was rare for a president to keep firing them so early—and so frequently.

What concerned me the most, of course, was its effect on the last man standing, Secretary Mattis. The "adults" had been walking a tightrope, translating Trump's impetuous demands into a more professional, nuanced process, with varying levels of success. McMaster's and Tillerson's oustings seemed guaranteed to sidetrack Mattis's ability to positively influence administration goals.

By now, I had been with Secretary Mattis for a year. We'd logged enough miles in our aircraft to circumnavigate the globe multiple times. Up close, I'd witnessed the challenging and, at times, frustrating circumstances within the Trump administration.

While some aspects of national politics are puzzlingly obscure, it's shockingly apparent when the political ground rocks below your boss's feet.

Losing Tillerson and McMaster was tough, but, at the time, I thought Tillerson's departure was the bigger blow. Contrary to popular belief, the former Exxon CEO was not an isolated and ineffective figure in the Trump administration. He had, in fact, performed a vital role in the national security team, at least as we saw it from the Pentagon's E-ring.

Yes, Mattis and McMaster had their differences, but McMaster's exit stripped Mattis of his last ally in the national security trio. The only firewall he had left at the White House was General Kelly, the president's chief of staff.

Although Mattis actively cultivated an "aww, shucks" public persona, behind the scenes he was a skilled diplomatic player able to effectively navigate through the chaotic Trump administration bureaucracy. The dynamics of his first year had enabled Mattis to operate in the role he was most comfortable with, as a "shadow warrior" able to go quietly about his work, while avoiding the media circus to the best extent possible. Conveniently, this also allowed him to avoid direct confrontations with the president on many pressing issues.

Tillerson and McMaster had been far more willing to take risks in disagreeing with Trump—Tillerson because of his personality, and McMaster due to the proximity of his West Wing office. From the phone calls I overhead, both seemed more willing than Mattis to challenge the president's decisions. They had staked out dangerous ground.

For the first time since joining the administration, Mattis was exposed and vulnerable. Back in January, Trump had singled Mattis out during his State of the Union speech to offer praise, recognizing that Mattis was "doing a great job." But that was January. Watching the news reports play out regarding McMaster's departure, I instantly concluded that it would be only a matter of time before Mattis appeared in the crosshairs. He had to choose his battles carefully. He would also undoubtedly receive more scrutiny—from both the press and other administration politicos—regarding his relationship with Trump.

Though it affected Mattis to only a lesser extent, Trump's chief economic adviser, Gary Cohn, also exited in March. Cohn departed over long-standing disagreements about steel and aluminum tariffs the administration planned to levy indiscriminately against allied and competitor nations. Cohn argued that tariffs would ultimately harm America's interests, a position Mattis agreed with but for different reasons. Mattis's concern centered around perceived economic attacks against allied and partner nations, generating further harm to the long-standing American-led international order.

Reportedly, Cohn's resolve was also shaken by Trump's handling of the response to violence at a "Unite the Right" white supremacy rally in Charlottesville, Virginia. It was yet another example of Trump's unartful tweeting wreaking havoc both in his poll numbers and within the administration itself.

Tillerson's, McMaster's, and Cohn's departures were compounded by a major loss within our own team. Sally Donnelly, Mattis's senior adviser, had departed two weeks before, leaving a sizable gap in our capabilities.

Donnelly enjoyed a good working relationship with the Pentagon press corps. This association provided a useful line of communication to find out what was on their minds, enabling us to douse potential media-related fires before they erupted into third-degree-burn major conflagrations. Her links were doubly important because members of the press loathed Dana White, Mattis's assistant for public affairs. To the press, White eagerly withheld updates on the military and access to Mattis. White was also more than willing to hold reporters accountable—behavior Mattis relished but the press pool resented.

Donnelly possessed a rolodex of contacts deeper than anyone I'd ever met. Need to get in touch with Jared Kushner at the White House? No problem. An obscure staffer at the state department? On it. The commanding general overseas? Here you go. Donnelly made it her job to connect with anyone and everyone who mattered, a skill set that enabled us to move quickly on Mattis's initiatives or requests for information.

Losing Donnelly, and her contacts, meant peeling away another layer of protection for the boss, a layer every bit as important as any Tillerson, McMaster, and Cohn had offered.

The lack of diversity in our office was also a problem: most of us were white, male, and military. The vast majority were also associated with the Navy or Marine Corps. Groupthink was a very real concern. Donnelly had offered a unique perspective. She didn't think like a military officer, which helped us translate military culture to "civilian speak," a handy skill.

A diverse office brings a great many strengths, not the least of which is a variety in background and ideas. Moreover, as secretary of defense, Mattis represented *all* branches of the armed forces. I'd like to believe that we still offered up unbiased information for Mattis to consider, but there was a sometimes-unhealthy disdain expressed for both the Air Force and the Army.

We were obviously (and visually) homogenous. A photo snapped while we walked to Johns Hopkins University back in January revealed a group of naval officers walking down the street: a retired Marine and three members of the Navy. At first, the picture reminded me of what the Marines say about sailors: Marines do the hard work. The Navy just exists to take Marines where they need to go.

There was a reason we worked hard to avoid being in the same picture frame as the secretary. We wanted to avoid highlighting the lack of diversity in our office. But there were certainly positive benefits to a military-heavy front office. Our shared background meant we largely understood Mattis's "commander's intent," the ability to receive minimal information and guidance but still get the job done to his satisfaction.

A large military presence also provides other benefits: a willingness to work near-limitless hours to get the job done, a bias toward action over discussion, and a built-in reluctance to talk with the media.

But I found myself wondering, at what cost? There were undoubtedly times where a slower, more deliberate pace would have served the secretary well. A greater civilian presence with a more diverse experience base would have increased our corporate knowledge and softened the civilian-military relationship concerns that plagued senior leaders in the Pentagon.

I felt this situation was a good reminder for all future leaders: every choice you make has tradeoffs—so think about what you are trying to achieve with the organization you are building. We were built primarily for speed and our ability to keep up with Mattis's furious pace. But that didn't make it the right choice.

Losing Donnelly also meant that we were losing our only consistently effective team builder. She rarely lost her cool, even during the most trying of challenges. She was the one senior member of the team who made time to walk around and say hello, especially to junior members of the office and around the Pentagon. She opened her door to assist others, including those in our office now seeking another line of work, selflessly giving of her time and contacts to ensure teammates found a place to land.

In short, Sally was the type of person you wanted to work for. She took care of her people. I was surprised to find myself thinking that our senior military leaders could learn a great deal from her approach to leadership and talent management.

The most damning part of her departure was the manner in how it developed, a reality that highlights some of the challenges we experienced in our own office.

The quickest way to exit Mattis's orbit is to have him believe that you've leaked material to the press. It's one of his few "unforgivable sins." Somewhere along the way, Faller, Sweeney, and White started a whispering campaign that Donnelly was leaking information. The assertion was doubly preposterous, because a large part of her role required staying connected with the press, especially since White hadn't forged good working relationships with them.

I witnessed this toxic campaign firsthand. Faller, Sweeney, and White had, at various times, pulled me aside, warning me not to be perceived as being too close to Sally. *Be careful,* they said. *The boss is upset with Sally. She's been leaking to the press. You don't want to get caught up in that.*

I knew Donnelly well enough to know that had they confronted her, she would have vehemently disputed their accusations. This struck me as quintessentially "DC" office politics. I had also watched similar techniques being used against others who had left Mattis's front office. It felt like that greatest and oldest of military tactics: divide and conquer.

It was also the most venomous kind of leadership. Maybe

Faller, Sweeney, and White thought their words would draw me closer into their orbit, but they only repelled me. *If you've done this to Sally and the others who left the team,* I wondered, *what are you saying behind my back?*

The experience reminded me of how Sweeney and Faller had turned on my predecessor, Justin Mikolay.

Mikolay was a fantastic writer but had a difficult time keeping pace with the torrent of speeches needed during his first few months. This was understandable, given that he held down the task of speechwriting by himself for the first few months of Mattis's tenure.

Rather than provide guidance or mentorship, Faller and Sweeney simply pushed him aside. Back in April 2017, I had been on the team less than two weeks when Faller made it a point to tell me that they were positioning me to take Justin's place. "Have you talked to Justin about this?" I asked. "No," Faller replied. "You get what we're trying to do here. He doesn't." Faller thought I'd appreciate that I was "his guy," but it only diminished him in my eyes. *Wouldn't we be better served by strengthening the team,* I thought, *not dividing it?*

This undermined every leadership lesson I knew. Then again, it's easy to teach leadership in a vacuum, like at the military schools I had attended in Annapolis, Colorado Springs, and Newport. This was the real world. I now worked with a relatively small number of officers on a high-powered, DC-based staff working for a powerful cabinet secretary.

I did what I considered to be the right thing after Faller shared his thoughts with me: I immediately passed them along to Mikolay so our speechwriting team could course correct.

The simple reality is that people rarely perform poorly on purpose. Rather, poor performance is usually sparked by a misalignment of expectations and subsequent lack of communication to address those differences. When a mistake is made, you talk about it openly and correct it. If a person routinely fails to perform as needed, you provide plenty of mentorship and opportunities to improve. They should be removed only after proving incapable of meeting the standards, and, even then, you should still work with them to find a suitable place to land.

I wanted to let Mikolay in on the conversations so he could respond appropriately. But his heart just wasn't in it anymore. He'd been ridden hard for the past eight months. He had been commuting for a total of two hours a day just to drive to and from the Pentagon. Ultimately, he decided it was time to return to his family and the private sector.

It was our loss. Along with Donnelly and Mikolay, I watched as others were pushed out. The worst part? Even as a Navy commander and chief speechwriter, I was powerless to do anything about it. I could only hunker down, work hard, and protect Bill Rivers and Nicole Magney, my two speechwriters, from meeting Mikolay's fate.

Thankfully, Donnelly received an appropriate sendoff for her efforts to shepherd Mattis through his confirmation hearing and for her year as senior adviser. The narrative was that her time had drawn to a close. That story offered a graceful—and appropriate—exit.

Her farewell reception in the secretary's dining room was standing-room only, a fitting testament to her positive, highly human influence as a leader. Senior leaders from around the Pentagon paid their respects and wished her well. Even Gary Cohn and Jared Kushner paid homage. It was noteworthy that team members who had previously left our office returned for the occasion.

Losing Tillerson, McMaster, Cohn, and Donnelly—all in one month—proved a difficult blow, especially given the challenges we were about to confront.

SIXTEEN

HEADWINDS

Your experience facing and overcoming adversity
is actually one of your biggest advantages.

—MICHELLE OBAMA

Mattis walked down the steps just outside the Pentagon's River Entrance as Ambassador John Bolton made his way across the last several feet of the parking lot. Both men had smiles on their faces, though Bolton's demeanor made his smile come across more like a grimace. As the cameras from the press corps clicked away, Mattis extended his hand to greet him. "Ambassador Bolton . . ." began Mattis, as Bolton simultaneously said, "Mr. Secretary, so good to see you." They didn't loiter outside; instead Mattis turned on his heels to lead Ambassador Bolton back up the steps. "Thanks for coming and it's good to finally meet you.

I've heard that you're actually the devil incarnate and I wanted to meet you," Mattis said as he and Bolton walked into the Pentagon. Bolton just chuckled as they passed through the doorway and made their way to Mattis's office.

It was March 29, and Bolton had recently been named to replace H. R. McMaster as Trump's third national security adviser in fourteen months. Widely considered hawkish, Bolton had been on television at various times to advocate for force against North Korea and overthrowing the Iranian regime. Bolton had served in three previous Republican administrations, including stints at the US Agency for International Development with Ronald Reagan, as assistant secretary of state with George H. W. Bush, and as ambassador to the United Nations under George W. Bush.

Other key replacements in the administration had also been named. Trump nominated Mike Pompeo, the Central Intelligence Agency director and former congressman from Kansas, to replace Tillerson at the state department. A West Point and Harvard graduate, Pompeo had reportedly formed a bond with the president by personally delivering the president's daily brief to the White House each day. He'd also broken tradition by becoming more active in decision-making discussions, rather than merely offering up an intelligence viewpoint when required.

Larry Kudlow had also joined the administration, taking Gary Cohn's place as Trump's chief economic adviser. A financial analyst with time on Wall Street with Bear Stearns, Kudlow had served in Reagan's Office of Management and Budget. He left during Reagan's second term, returning to Wall Street before leaving to become a host on CNBC.

Bolton, Pompeo, and Kudlow—despite his being a longtime supporter of free trade—were reported as being far friendlier to the president's "America First" policies than the officials they were replacing. Conversations among Mattis's front office team members were cautious but optimistic.

Trump certainly deserves to have appointees that support his initiatives. But one aspect of their shared backgrounds gave me cause for concern: all three had political backgrounds, whereas Tillerson, McMaster, and Cohn did not. Mattis had not only lost his support structure in the administration, but those three men's replacements would be far more skilled at offsetting Mattis.

The other significant shoe to drop was Bolton's hiring of Mira Ricardel as his deputy national security adviser, the same Ricardel whom Mattis clashed with over political appointee jobs during the administration's early days. Mattis and Sweeney had believed her to be safely sidelined with a job at the commerce department.

Now she was back.

I had learned a lot during my first year on Secretary Mattis's team. One of the first lessons on how to succeed in Washington, DC, came from a conversation with two special assistants in Deputy Secretary of Defense Pat Shanahan's office. Their blanket advice? "Always treat people well on your way up the ladder, as they'll be the same people you see when you inevitably come back down." Another, more cynical take would be, "never make an enemy."

Mattis always encouraged those around him to heed President Lincoln's call to "listen to their better angels," especially when dealing with others. Unfortunately, Sweeney's challenging relationship with Ricardel now took on ominous proportions, with Ricardel now in an influential position from which she could affect the Department of Defense.

One of the earliest indications of the shift within the National Security Council was the significant reduction in communication between the Pentagon and the White House.

Under McMaster the NSC had routinely included the Pentagon on correspondence circulated among federal agencies, but this conduit dried up. So too did the transcripts of Trump's phone calls with world leaders. Pentagon leaders were also held out of committee meetings typically hosted at the White House. We were notified that other departments were included as needed, but Defense was now increasingly held at arm's length. Perhaps it was merely coincidence, but Mattis was also no longer being invited over to the White House to meet with Trump as often as when Tillerson and McMaster were in the administration.

I personally witnessed a similar change in how the administration's message was crafted. For the first ten months or so I'd taken the de facto lead for coordinating defense-focused messaging with the White House and other agencies. Mattis was laser-focused on core issues and expected us to be planning three to six months out from any significant events. The rest of the administration didn't seem to be planning that far ahead, so I took the lead when events came up that required coordination across agencies, like congressional briefings or Pentagon briefings for President Trump.

This changed with the swap-out of leadership at State and

the NSC. We were still collegial and worked well together, but the NSC in particular wanted to drive the message rather than defer to Defense. From my vantage point, it seemed like further evidence that the Pentagon was being iced out.

Mattis worked to maintain a "steady as she goes" mind-set for the department as we continued to tackle big issues that still lingered. The secretary also remained sensitive to aligning our message with President Trump during this period. My interpretation of our interactions was Mattis's continued desire to ensure we didn't make any easily avoidable mistakes that would highlight a policy divide between the White House and the Pentagon.

During a Small Group meeting in his office on Friday, March 23, Mattis reminded us of the need for alignment. "Small Group" was a meeting held every Monday, Wednesday, and Friday morning in Mattis's office. Unlike the collegial Large Group meeting held in the secretary's conference room, Small Group included only a small subset of senior officials.

This day Mattis asked Dana White to ensure she had "new, solid White House talking points. The White House is not to be trusted right now—it's too undisciplined at the moment" due to its high-level personnel shake-ups. He reinforced the need for proactively ensuring that we remained aligned with the latest language from Trump and senior administration officials. "Let's not walk into an L-shaped ambush," he said, referencing a military term describing a mistake that would land us in the kill zone and cause us to take heavy casualties.

North Korea was still a leading topic, and President Trump was openly musing about holding a meeting with North Korea's

Kim Jong Un and curtailing exercises between the US and South Korea, a recurring request from the North Koreans. "Don't take away the president's decision space," Mattis said. He also cautioned against sharing too much in a public hearing with Congress. "We owe candor—but we don't reveal operations. Using his favorite advice from Kissinger, Mattis said, "We also won't tell the enemy what we're not going to do."

Mattis pulled me aside as the meeting ended. "Bus, I need you to get with Stephen Miller. I saw him recently at the White House. He's got some good ideas for language we can use for North Korea."

Stephen was even busier than I was, so we coordinated an opportunity to speak on the phone along with Matt Pottinger, an Indo-Pacific representative at the National Security Council. While I had worked regularly with Stephen during my time on Mattis's team, we'd actually never met in person. Trump kept him close by at the White House, and Mattis did the same with me at the Pentagon, making linking up in person during the workday difficult.

Miller's guidance on the phone was every bit as colorful as the messages I'd watched him deliver on television. Regarding the Korean situation, Miller said, "We must counter North Korean rhetoric. This is a repressive regime that murders innocents."

He sounded like he was shilling talking points on a Sunday show rather than speaking with an administration colleague from across the river. "Bus," said Miller, "we must highlight the depravity of the regime." He was comfortable including tougher language with the understanding that we wanted to maintain the "maximum pressure campaign" that Tillerson had led diplomatically before exiting the administration.

Miller continued, "We need public and international support for our maximum pressure campaign as we attempt to reach the 'international left'—portray [the North Koreans] as racist, anti-women, anti-gay, ethnocentric fascists." Heck, I was willing to give Miller credit just for finding a way to work "ethnocentric fascists" into a sentence.

"This is a country with prison and labor camps," he said, "that uses public execution, and with a dictator who murdered his brother in an international airport." It wasn't lost on me that we were developing a coordinated message that would soon become the official stance of the United States of America.

Beyond the conversation with Miller for new North Korea talking points, Mattis also remained adamant about following through on the department's obligations to serve as good stewards of taxpayer dollars, a promise he had made to Congress when seeking a two-year budget deal.

Deputy Secretary Shanahan said during a Small Group meeting what we all knew to be true: that "the military manages expenditures, not results." He made a good point. Congress authorizes a budget for the military, and then it becomes our job to spend each account down to the last penny to justify the same amount—or more—the next year. Shanahan wanted to break that cycle, creating the Pentagon's Reform Management Group to identify ways to save money across the next five-year plan, known as the Future Years Defense Program (FYDP), pronounced "fiddip" for short.

Mattis directed me to draft a message to the military about our fiscal responsibilities.

"I am writing directly to you for help in taking proactive steps to ensure our military is ready to fight today and in the future," it stated. "I need your help to promote a culture of performance where results and accountability matter on every expenditure. . . . This is critical to strengthen the trust and confidence that the Congress and the American people have for our team." Mattis released the message on March 26. When writing a message for the secretary we always assumed it would leak . . . and sometimes we wanted it to leak to help get the message into the public debate.

The rest of the spring remained a whirlwind. It felt like we were putting out one dumpster fire after another. On April 5, President Trump ordered Mattis to send troops to the US-Mexico border. Ken Rapuano, the assistant secretary of defense for Homeland Security, took the lead to assess options along with members of our general counsel. Mattis was concerned about the legality of the action, the limitations that we'd be placing on our troops, and the overall optic of involving troops in domestic border control actions. He ultimately ordered four thousand members of the National Guard to the southern border using Title 32 duty status, the law that governs use of the Guard for federal active duty.

The parade that Trump had directed us to plan back in July 2017 had evidently raised its head again. As Faller noted, it had been tasked out for cost analysis. Mattis, reflecting all our thoughts, said, "I'd rather swallow acid," in response. I certainly wanted to avoid the sight of tanks rolling down Pennsylvania Avenue, let alone repurposing money for that rather than military readiness. As one of my sailors once told me, a parade was "all show and no go."

The chaos in the administration did provide a form of top cover. Although reports of a Mattis-Trump rift started appearing in the news, the departure of sixteen senior administration officials over the next five months meant that the reports never became the focus.

The press continued to fixate on long-running stories about David Shulkin at Veterans Affairs, Hope Hicks at the White House, and Scott Pruitt at the EPA—not to mention the perpetual Mueller investigation. Having watched the administration's revolving door spin wildly for a year now, I regretted the media scrutiny its victims faced. It seemed difficult to leave the administration with one's honor intact unless you simply set an egg timer and then walked away when it went off. Anything else seemed destined to be spun as "being fired" by Trump.

This was a difficult period of time for the front office team. Faller risked being forcibly retired from the Navy because he hadn't been cleared yet from the "Fat Leonard" scandal rocking the Navy. A company named Glenn Defense Marine Asia had traded money and gifts for classified information regarding ship movements. Faller, having previously accepted ten-thousand-dollar-a-night luxury hotel rooms and attended extravagant company dinners, had been caught up in the mess. His stress level was through the roof—and he shared that stress with the rest of us in the office.

The honeymoon that had existed following the writing of the unclassified National Defense Strategy and some other "heavy lift" projects had worn off. I was in Mattis's office one evening to work on his budget testimony for the next day. Mattis looked exhausted. I had brought a fresh copy of the sixteen-page draft with me and he wanted to sit down and review it line by line. At one point he gestured to a quote I had in the draft about Congress's responsibility to "raise and support Armies" and to "provide and maintain a Navy."

Mattis looked up at me, the bags under his eyes bigger than usual and his hair falling limply forward on his forehead, a sure sign that he was exhausted. "Hey, Bus, these don't look quite right. Let's move the quotation marks here," as he used his pen to indicate where he wanted them. I dutifully agreed to make the changes.

The next morning, he walked down the hallway to my desk. "Bus, do you have the updated statement?" I reached down to my desk, "Yes, sir—here it is." I handed the fresh copy over and he started to walk away, flipping slowly through each page. Then he stopped, paused, and turned right back around. "Bus, this quote is wrong." He was pointing to the one he'd asked me to change the night before. "This is a quote straight out of the Constitution. We can't afford to mess things up like this. You need more eyes on this before I see it. Remember, even Hemingway had an editor."

Frankly, I wasn't quite sure what to do in the moment. My first thought was to point out that he had directed that very change last night. But that didn't seem appropriate, especially as he was tired and now visibly agitated. Instead, I took the most direct path I could to achieve a speedy resolution. "Got it, sir. I can make the change for you right now."

Mattis walked over and stood by the printers near my desk, saying, "Okay, I'll wait." I unlocked my computer and began to navigate to the speech folders buried within our network. Finally locating the speech, I opened the file and got to work. Mattis grew impatient and just grumbled, "I don't have time for this," along with a few choice comments, before he walked toward his office. "Just bring it to me when you've fixed it." It was the most agitated I'd ever seen him in private.

It was one of those moments that I wish I could have back. My primary goal as chief speechwriter was to ensure Mattis had whatever he needed just the way he wanted it. My team played with speech content all the time to ensure he had the correct phonetic spelling for complicated names and to hit the right voice inflection at the right time.

It was all part of the behind-the-scenes operations in the speechwriting world. But Mattis seemed to take my comment as an admission of guilt, which meant that he walked away thinking I was in error, always a dangerous place to be. He was now convinced I needed several people to review my drafts before he received them, a decision that would create an entirely new problem moving forward.

It was around this time that Faller pulled me aside to discuss my future. I was still seeking a way to serve as a leader in the defense department after declining to accept the pathway to aircraft carrier command. Since the door to the way forward in the Navy was shut, I had submitted my paperwork to retire after twenty years in the Navy and then remain with Mattis as a political appointee. I was disappointed that my dream of being an air wing commander had dissolved, but thankful that avenues were available for me to continue making a difference to the nation.

Faller, however, was concerned that I might retire and then decide to leave the team. One afternoon as we walked in the hallway past the conference room, he told me that the Navy had forwarded my retirement letter to him for endorsement. "Bus, I need to know what your intentions are. I'm not inclined to sign your letter if you're not willing to stay here." I assured him that I was happy to stay. "Sir, I've already told Chief [Sweeney] that I'm excited by the opportunity to continue to serve as a civilian appointee." Faller visibly relaxed. "Really? Okay then, I'll endorse your request for retirement. We need you on the team."

So I was rocked back on my heels by a follow-up conversation with Faller a few weeks later. I had stopped by his office to drop off some draft speeches and asked Faller how he thought things were going. He was blunt and didn't mince any words. "Bus, not taking the next, hardest job (the aircraft carrier pathway) was a mortal wound in your relationship with the secretary of defense."

This was what he'd warned me about—that Mattis loses respect for people who turn down the toughest jobs, no matter the reason.

Faller had cautioned me about Mattis's worldview, but I'd hoped that "staying in the fight" at work would ultimately carry the day. The toughest part for a type A personality like mine was Faller's answer after I asked what I could do to improve the relationship. "There's nothing you can do. Just keep working hard."

This was tough medicine to take. I was already leaving the

house at 5:30 a.m. and returning after 8:00 p.m., and typically spending one day of each weekend at work. During the week the kids were already in bed when I returned home, so I tended to see them only on the weekend. I was worn out, more emotionally than physically. And I was a burden to Sarah, who was tired of hearing me talk about work. I was absolutely guilty of bringing my work home with me, and the stress that went along with it, but couldn't seem to break the cycle. It was a tough time for the family. The only answer seemed to be the one that had made me successful to this point in my career: Stay in the fight. Don't give up.

I'd tried to talk with Mattis in person for some mentorship and to discuss opportunities to shape a civilian career with a focus on continued service. We were both in the Pentagon one weekend during the winter while I was working on the unclassified national defense strategy. He walked down to my desk to say hello and check on me. As he turned to walk back to his desk, I asked if he could spare a few more minutes. He obliged, so I asked, "Sir, I know you made a significant impact during your four decades in uniform. Do you think I can have the same level of influence as a civilian?"—a reference to my new career path.

He didn't pause to consider before replying, "No, you can't. As a military officer in uniform you'll always be relevant. As a civilian, you're usually cycling into and out of positions of responsibility depending on how the winds blow. You can't have the same impact." I appreciated his candor but was surprised by his response. What about the leaders he respected? Henry Kissinger,

Condoleezza Rice, George Shultz, and countless others? Each made incredibly meaningful national security decisions as civilians. Wanting to understand more, I asked if he would consider sparing fifteen minutes for an actual mentorship session. "Sure, Bus," he said, "anytime. Just come on down."

Mattis remembered my request. Two weeks later he brought Stoddard, me, and the Marine lieutenant colonel into his office for some mentorship. Stoddard and the Marine had worked for him before, so they were trying to avoid this session. They said it'd be a waste of time—Mattis wouldn't offer a conversation or personalized thoughts. They were right.

At the appointed time, the three of us piled into his office. "Mentorship" consisted of handing over some letters he'd written previously to help us better understand his worldview. His talking points were what he provided to each class of new one-star officers and senior civilians. It was clear that his heart was in the right place, and I appreciated his generously making time for us, but I left with the uncomfortable feeling that he'd spent so long as a general that it was tough for him to relate to us—he'd lost the perspective of what it was like to be Lieutenant Colonel James Mattis.

At the end of April, I transitioned out of uniform, retiring as a Navy commander with twenty years of commissioned service.

It wasn't the career path I had imagined when joining Mattis's team in the Pentagon. To his credit, Sweeney had met me for a beer during the winter to discuss my next steps. Meeting at a

BBQ restaurant near the Pentagon, Sweeney had asked, "Okay, Bus. What's your plan?"

I had shared with him my desire to continue to serve. I suggested that I continue in the office as a civilian political appointee, a path that would enable me to contribute while providing a path to a leadership position down the road. Sweeney agreed and asked me to stay with the team. I gratefully accepted.

A big part of the military's ethos is to take life as it comes while maintaining your "military bearing," a term that refers to a state of mind similar to stoicism. Stay focused. Don't let setbacks affect your attitude. Move forward and stay positive. *Always* stay positive. It was a mind-set I had had ingrained in me over the past nineteen years, and it helped carry me through this period of time. While I wished that things had gone differently, I was nonetheless excited about the opportunities that lay before me. I would still be in the fight, albeit as a civilian.

So now my time as a naval officer was drawing to a close. I was honored that Mattis had invited my family to his office for the presentation of my "end of tour" award. He was presenting me with the Defense Superior Service Medal, an award for "superior meritorious service in a position of significant responsibility"—a level of award normally reserved for admirals and generals. Mattis was presenting the award in recognition of my work with him and the staff "during a time marked by historic national security challenges." I felt incredibly humbled. Sarah dressed the kids up in their Sunday best, and we made our way to the Pentagon.

As focused as Mattis usually is on business, he really comes alive when families are involved. His head of protocol escorted us into his office as members of the front office team lined the hallway. Mattis greeted the kids, bending over to shake their hands. He then walked the family around the room, showing off his keepsakes. A Marine, he appreciated that my sons gravitated to a nickel-plated revolver in his display case.

He then led all three kids over to his small round table, where he presented each with a gift, handing the boys calendars from the Royal Tank Museum in Jordan. He gave our daughter a beautiful "Colombia By Colors" book that he himself had received from Luis Villegas, the defense minister from Colombia. My daughter loved it so much that she carried the book around the house for weeks afterward.

Mattis was incredibly kind, not only to take this much time out of his schedule but to make my family feel like a part of the team. After the award ceremony, he again walked the kids around his office, this time to his General Grant desk located against the wall. Mattis was beaming. "Okay, kids. You see that big phone right there? If you push the big button it goes directly to the president. Who wants to call President Trump?"

Sarah patted my arm as Mattis was playing with the kids. "Look," she said, pointing to the right side of the desk. There on his desk was a Christmas card that our daughter had drawn for him. I had seen it there months before but he still had it, alongside a picture of him with a former staffer, and a framed quote that said, "Avoid trivia." It was a great reminder that despite all the pressures he faced, the boss still had a soft side.

Stoddard eventually ushered us out of the room so Mattis could resume his schedule. "Thank you, Mister Mattis!" the kids exclaimed in unison as we left.

It was Friday, April 27. I was walking out of the Pentagon for the last time in my uniform.

Monday I'd be coming back in a suit and tie as a political appointee in the Trump administration. My attire didn't really matter. I'd be working every bit as hard as before. But events with lasting consequences were just around the corner.

SEVENTEEN

NEW TEAM

Alliances are difficult precisely because there is
no "boss" in them. They are a partnership. And
partners are equals, by definition. One
cannot give orders to a partner.

—PETER DRUCKER

No matter how senior your position, meeting dynamics are always different with your boss in the room. The setting feels more formal. There's less cross-talk and open discussion, and attendees are naturally biased toward agreement with the most senior person present. Especially when that person is the president of the United States.

It was May 11, and I was once again preparing a brief for senior administration officials. But this gathering would be different from the first two held at the Pentagon for President Trump. Today, Mattis was hosting a newly appointed team of senior counterparts from the administration, which meant a much greater chance of engaging discussions and a freer flow of information—the first opportunity for Mattis to host Trump's replacements for Tillerson, McMaster, and Cohn.

Our staff in charge of protocol had already completed the seating arrangement. Mattis would be at the head of the table as host of this morning's meeting. Secretary of the Treasury Steven Mnuchin and Chief Economic Adviser Larry Kudlow sat to his left. To Mattis's right were Secretary of State Mike Pompeo and National Security Adviser John Bolton. Pompeo was the most recent addition to this group, having been confirmed by the Senate on April 26.

Everything looked good in the conference room, so I headed back to my desk in Mattis's office suite, taking the stairs just inside the River Entrance up to the third floor. This was one of my favorite stairwells in the building, not only because it was more ornate—with wood paneling running along the sides and large oil paintings—but because of what I saw on the wall halfway between the second and third floors.

There, in crisp black letters against a white wall, was the Preamble to the Constitution.

> We the People of the United States, in Order to form a more perfect Union, establish Justice, ensure domestic Tranquility, provide for the common defense, promote the general Welfare, and secure the Blessings of Liberty to ourselves and our Posterity, do ordain and establish this Constitution for the United States of America.

The quote served as a tangible reminder of the oath to support and defend the Constitution.

I quickly made my way back to my desk to grab a folder and notebook. I needed to hustle. Mattis was hosting Pompeo and Bolton in his office for breakfast and they were expected to enter the conference room in about ten minutes, so I grabbed my things and made my way forward to let Admiral Faller know we were ready before heading back down to my place in the control room.

Soon the others joining today's meeting began to arrive. Deputy Secretary Pat Shanahan was taking part, as was Chairman of the Joint Chiefs General Joe Dunford, Vice Chairman General Paul Selva, and a few senior Pentagon staff members. At the appointed time, Mattis arrived with Pompeo, Mnuchin, and Bolton in tow.

Mattis led off, working his way through a succession of slides that mirrored some of the information he'd provided to President Trump during the first meeting: the disposition of American forces around the world, the return on investment from American presence abroad, and the benefits of strong international alliances and partnerships.

As a staff, we'd also put together a new slide for him that he'd previously shown Trump. On the left side were a lot of gears with each one representing a department or an element of national power, except that they were disjointed and didn't mesh properly, a broken process Mattis lamented as "chipping gears." He wanted to contrast that with the right side of the slide showing gears perfectly meshed and aligned. The main gear that turned all the others was the economy, America's engine of national security.

The others listened as Mattis walked through each slide. Body language in the room was positive—just a group of senior leaders gathered to discuss the way forward.

The door opened about fifteen minutes into Mattis's presentation, and in walked Deputy National Security Adviser Mira Ricardel. *Oh boy,* I thought, *Ricardel can't stand Mattis or Sweeney,* who was also in the room. I was mildly curious to see if Ricardel was going to challenge some of Mattis's assertions during the meeting, but she remained silent. She was likely remaining deferential since Bolton, her boss, was also present.

A few minutes later, Larry Kudlow, Trump's chief economic adviser, walked into the room and took his seat.

Bolton spoke after Mattis. "Thanks for hosting this and for the introduction," he said before jumping into his long-term and short-term concerns. I was pleased to hear that Bolton's concerns were aligned with Mattis's, which meant they were also aligned with the National Security Strategy and National Defense Strategy. China, Russia, North Korea, Iran, and terrorism were at the top of his list. To me, Europe seemed to be flexing its collective political muscles, taking advantage as the US appeared to be retreating from its decades of international leadership. Bolton also discussed India's importance in the Indo-Pacific region.

I'd never really listened closely to Bolton's speeches in the past. I only knew him by his reputation as an unabashed defense hawk usually portrayed as comfortable with using military force. In the conference room, however, I found Bolton to be incredibly reasoned and articulate about the threats facing America. I also had the sense that his understanding and appreciation of history rivaled Mattis's.

One thing was clear: as a longtime Washington hand, Bolton was well connected and politically savvy.

Pompeo spoke third and broke his brief remarks into three parts.

The first centered around the "need to integrate the economic element" into everything the administration was doing. He said, "State should take a central role to lead the effort," but that he was still waiting for senior economic advisers to be named to his department. It was well known that the Trump Administration had significant vacancies in political positions across a wide spectrum of government agencies.

Pompeo's second point was to underscore the urgency of the North Korean nuclear and intercontinental missile threat while acknowledging that "China has a piece of it."

Pompeo's final point centered on counterterrorism or the "struggle against Islamist terror." He warned against focusing solely on ISIS as opposed to terrorism's numerous other threats. Instead, the administration needed to be "telling the story of American exceptionalism around the world . . . but for eighteen years it's been poorly executed," a challenge he and the state department were taking on.

Mattis interjected. "There is a danger," he said, "of immediate concerns overtaking issues of long-term strategic importance."

I agreed. America's looming strategic challenges were in danger of being overrun by more short-term, and sometimes less important, issues. Senior leaders in the administration needed to shift gears and consider how to get the whole government engaged on long-term issues, especially with leaders swapping in and out of significant roles. My view was that the White House could make significant strides by aligning priorities throughout the administration, ensuring that each department was moving in the right direction. Focusing primarily on the challenges of the day meant losing steps on bigger issues.

Mnuchin spoke fourth and came out of the gate strong. While Bolton and Pompeo came across as collegial, Mnuchin's words and energy level made him seem ready to dominate today's conference.

"The problem isn't that we don't already do these things," he said, "but rather the problem is conflicts." He then mentioned that "Rex [Tillerson] is a terrific person who worked very hard, but he didn't embrace the president's vision" which led to "obvious conflicts and nonalignment." He then pushed back on Pompeo's remarks, saying that it wasn't State's place to pursue an economic role, a comment protecting his turf at Treasury.

What really caught my ear was Mnuchin's use of language that made it seem as if he was speaking for the president at the meeting, as when he said, "The president's intent for Defense is . . ." or "Peter Navarro thinks we are in another Cuban Missile Crisis" when it comes to our economic relationship with China. His comments weren't constrained to his role at Treasury but were far more expansive, as if he'd seen the recent departure of Tillerson and McMaster as an opportunity for Treasury to exert greater influence over the other agencies represented in the meeting.

The last to offer opening remarks was Larry Kudlow, who

seemed to sense a power struggle with Treasury. He wanted to ensure he was heard as the president's chief economic adviser, not Mnuchin.

Kudlow was largely focused on America's economic relationship with China, saying that "the president's instincts are 100 percent right with respect to China. They've been getting away with murder for the past twenty-plus years." He reinforced his position as a believer in free trade. "If China opens its markets," Kudlow remarked, "then all sides will experience significantly faster economic growth." The only problem is "that I don't know how to get there with China."

The floor was now open for discussion. Things got interesting, especially from the perspective of watching how senior leaders jockey for influence.

Bolton jumped right in, saying that the "problem is that all of the departments have different priorities." "To serve the president," he said, "departmental efforts should be integrated." He wasn't wrong, but the way he said it gave me pause. His comment seemed to indicate that as national security adviser he should be the integrator and therefore the de facto lead. After a year within the administration, I thought he was probably right. Someone needed to be in charge of coordinating the administration's efforts.

Bolton looked over at Mnuchin. "Steve, there are differences, and that's okay. We have to give the president crisper alternatives."

Around the table it went. Bolton was making some compelling points, not the least of which was that "the administration was losing time" by merely bouncing from distraction to distraction. Mnuchin continued to try to wield the most influence by making sweeping, declarative statements as if he was speaking for the White House. Kudlow was also attempting to assert himself by saying that he and Bolton needed to do a better job with the interagency process, implying that as chief economic adviser he was a key player in how things ran in the administration. For the next five minutes, Mnuchin and Kudlow went back and forth, cutting each other off to get their word in.

It was as if the treasury secretary and chief economic adviser had started their own trade war in the Pentagon.

Mattis finally had enough. He cut Kudlow off mid-sentence. "I think we're all there, Larry . . ." Rejoining the conversation, Mattis employed tired soundbites rather than actually engaging in an in-depth discussion. He seemed weary.

He mentioned that the administration needed to "provide both security and solvency" and that "the economy is the engine for national defense." He warned that Trump's decision on the Trans-Pacific Partnership (TPP) was a mistake. "Walking out of the TPP without a replacement is a position that the Chinese have exploited for over a year," a reference to China's growing economic sphere and pursuit of the "One Belt, One Road" trade initiative. The Trans-Pacific Partnership had ultimately fallen apart without US participation, giving China an opportunity to claim the mantle of an increasing global leadership role.

Mnuchin jumped back in, confirming that "the administration has been lousy with integrating each of the pieces to make a holistic policy." Bolton agreed. "One way to start is with people sitting down and using the interagency process." *Touché,* I thought, as Bolton pivoted back to a National Security Council–led position.

The discussion swirled as the talks shifted to tariffs.

Kudlow, a longtime believer in free markets, commented that "with steel and aluminum tariffs we hit our friends just as hard as our allies." Mattis chimed in, "Even harder . . ." He followed up, "The US is a global reserve currency. Overuse of sanctions means nations will find another way." That seemed a good point. The dollar was the leading currency for trade around the world, but if you forced your will too strongly, nations might just throw their hands up and start shifting to another currency and begin bypassing the dollar altogether.

At this point, I noticed Mnuchin growing even more agitated, darting anxious glances around the room as he was increasingly shut out of the conversation.

I also noticed an interesting shift in the dynamic that occurred about halfway through the meeting.

As a former commanding general, Mattis was used to controlling the room and the conversation, especially when seated at the head of the table. But today I watched as Pompeo, Mnuchin, and Bolton—peers within the administration—all cut Mattis off midsentence at various times. I fully expected Mattis to say something about it or to reassert himself, but he never did. When they cut him off, he just stopped talking.

I was shocked at the rudeness of it, but Mattis's inability to control the meeting also reinforced what had been nagging at me since McMaster's firing—the balance of power in the administration had shifted. Today's unruly scene only reinforced that fact.

The meeting petered out about an hour and forty-five minutes after it started. Sensing things were rapidly coming to a close, Mattis thanked everyone for coming. Gathering his things, he turned and walked out of the room and down the hall, fully expecting the others to flow out of the room behind him.

They didn't.

Instead, the other principals and uniformed members remained behind and clustered in small groups to continue their conversations. That by itself isn't too noteworthy—leaders usually congregated afterward to follow up on issues raised during a meeting—but what happened next is.

Mattis came back.

I'd never seen anything like this. Mattis makes a decision and sticks with it, come hell or high water. But this time he didn't. He must have made it down the hall before realizing that no one else had followed him out, then turned around to come back to the room.

I watched as two minutes after Mattis left the room, he returned, awkwardly standing in the doorway and watching the scene before him. He didn't say a word to anyone. He just stood there by himself. A few people glanced up and saw him standing there, but they didn't invite him into their conversation.

After another minute, Mattis slowly turned and walked back out again.

Alone.

EIGHTEEN

SUMMER OF SURPRISES

A Scout is never taken by surprise; he knows exactly
what to do when anything unexpected happens.

—ROBERT BADEN-POWELL

With Mattis almost completely shut out, June 2018 unfolded as
the most challenging month yet for those of us trying to keep the
Pentagon and White House together.

First, there was a crisis with our allies. On June 6, we had
flown to Brussels for the latest NATO meetings, followed by a
quick stop in London.

The Brussels visit was particularly important, as it was the last
meeting of NATO's twenty-nine defense ministers before July's
much-anticipated presidential-level summit. Trump was scheduled to attend, and allied ministers were increasingly nervous:

What would the president do? Trump's fiery May 2017 visit and his consistently alarming language since then had opened fissures in an alliance where public unity is considered paramount. But he had also spoken positively at times about the alliance's role. Which Trump would visit Brussels next month?

NATO's concern thrust Mattis back into his role as "Reassurer in Chief."

Once we arrived in Brussels, Kay Bailey Hutchison, America's ambassador to NATO, cautioned Mattis that "there has been a change in tenor here at NATO . . . it's important to tread more carefully." Allies were expressing their frustration to her about their nations' public treatment at the hands of Trump's administration.

In their view, the president only discussed areas where he felt they were falling short. But, as Hutchison put it, "there are all these areas where we've asked for a lot and received a lot," such as for sanctions against North Korea, or additional funding and troops for the counterterrorism fight. Hutchison believed it was important to "emphasize alliance unity and solidarity . . . and our collective strength."

Mattis concurred. Looking over to me, he said, "Bus, add a paragraph or two in my remarks to acknowledge the commitments that the allies have made . . . make sure we recognize right up front a list of nations who are on track to meet their financial commitment."

That was a good idea. After beating the drum about "burden sharing" for the past year, this visit presented an opportunity to recognize those nations now spending 2 percent of their GDP on their military.

Mattis emphasized to me that his closeout press conference at

NATO also needed to acknowledge the progress nations had made since the 2014 agreement to increase spending. The secretary clung to the idea that showing progress would placate Trump, especially if we credited him directly. The message was one of, "Look what we've accomplished because of President Trump! This *never* would have happened otherwise." It was a message that Secretary General Stoltenberg, the head of NATO, also embraced, in an attempt to show European progress on this issue.

I dutifully added the language, and Mattis sold it on our last day in Brussels. "In 2014," he said, "only three nations' military spending was at 2 percent of GDP . . . By 2017, all nations had reversed the downward trend."

Putting it in the stark terms that Trump appreciated, Mattis added, "Last year, we also saw the largest across-NATO increase in military spending in a quarter century . . . I salute the fifteen allies who are on track to reach 2 percent by 2024."

Behind the scenes, we openly admitted that we needed to do whatever it took to preserve alliance unity, while simultaneously appeasing a president desperate for positive talking points. We just weren't certain whether or not it would ever satisfy the White House.

Before returning to Washington, we stopped in London for Mattis's participation in Queen Elizabeth II's ninety-second birthday celebration and the annual "Trooping the Colour" ceremony. A tradition carried on for more than 260 years, it was an impressive display of royal pageantry with around two thousand troops participating. Only a small delegation accompanied Mattis to the parade. Most of us worked from the hotel, catching back up with Mattis as we boarded the E-4B for the flight home.

On board, I made my way over to my laptop in the plane's conference room, beginning my pretakeoff routine scan of the latest online headlines.

A Twitter post seized my attention. It contained an alarming photo of President Trump seated at the Group of Seven (G7) Summit, arms crossed defiantly while all the other leaders stood clustered together, facing him with what could only be described as a unified front.

The G7 represents most of the world's largest economies—Canada, France, Germany, Italy, Japan, the United Kingdom, and the United States. The photo had the appearance of an intervention. Shinzo Abe, Japan's prime minister, stood with arms crossed, a sour look across his face. Germany's Angela Merkel had both hands planted firmly on the table immediately before Trump as she leaned in defiantly. France's Emmanuel Macron stood next to Merkel. It was a powerful image.

I printed the photo and handed it to Pete Verga, our deputy chief of staff. Verga, a retired Army lieutenant colonel and longtime Pentagon official, had joined us on this trip.

"Pete, take a look at this." Verga studied the photo, saying, "Looks like an obvious Photoshop job. No way this is real." He handed it back to me. I chuckled. "Really?" I said. "Then why was the photo sent out by Germany's official press account?"

Pete did a double take. "What? Hand that back." He took a closer look. "This sure doesn't look good."

No, it didn't. The press had a field day. The consensus, as *The*

Guardian put it, was that "Donald Trump has left the G7 network of global cooperation in disarray."

Trump then fired off a tweet aimed at Justin Trudeau, Canada's prime minister, calling him "very dishonest and weak." Another tweet added, "I have instructed our US reps not to endorse the communique," overturning his previous decision to sign the summit's mutually agreed upon resolutions. It was the latest image of a president breaking yet again with another long-standing international tradition.

Just like that, the goodwill Mattis had generated in Brussels evaporated.

The flight back to Washington was sobering. Mattis was obviously bothered as he chewed on this latest development. Nonetheless, we stayed focused on the task at hand. He pulled several of us into his cabin to debrief the trip to Europe. He rarely expressed displeasure with the president outside of his closest advisers, and this time was no different.

Rather than stew on something he couldn't control, Mattis slipped back into what he called his "Joe Friday" mode—ignoring distractions and emotion to focus on "just the facts."

At the top of his list was a concern that "the European Union has embraced Putin [Russia]," mentioning that Chancellor Merkel "talks to Putin two times a week, for one to two hours at a time." He was concerned that American actions were causing Europe to take a more pro-Russia stance.

He linked his personal mistrust of Russia directly to Putin. "Putin violated the intermediate nuclear forces treaty," Mattis said. "There's no trust anymore while Putin is in power." He continued, saying, "The Russian Federation is incurring a strategic deficit. Their actions may work for a short time, but to what purpose? China just wants a subordinate . . ." Mattis was alluding to recent Chinese overtures toward Russia, but while China grew ever stronger, Russia seemed teetering on the verge of collapse. Mattis just shook his head. "Russia is simply out to undercut the rules-based order."

His aimed his last request at me. "Bus, get me [President] Reagan's speech on free trade. Reach out to Peggy Noonan, she might have it." I didn't personally know Noonan, who had been one of Reagan's speechwriters, but I managed to locate the text online.

It was a tense flight home.

Just a few days later, after we'd had only a weekend to recharge, we faced our next surprise. At 4:00 a.m. eastern time, President Trump, attending a game-changing summit in Singapore with Chairman Kim Jong Un of North Korea, declared an end to the "war games" between the US and South Korea. Responding to a question from a member of the press regarding security assurances the US exchanged for promises of North Korean denuclearization, Trump said, "We will be stopping the war games, which will save us a tremendous amount of money." It was an alarming, and seemingly ad hoc, decision. He caught the Pentagon flat-footed.

As the two leaders had prepared to meet in person for the first time to discuss potential denuclearization of the Korean peninsula, two views had dominated Mattis's personal staff's thinking. The first held that the president might actually pull off what no other US president had done—convince Pyongyang to forgo their nuclear weapons and rejoin the international community.

The other half felt Trump's was a fool's errand. Kim was toying with Trump's seeming desperation for a big "win" to continue strengthening his nuclear posture under the guise of peace talks. It was a plan North Korea had used to its benefit with past administrations. This second camp was concerned that Trump was boxing himself in—a splashy, bold announcement would give Kim more leverage in negotiations.

Both options represented a false choice. Trump was likely to get the splashy news cycle that he craved, *along with* a cessation of immediate nuclear testing and a pathway for North Korea's rejoining the international community . . . but North Korea might continue developing nuclear weapons behind the scenes.

I was concerned, however, by the president's propensity to make concessions in private in order to get a much-sought-after splashy public announcement, just as he had when declaring premature victory on the "savings" for the F-35 Joint Strike Fighter program. The summit with North Korea wasn't part of a grand strategic plan within the administration, so his actions had to be taken at face value—and with a grain of salt.

Now Trump had surprised us all by declaring his intention to stop military exercises with South Korea, and it was not at all clear that the world would take this with that same grain of salt.

Military exercises with South Korea are crucial to preserving the readiness of US forces stationed on the peninsula, ensuring our forces can properly mesh should conflict arise. And it turned out that Trump hadn't even gotten what he'd hoped for in return for this deal. A reporter's very next question to Trump revealed that the joint statement signed by North Korea didn't mention the "verifiable or irreversible denuclearization" of North Korea. We had traded necessary troop exercises for a verbal assurance by an authoritarian dictator.

After a few more minutes, another reporter followed up on Trump's statement regarding war games. "When you said you were stopping 'war games,' so you are stopping the exercises with South Korea?" Trump's response confirmed the change, as he said, "I think it's inappropriate to be having war games."

That's how Trump notified his Department of Defense that its war games with South Korea were suspended. There was no beforehand heads-up from the White House. I suspected that Trump was simply "winging it" at the podium, and now we were all forced again to react. But Trump sometimes spoke in vague, ill-defined terms. Plus, his declaration had been made during the question-and-answer period with reporters and not during his prepared remarks. What did his declaration actually mean? *No one knew.*

The next day, Faller announced we had to "find out what it costs to do war games with South Korea." The White House wanted to retroactively use the president's declaration as a way to show we were saving taxpayer money.

Later, during our Large Group meeting, Mattis reassured the audience of senior department officials, saying, "What you're seeing play out in the news is the normal fleshing out of broader ideas . . . this isn't historically different. It's important for us to send a message of calm throughout the department." Mattis wanted to maintain our focus on the task at hand, reminding leaders to "stay focused on defense. When it comes to the media, think before you speak. The [North Korean] summit will *not* serve as a distractor . . . steady as she goes, everyone."

With that, Mattis stood up and left.

—————

That afternoon I sat in on Mattis's meeting with three top members of the press: the *Washington Post*'s David Ignatius, *The Atlantic*'s Jeff Goldberg, and CBS News's John Dickerson.

The press was naturally curious about the recent upheaval, to which Mattis responded with "I'm not trying to put lipstick on a pig for you" three times in the first twenty-five minutes. His insistence made it seem like that's *exactly* what he was trying to do.

Ignatius noted, "Our allies are extremely unhappy. When does all this become a security issue?" Mattis agreed, "Yes, you might even say our allies are in a fury." He continued, "We in the Pentagon are seen as the Department of Reassurance." The phrase had now become a common refrain, both publicly and privately.

Dickerson followed up with, "So, what *is* the Trump policy?" and Mattis replied, "America first does not mean America alone. You know, Reagan was seen as crazy early in his first term." Ignatius jumped back in, "But do you think the country will be stronger for [Trump's] policies?"

Mattis didn't hesitate.

"No, I don't. I've been reading Reagan's speech to business leaders on trade recently." He was referring to the Reagan speeches he'd asked me to retrieve for him. "I do not think Trump's policies will make America stronger, although we will appear stronger in the short term."

I was surprised. Mattis always carefully shielded his thoughts, especially if they didn't align perfectly with the president's. Was it an accidental slip-up? (unlikely) A statement to indicate his level of trust for these senior press representatives? (maybe) Or a harbinger of his sheer exasperation and an opportunity to lodge his disagreement, even if in an "off the record" capacity? (likely)

Two days later, Mattis conducted damage control in a phone call with Japanese defense minister Itsunori Onodera. Onodera wasted no time, asking Mattis for his "candid evaluation of the US–North Korea summit." Like the defense department, our Pacific allies had been blindsided by Trump's pronouncement.

Mattis played the role of the good soldier, saying that it was "obviously a breakthrough with legitimate reasons for the way forward." Onodera asked which exercises would be suspended, to which Mattis replied, "We're still working to determine exactly what we will suspend," vowing, "There will be no impact on US-Japan exercises."

This call mirrored so many others that Mattis had taken over the past year and a half from alarmed allies seeking reassurance for the way ahead. Mattis, in fact, was concerned. We all had reason to be, as the surprises weren't yet finished.

The next complete surprise came the following week. President Trump took to the stage in the East Room of the White House to announce that he was directing General Joseph Dunford, chairman of the Joint Chiefs, to establish a sixth branch of the armed forces: The Space Force. I was at my desk, watching the television, dumbfounded by Trump's announcement.

Trump had been raising the idea of a separate Space Force for about a year. Each time, Mattis had helped convince him that the US Air Force—which owned the space mission—was still the right organization to lead our efforts in space. Mattis, in particular, wanted to avoid the additional bureaucracy and cost that would accompany a separate force.

Mattis's nervousness had only grown, especially in light of recent surprises. The week before Trump's announcement, Kevin Sweeney had asked me to reach out to the White House to see if any more bombshells were coming our way. One of the White House speechwriters, Ross Worthington, emailed back. No, no announcement of a Space Force. Trump would only be signing "Space Policy Directive 3," a minor announcement regarding traffic management in space.

Sweeney was relieved when I relayed the message.

Mattis had made his position very clear, both privately to the president as well as to members of Congress who wanted a new branch of the armed forces. Mattis had written a letter to Ohio Representative Michael Turner, a proponent of a separate Space Force, the year before to say, "I strongly urge Congress to reconsider the proposal of a separate service Space Corps . . . I do not wish to add a separate service that would likely present a narrower and even parochial approach to space operations rather than an integrated one we're constructing under our current approach."

Later in the letter, he added, "I believe it is premature to add additional organizational tail [a term for administrative functions] to the Department at a time [when] I am trying to reduce overhead. The creation of an independent Space Corps, with the corresponding institutional growth and budget implications, does not address the specific concerns nor our Nation's fiscal problems in a responsible manner."

Although we had heard grumbles from the White House, and particularly Vice President Pence's office, the push to create a new armed service had seemed to fade away. Until today.

With Pence standing to his right, Trump stated, "My administration is reclaiming America's heritage as the world's greatest spacefaring nation . . . But our destiny beyond the earth is not only a matter of national identity but a matter of national security. So important for our military. So important. And people don't talk about it. When it comes to defending America, it is not enough to merely have an American presence in space, we must have American dominance in space. So important."

Trump continued, "Very importantly, I'm hereby directing the Department of Defense and Pentagon to immediately begin the process necessary to establish a Space Force as the sixth branch of the armed forces. That's a big statement. We are going to have the Air Force and we are going to have the Space Force. Separate but equal. It is going to be something. So important. General Dunford, if you would carry that assignment out, I would be very greatly honored also."

Trump surveyed the audience in front of him, looking for Dunford. Unable to find him, the president turned backward. "Where is General Dunford?"

Dunford, seated to his left the entire meeting, piped up with, "Right here."

Trump now turned in a full circle before spotting him. "General." Dunford was expressionless. Trump pointed at him. "You got it?" Dunford nodded, emotionless. "I got it, sir."

"Let's go get it, General."

A few minutes later, at 12:45 p.m., the secure phone line rang. The caller ID flashed.

It was General Kelly, White House chief of staff, calling to let Mattis know *after* the official announcement that Trump had just ordered the creation of a Space Force.

———

June also proved to be my most difficult month with Mattis and our staff. Stress levels were again running high within our office. Tempers were easily inflamed. The smallest issues easily became egregious sins. I found myself in a similar emotional state, invariably reaching home each night in a foul mood. Mattis's being out of alignment with the White House, in turn, only elevated stress levels for his front office.

Like the winter before, we were trying to accomplish too much. The veneer of civility had worn away.

Faller and Sweeney were now yelling at everyone, seemingly in an effort to restore a relationship between a president and his secretary of defense that was never coming back.

One day I paused as I passed by an office with its door closed. It belonged to Mattis's principal and junior military aides, and someone was clearly agitated. When the yelling continued, I decided to open the door to find out what was going on. There, crammed into a small office, was Faller with our staff's military officers. He was furious and not afraid to share that fact. The sin committed by the assembled members? They wanted to ensure a Marine gunnery sergeant in our office, an enlisted member in the armed forces, received the same opportunity to see Mattis when checking out as everyone else did. The yelling continued, with Faller finally proclaiming, "I don't have time for this s—t!" He left the office, slamming the door behind him.

This elevated level of stress directly affected my speechwriting team: Faller and Sweeney wanted to increase scrutiny on Mattis's speeches. As Faller relayed it to me, more eyes on a speech before Mattis delivered it meant greater alignment with the White House.

This newest development was undoubtedly an unintended consequence from back in March when I had failed to push back when Mattis thought I'd erred in crafting his speech for Congress. It had festered, and was now magnified because of our misalignment with the White House.

Sweeney pulled me into his office. "Bus, we need to talk about the speech process. There have been some recent changes with Dana [White, the Pentagon spokesperson] taking a more elevated role. She's going to own more of the speech process." The decision placed me in an obviously unwinnable position.

Speechwriting is an odd beast. This was my second time in that role during a twenty-year military career. By no means an expert, I had nonetheless learned valuable lessons along the way, perhaps the most important being that a lead speechwriter needs *direct access* to their boss, plus *direct feedback* on what worked—and what didn't. It just doesn't work any other way. I had enjoyed that level of access for over a year, but now our consistently successful process was falling apart.

In aviation terms, I was being forced into a "graveyard spiral," a dangerous corkscrew downward spin that usually results in your plane crashing, killing all on board. I didn't want my speech team to be the next crew caught in a graveyard spiral.

Here's how the new process faltered.

Previously, my team would compose a draft, and I would edit and finalize it before passing it forward to Sweeney. But now six people were placed between Mattis and me, each person inclined to "add value" by inserting language that really didn't work or didn't sound like Mattis. If I dared to fight their edits, I was informed I wasn't being a team player vis-à-vis leaders senior to my position. If, however, their additions remained, Mattis often complained that the language didn't sound like him, reinforcing his view that something was wrong with our speechwriting process (i.e., me).

You can guess how many times someone volunteered that *they* had authored the offending language. Zero.

It was an untenable position. I talked to Sweeney about it, but he remained unreceptive.

I felt the only way to right the ship was to take ownership and chart a way forward. On June 20, I stayed up all night to author a succinct one-page document that outlined what was now broken with the speechwriting process and how to fix it. Emotionally drained but ready to lead a restoration of our old process, I emailed it to Sweeney and the front office team at 5:16 a.m. without copying Mattis. Faller and Sweeney had made it clear that staff was *never* to email Mattis directly.

Things quickly escalated. Sweeney simply emailed it back out to Faller, Dana White, and others, asking them to "Pls review Bus's memo, talk and provide me a recommended way forward."

Later that morning, Sweeney smirked as he told me in the hallway, "You know, Bus, I never even read it [the memo]." I found myself questioning whether or not he really wanted to see a positive change in the process.

Faller weighed in via email, writing, "We have never had any well-established process/processes." He went further. "In my view Dana White should be the Director of Communications for the DOD and has grown into that role very well."

That presented two problems. First, I had been presidentially appointed to my role as director of communications. The second was that Faller had been pulling for Dana to assume my role for a while . . . and, to make things even more awkward, his daughter was White's special assistant. Faller's email presented an obvious conflict of interest and what I felt to be a serious ethical breach.

I leaned back in my desk chair, wearily staring at the Washington Monument jutting up above the skyline across the Potomac. *Well,* I thought, *this is certainly a steep dive to recover from.*

I hoped that I could pull up before hitting the ground.

NINETEEN

BULLETPROOF

The press is not the enemy, and to treat
it as such is self-defeating.

—ROBERT M. GATES

On June 25, we were airborne once more for the second stop of
Mattis's fourth trip of the month. We spent one day in Alaska
with Senator Dan Sullivan before taking off for Beijing. I was
sitting at my workstation in the conference room with my ear-
buds in when Will Bushman grabbed my attention. "Hey, did
you see the article from Kube?" I quickly scanned the news tabs
already open in my browser. "Nope. Can you email me the
link?" Will nodded. "Sure. Heading your way."

The email hit my inbox a minute later. The link took me to
an article by Courtney Kube, an NBC national security reporter.

Titled "Mattis Is Out of the Loop and Trump Doesn't Listen to Him," the article walked through Mattis's eroding relationship with President Trump.

Kube laid out how Mattis, once a star of Trump's cabinet, had fallen out of favor in recent months. She even correctly identified—evidently through senior White House officials—that losing Tillerson and McMaster back in March had pushed Mattis further into the line of fire while diminishing his role. *This is the article we all should have seen coming a mile away. Why are we acting so surprised?* Dana White was quoted as saying that Courtney's reporting "is pure silliness," a remark that Mattis told us that he loved when he later walked into the conference room.

"Well done, Dana," Mattis said, standing in the doorway. "We won't even dignify reporting like this." Dana just nodded. "Yes, sir. You won't be seeing much of Courtney for a while. We can't have her around if she's writing stories so off the mark." Satisfied, Mattis turned in to his personal cabin to get back to work.

Mattis's relationship with what he termed the "mendacious press" fascinated me. He understood the key role that members of the press played but at the same time recognized the peril they presented, as getting caught saying anything counter to Trump was a guaranteed ticket to finding your status diminished in his volatile administration. It was a careful dance, especially for a secretary of defense with such deep ethical convictions.

I glanced back down at Kube's article: Finding out about canceling exercises with South Korea after the fact? Check. "Blindsided" by creation of a Space Force? Yes. Diminished contact between Mattis and Trump? Uh-huh. The statements in her article were deadly accurate. Mattis's interaction with White had the appearance of theater for the sake of those of us on the core team: *we* define reality, not the press or anyone else.

Frankly, I thought Mattis's first year was near pitch perfect regarding interactions with reporters. While he could have expended more time and attention on members of the press, that would have elevated his risk level, especially since Trump could—and did—quickly reverse course on decisions within even an hour. Mattis's solution was to avoid speaking to the press except when absolutely necessary. When he did speak, he wisely focused solely on his area of expertise: running America's military.

He wouldn't hesitate to refer reporters to the White House, Department of State, Department of Homeland Security, or other relevant agency to avoid speaking out of turn. It was both deferential (in a good way) and politically savvy. No need, as Mattis had said before, to "walk yourself into an L-shaped ambush."

When the press found a point of disagreement during the first year, Mattis would usually respond by deflecting, saying, "I provide the president with my recommendations. I owe him confidentiality regarding what we discuss." It was an elegant way to bypass a question he shouldn't—or didn't want to—answer. He saw talking to the press as a zero-sum game.

Mattis also went to great lengths to emphasize the importance of a unified front, which he routinely referred to as "transparency and alignment" within the department. While he didn't discuss it as openly, he also fought to ensure that we were aligned with the language coming out of the White House or state department. I had learned early on that one of Mattis's first questions regarding a draft speech was whether or not the relevant official had either reviewed it or offered input. Telling Mattis "no" more than a few times would likely earn an expulsion from his team.

A large part of my role as communications director was to seek input from all relevant international, administration, and expert stakeholders to ensure their thoughts were appropriately reflected in the draft, and that they'd had the opportunity to see the final product. Major policy speeches were provided to Cabinet Affairs, the Office of Management and Budget, or the National Security Council for coordination and review. We worked to inoculate ourselves as best we could.

Mattis had emphasized the importance of transparency and alignment during a Senior Civilian Offsite meeting held at Washington's National War College back in March, a large conference with all senior Pentagon civilians invited to attend. During his opening remarks, Mattis stated that because of our business schedules, "We may pass like ships in the night, but the issues we face are too grave not to have a unified team. I come from out west and we have a saying—each of us needs to 'ride for the brand.' Washington, DC, is often a corrosive town. The Department of Defense has to be different. I expect us to take responsibility and maintain our trusted relationships."

He then distributed a collection of select speeches, memos, and letters he had released during his DOD tenure. "These readings show my thinking on how to lead in this mission." It was all part of ensuring that department leadership spoke with one unified voice.

White had pulled me aside early on during my tenure with Mattis. "Never forget, Bus. The press is the enemy. They are not your friend." I couldn't have disagreed more. The press wasn't the enemy. Oh, I knew better than to talk much with the press—that, after all, was White's responsibility. I knew that the press, like many organizations in Washington, could be transactional, but that didn't make them "the enemy." Heck, most of the people on Mattis's own team were transactional. It seemed a better way to look at the situation was that we were all actors on a stage, playing our assigned parts to the best of our ability. The press was no different. They wanted the scoop, to find newsworthy information to share with their readers. We could have been far savvier in our approach to foster better relationships.

A downside of Mattis's perception of the media was the culture of fear that trickled down from the secretary into each of the services. Mattis made clear during several Large Group meetings with his boardroom leaders that "no senior defense official ever speaks off the record." He also abhorred leaks, the passing of unapproved information to members of the media.

Navy Captain Jeff Davis, director of Pentagon Press Operations during my first year, explained to me the difference between a leak and providing "background" information. A leak is the passing of sensitive information without your boss's awareness. Background is when you have your boss's permission to provide sensitive information to the press but on the condition that you won't be named.

Simple. If you're sharing information *without* explicit approval, you're leaking to the press.

Mattis's direction created a chilling effect. Each of the military branches clamped down on their relationships with members of the press, and in some cases stopped communicating with the press altogether. The media complained loudly about the near-instantaneous evaporation of "background" information. They had already seen their access to senior leaders dry up. Now Mattis had declared war on leaks, curtailing even more of their life-blood: information.

We overshot the mark. We didn't need to be discussing vulnerabilities or readiness issues in the public domain, but the press serves an important role in informing the American public. Failure to provide background material and context increased the risk of the press reporting data incorrectly, drawing even *more* of Mattis's ire. It was—and is—a tricky affiliation to manage.

Members of the press were surprised by Mattis's direction because he was widely known in defense press circles to have been a "chatty general," especially while leading US Central Command. Several members of the Pentagon press pool shared with me that Mattis had been notorious as a general for spinning his version of stories or talking about senior leaders. They thought it was ironic that he had a problem with others talking to the press now that *he* was the one running the show.

Mattis's relationship with and his availability to the press varied from month to month. During positive times, like the successful release of the National Defense Strategy, Mattis was more willing to engage with the press. During stressful periods, he might confide that "I don't trust this group" of traveling reporters, or snipe, "You know, we defend stupid people's right to free speech too."

He did, however, maintain a sense of humor about it. Once, during a planning meeting for a trip to NATO, White told Mattis that a couple members of the press wouldn't make the trip because they had contracted the flu. Mattis's response? "Ha, there *is* a God . . . biological warfare *can* have a useful purpose." It was said in jest, smiling widely, but there was no mistaking the hint of truth—and resentment—in his remark.

Mattis zinged the press in July 2017 by granting his first exclusive interview to a high school student named Teddy Fischer. Teddy, a student at Mercer Island High School near Seattle, Washington, had spotted Mattis's phone number when it was inadvertently caught on camera. Demonstrating two of Mattis's most prized character traits—initiative and aggressiveness— Teddy had left a voicemail on his cell phone, which Mattis surprisingly returned, granting the high schooler an interview that went viral. *It's ironic,* I thought, *that Mattis didn't tell anyone on his staff he was going to give the interview.* Trump wasn't the only one who could find ways to keep his team on their toes.

Despite Mattis's frustrations, the press was actually quite protective of him. After all, they were the ones who had billed Mattis, Tillerson, and McMaster as the "adults in the room." Later, they were the ones who dubbed Mattis the "last adult standing."

On the day the Kube story broke, I realized suddenly that the press was protecting him again. Wanting to understand why, I made my way back to the press cabin during a lull in the eleven-hour flight from Eielson Air Force Base (Alaska) to Beijing. Kneeling down next to Gordon Lubold, a reporter from the *Wall Street Journal,* I got straight to the point. "Gordon, I'm curious about something. No one has asked the secretary about Courtney's article. That seems odd." Gordon thought about it for a second. "Not really. Look, at the end of the day we're all Americans. If Mattis goes, who's left? There are things we wish were different [in their relationship with Mattis] but he's defending the nation in more ways than one. We all know that."

I had long suspected this was the case. There had been ample opportunities to find chinks in Mattis's armor or to go after him for a perceived slight. Heck, during a press gaggle at the Pentagon Mattis had grown testy with Idrees Ali, a reporter from Reuters, telling him, "Don't f—k with me on this one," in response to a follow-up question. We expected the media to make hay over this outburst but they didn't. In fact, though they routinely pried into every perceived Trump administration issue, they just as routinely gave Mattis a pass, making my job as communications director much easier than it might have been.

This was apparent another time when Mattis made a tech-related trip to the west coast. The trip had been important to aid the secretary's understanding of how technology was changing the character of war, especially leading-edge technologies like artificial intelligence (AI), machine learning (a subset of AI), and big-data analytics.

His first stop, however, had been to visit a nuclear-powered ballistic missile submarine, the USS *Kentucky*, stationed in Bangor, Washington. During a short speech followed by a question-and-answer period, Mattis thanked the sailors for being in the Navy, saying they'd never regret their service.

"That means you're living," Mattis had said, "That means you're not some p—y sitting on the sidelines, you know what I mean, kind of sitting there saying, 'Well, I should have done something with my life.' Because of what you're doing now, you're not going to be laying on a shrink's couch when you're forty-five years old, saying, 'What the hell did I do with my life?' Why? Because you served others; you served something bigger than you [sic]."

A cabinet member using rough language would normally make the news. Not this time. His remarks made a very brief appearance but it only seemed to bolster, not detract, from Mattis's credibility. The press had our backs.

Gordon Lubold's response about rooting for Mattis was echoed by other members of the press seated nearby on the trip. They confirmed my suspicion regarding a story that had broken the month prior and been promptly deflected away from Mattis: the massive corruption at Theranos, a company Mattis had spent years guiding as a member of the board of directors.

John Carreyrou's *Bad Blood: Secrets and Lies in a Silicon Valley Startup,* a book detailing the scandal, had been released on May 21, 2018. Mattis made several unfortunate appearances in the book, first as a Marine general looking to circumvent testing protocols to rush unproven blood testing equipment to the battlefield, and later as a member of the board of directors for three years, serving alongside his longtime mentors George Shultz and Henry Kissinger.

The company's founder and CEO, Elizabeth Holmes, had deliberately misled investors about blood testing equipment that purportedly rarely—if ever—worked, driving Theranos's valuation to an estimated $9 billion. Mattis had remained on the board until January 2017, more than a year after a *Wall Street Journal* investigative report had highlighted significant concerns with the company. Mattis, as a member of the board of directors, had doubled down, telling the *Washington Post* that "I have the greatest respect for the company's mission and integrity."

By the time of the book's release, the company had collapsed after being confirmed as a fraud.

It was a nightmare scenario: a made-for-television scandal involving a retired Marine and current secretary of defense. Mattis's current head of security, Jim Rivera, had even been the head of security for Theranos, personally escorting Holmes. But no one touched the story, beyond a few small articles that never gained traction. We dodged a bullet just as Gordon had said we would—no one wanted to risk taking down Mattis.

The situation reminded me of the *Saturday Night Live* skits from the 1990's when comedian Darrell Hammond played the role of President Bill Clinton, announcing, "I am bulletproof" after surviving impeachment. It was a formidable reminder of the Fourth Estate's power to determine where to focus its attention . . . and where not to.

It was also noteworthy that despite Mattis's lukewarm relationship with the press, he still focused a significant amount of his attention pursuing what they published. Every morning at 5:00 a.m, the Pentagon public affairs arm produced the "Morning News of Note," a fifty- to sixty-page collection of articles pulled from leading newspapers and blogs. Mattis underlined areas of interest, jotting down questions in the margins. He'd then hit White or others with questions he had from the articles. It was a great system, but I was always struck by his presumption that whatever the reporter had said was accurate. Convincing him otherwise required proof that could tie up staffers for hours (or days).

This diligence in pursuing the media's assertions reminded me of an excerpt from former defense secretary Bob Gates's book *Duty: Memoirs of a Secretary at War*. Gates made the point of how very isolating it can be, occupying the top spot in the Pentagon—and how easy it is to live in an ivory tower.

Gates had also pointed out that he only learned about the widespread neglect occurring at Walter Reed Army Medical Center because he had read reporter Dana Priest's article in the *Washington Post*. Likewise, President Ronald Reagan admitted to being heavily influenced by what he read in *Human Events*. To my knowledge, members of the defense press community never realized the direct influence they wielded with Mattis.

When it came to the press, one of my concerns was about how Mattis would handle the widening policy chasm between him and Trump. Dana White had already had to deny reports that the department had been caught flat-footed by the cessation of military exercises with South Korea and the creation of the Space Force, an assertion we knew to be true. It would be political suicide to admit that Trump was catching us off guard, but anything less than complete honesty with the press would imperil Mattis's reputation as an ethically spotless leader. The last thing Mattis needed was to say something untrue on the record just to preserve his relationship with the president and his place in the administration.

It was a tightrope he'd be forced to walk in the very near future. As Mattis reminded everyone during the Large Group meeting on June 21, "Alignment, alignment, alignment . . . not an inch of daylight between us [the White House and Pentagon] right now."

It was a timely reminder. We had an incredibly important trip to prepare for.

TWENTY

CHINA

The rise of China as a new power is another great
challenge for the US. Our failure to properly handle
Germany and Japan earlier in the 20th century
cost us and the world dearly. We must not
make this same mistake with China.

—STEVE FORBES

Despite the recent challenges, one bright spot was Mattis's visit
to China at the end of June. Mattis would be the first US defense
secretary since Chuck Hagel in 2014 to make the trip, but he
wasn't the first in the administration. Trump and Tillerson had
both visited China the previous year. Trump, in particular, had
been effusive with his praise of Chinese President Xi Jinping,
and China had supported Trump's aggressive stance against North
Korea's nuclear testing. This provided us with some easy points
of alignment with the White House, though on the whole there
were plenty of areas for concern.

During the intervening four years since Hagel's visit, China had pursued an aggressive military buildup, creating artificial islands in the South China Sea while aggressively pursuing regional hegemony through its "One Belt, One Road" program, a development strategy providing countries with investments and infrastructure—but with strings attached. A number of countries have defaulted on their loans, enabling China to exert significant influence on them, leading others to believe the program is actually a front for increased dominance.

It's hardly a secret that China actively steals a tremendous amount of America's intellectual property. For years, security experts have warned us about China's industrial espionage habits, whether through cyberattacks or the forced technology transfers required for businesses to operate in China. In short, an aggressive China remains unapologetic for its efforts to surpass the US as the world's preeminent economic and military power.

Mattis had been thinking about his Chinese trip for some time, as indicated by the contents in the envelope I had couriered back from Henry Kissinger in New York City. Kissinger continued on this theme during a Defense Policy Board meeting in the Pentagon on January 18. The meeting's primary focus was the National Defense Strategy that would be unveiled the next day, but the conversation eventually turned to America's place in the Indo-Pacific region.

I sat in a chair placed just behind Henry Kissinger. The then-ninety-four-year-old Kissinger's thoughts were clear and salient, and he retained his trademark strong, distinctive gravelly voice.

Kissinger took a different view than most regarding China and Russia, asserting that "neither are after world domination, at least in the traditional sense." Kissinger warned that "China would never accept a vacuum on the Korean peninsula, as it recalls the instability of the 1950s," cautioning Mattis to keep our expectations in check with regard to Chinese support for North Korean denuclearization. Kissinger said, "We must analyze China in light of its historical experiences, not through our personal ones," a historical experience where the Chinese believe they are "being constantly castigated as the villains with unlimited aims."

Kissinger's points were well spoken, though he also had a well-known reputation for being a Russian and Chinese apologist. Frankly, I didn't have the depth of knowledge to make an informed decision about his remarks. But as a fighter pilot who had spent six years on an aircraft carrier patrolling the South China Sea, I had witnessed firsthand China's aggression against other nations in the region.

China's actions didn't align with international rules and norms, or with its own rhetoric of peace. It reminded me of the story about the frog and a pot of water. Throw the frog into boiling water, and it immediately jumps out. However, put the frog in lukewarm water and turn up the heat, and the frog gets cooked. China was very comfortable operating in the "gray zone" of conflict. Its aggressive actions were all below the threshold requiring a strong response. But, over time, they add up, while chipping away at US prominence in the region.

To continue preparing for the trip, we scheduled three in-depth planning sessions. The first, on June 12, served as a dedicated opportunity for Mattis to share with a small group of staff and policy representatives what he needed to study up on China. His zeal to prepare was inspiring. He asked for his notes from a different discussion he'd had with Henry Kissinger and maps of China during European colonization from 1850 to 1945, and he emphasized having the National Security Council review and "clear" all of his talking points for meetings with his Chinese counterparts, ensuring they aligned with the White House's position.

As always, Mattis sought alignment. Trump had vacillated in his previous remarks about China. During the campaign he had taken a hard line, but that had recently softened, especially during his state visit to China at the end of 2017. To ensure we had the latest talking points, Mattis emphasized that, "State and National Security Council framing principles need to be at the top level of what [I] would say." He wanted to "focus on common ground and avoid anything that could be disruptive to [his] visit." He asked senior Pentagon leaders if he should zero in on reciprocity in our trade relationship. John Rood, the recently appointed head for Policy, waved him off. "Reciprocal trade should be an issue raised by the White House. You should remain consistent with the message you gave in Singapore of America's continued resolve in the region, but also a message of reassurance."

Mattis nodded, saying, "Okay, let's focus on a nonpersonal, philosophical approach." He went so far as to inform our head of protocol, the person responsible for gifts, that he wanted to present a Remington pistol as his gift to the Chinese. Some said it would serve as a reminder of his heritage from growing up in the west. It could also be viewed as an unmistakable warning.

At our next prep meeting on Monday, June 18, Mattis continued asking questions and refining his talking points. When time allowed, Mattis would work through the language he planned to use once in country—another reason I, as his speechwriter, cherished the opportunity to sit in on these sessions. Hearing Mattis work through his talking points enabled me to provide draft remarks that were far closer to what he wanted to use.

Mattis struck upon the concept he wanted as the anchor to his trip: "competitive coexistence." As Mattis put it, "We are two great powers that will periodically step on each other's toes . . . but we will cooperate where we can and confront where we must," a line similar to one he used regarding Russia.

David Helvey, an Indo-Pacific senior leader in Policy, reminded him to "think of a good toast. Remember, it's the Year of the Dog." Mattis looked over at me and just nodded. *Got it. The Year of the Dog.* Maybe we could ask them to make it the Year of the "Mad Dog," the media's nickname for Mattis that Trump liked so much.

Our last prep meeting for China, called a "murderboard"— a military term for a tough, critical review of the secretary's preparation—occurred on Friday, June 22. This meeting presented an opportunity for Mattis to practice his remarks, discuss any last-minute changes, and answer tough questions before he could slap the table and proclaim, "So let it be written, so let it be done."

For this meeting, he'd invited three heavy-hitting China scholars: Dan Blumenthal, the director of studies at a Washington think tank called American Enterprise Institute; David Finkelstein, vice president at CNA Corporation; and Dave Rank, a senior adviser with the Cohen Group with experience at the US embassy in Beijing.

Mattis waded through his talking points, reinforcing his desire to develop a "hotline as we build our military relationship" to keep the lines of communication open and prevent misunderstandings.

At one point, he leaned back in his chair, pushing away from the conference table. "It's about competitive coexistence. How do we live together? We're not going anywhere . . . we're two Pacific powers." He mulled it over. "You know, I'm a man of war . . . but I come in peace. I've done it the other way and trust me, no one wins."

Personally, I liked that line of thought, as it reminded me of the tough talk he'd used as a four-star general. The only question was whether that type of language would achieve the desired ends for his first visit to America's primary strategic competitor.

As Mattis had emphasized in the National Defense Strategy, America faced three types of primary threats: the *urgent* threats of North Korea, Iran, and terrorism, the *powerful* threat posed by Russia's military, and the threat of political *willpower* demonstrated by China. China was "shredding trust in the South China Sea," as their successive implementation of five-year national development plans, their "Made in China 2025" initiative, their "One Belt, One Road" initiative, and a rapid military buildup left no doubt as to their intentions.

I was really looking forward to this trip. The last few months had proven to be a rough patch. I saw this trip as a chance to hit the reset button with Mattis and Faller. This trip was viewed as a "heavy lift" for the staff with the potential for positive outcomes. Working hard here could go a long way toward mending fences.

Plus, I was on the itinerary to join Mattis for several of the in-person meetings, as well as to attend the dinner hosted by

General Xu Quiliang, the vice chairman of China's Central Military Commission. Sitting in would provide a wealth of background knowledge for our next visits to NATO and the Indo-Pacific.

That is, of course, until *you're the only member of the delegation pulled off the China portion of the trip*. I was obviously in a tough spot based on the changes to our new speechwriting process. I'd watched others in the front office endure similar indignities—when your stock goes down, and Faller and Sweeney start to make life uncomfortable. Perhaps I was foolish to believe I could fight my way back up through continued effort and a "never give up" attitude. But my stock had been incredibly high only a few months previously, and I believed it to be in the realm of possibility.

Faller pulled me aside the day before our scheduled departure for Alaska, China, and Japan. There wasn't much fanfare either, as Faller was still fuming over our exchange about the speech process from a few days before.

"Bus, you're not going in to China. I'm sending you to South Korea instead to wait for us." That was that, and he just walked away. I was now out of uniform and serving as a political appointee, but twenty years of military discipline is hard to break, so I simply replied with a "Yes, sir." It was a bitter pill to swallow.

It got worse once we were airborne. Not only was I going to bypass Beijing and head to South Korea . . . I was the *only* member of the delegation not deplaning in Beijing. I wasn't just benched, I was in the penalty box. But why?

Faller pulled me aside during the eleven-hour flight. "Bus, I want you to know that this wasn't my idea. The boss directed me to pull you off the China portion." I wasn't sure how to take that.

Should I feel glad that Faller provided that explanation? I'd caught him previously lying to staff members, so was this even the truth? If *Mattis* had pulled me off, what did *that* mean? This is why trust between members of a team is critical, and why the absence of trust can be so corrosive. By this point, it was hard to know who to trust.

Before we left our hotel in Alaska for Beijing, I had chatted with Major Trevor Williams, Mattis's new aide de camp, to see if I could steal a few minutes of the boss's time before we left. The deteriorating situation with the speech team was chewing me up. The growing divide wasn't serving the boss well either. Every bone in my body said I just needed to cut out all the middlemen and discuss the situation directly with Mattis. Frankly, I'd reached the point where I'd gladly offer my resignation if that's what he needed. It just didn't seem fair to him, the team, or my family to even try to live with the untenable status quo.

Trevor had merely shrugged. "Sure, man. You do you. He's just in his room waiting for us to depart the hotel."

I walked farther down the hallway, knocking on the boss's door. "Come in," came Mattis's voice from the inside. The door was already cracked open, so I simply pushed through to walk inside.

There, standing in front of his bed, was Mattis with a dress shirt and black socks on but no pants. *Awesome,* I thought, *could this situation get any more awkward?*

Mattis glanced over, not missing a beat (this wasn't necessarily unusual, nor my first conference with the boss while he was absent pants). "What's up, Bus?"

I pressed on. "Morning, sir. I just wanted to chat with you about a few things before we left the hotel." Mattis pulled his slacks on. "Ah, okay Bus. Let me finish getting ready and take my suitcase down to the luggage room, then we can talk." I nodded. "Sounds good, sir. I'll see you in a few." I walked back out of his room and down the hall to wait for him.

A few minutes later, he walked past with his suitcase. Mattis's popular image in this regard is entirely accurate—Mattis always wanted to carry his own luggage. He was incredibly self-reliant that way.

But things grew ever more awkward as he walked back down the hallway toward me, stopping to pop his head into the communications room where our computers were set up. Speaking in an abnormally loud voice so I could hear him from fifteen feet away, he addressed Faller and Pete Verga, our deputy chief of staff. "Bus has asked to see me. Can either of you tell me why?" My face didn't change an iota but I was cringing on the inside. *Well, he just dialed the awkwardness up to a ten.*

He then turned and walked to his room, saying, "Okay, come inside Bus." Unfortunately, Pete Verga soon walked in, right as I was beginning to talk. I paused. I needed to bare my soul privately with Mattis, not with an audience. Verga would understandably try to run interference for the boss, making the situation even more awkward.

So I punted.

"Sir, I just wanted to let you know that Stephen [Miller] and I had a chance to talk. We're looking good for next month's NATO Summit." Mattis did a double blink. "Is that all you needed?"

I didn't hesitate. Believing discretion the better part of valor in this circumstance, I simply nodded and said, "Yes, sir. I know how important the NATO Summit is to you and wanted to let you know right away." His expression said I wasn't fooling anyone, but he let it go. "Oh, okay, Bus. Thanks. See you in a bit."

Now airborne aboard the E-4B, it wasn't a surprise when Mattis walked into the conference room and motioned to me. "Bus, do you have a few minutes?" He obviously wanted to follow up on our aborted conversation. I followed him from the conference room and into his personal office on board the plane.

"Bus, I know we didn't have much time together this morning. Was there anything else you wanted to discuss?"

I nodded. "Yes, sir, there is. From what Admiral Faller and Chief Sweeney have told me, I'm concerned that the speechwriting process isn't giving you the product you deserve. I have some ideas on how we can get it back to where we're batting a thousand again. That being said, we haven't had a chance to talk about it and I was hoping to get your thoughts."

Mattis retreated half a step. It cuts against his public image, but Mattis is actually conflict-adverse in dealing with people he sees on a regular basis. I always chalked it up to our shared backgrounds as naval officers. In most Navy and Marine Corps units, the commanding officer (in this case, Mattis) takes the "good cop" role, while his executive officers (Faller, Sweeney, and Verga) handle "bad cop" tasks. My approaching him directly about an issue was not something in his comfort zone.

"Oh, no, Bus, no. Things are going really well with you and the team. You, Nicole [Magney], and Old Man Rivers are doing a great job." *Really? Then why are Faller and Sweeney always on my case?* I paused for a moment, weighing my next move. "Well, sir, there's been a lot of changes to the speechwriting process lately which seem to be causing more issues than they're solving. I don't think this new process is serving you well."

Mattis just waved me off. "No, no, everything's fine. Okay, Bus. Thanks for coming by." He started to turn and walk back to his desk, "See you in a bit."

Okay, so the direct route isn't going to solve anything. I knew that flights represented the best opportunity to talk, as he was usually incredibly busy when we were back in the Pentagon or in a host country. Mattis's reassurance rang hollow. Actions speak louder than words, and the actions of the past two weeks didn't provide much confidence in where things were headed.

I returned to my seat for the rest of the flight into Beijing while working on speeches occurring after our return.

It was sunny and incredibly hazy in Beijing. Mattis and the delegation left the airplane for twenty-four hours in China, while I dutifully proceeded to South Korea. Our takeoff was delayed by an hour because of a torrential downpour. *I wonder if it's true that the Chinese "seed" their clouds to make it rain to clear the air for visiting dignitaries?* If not, the timing was conspicuous. The rain cleared, and the flight crew got us airborne for the quick flight to South Korea. I have to admit, it was humorous to have the entire E-4B to myself. The place was a ghost town. Just me and the flight crew.

The next twenty-four hours passed quickly. I used my time in South Korea to talk with officers at the Seventh Air Force, the headquarters for all US military air operations. They confirmed our suspicions that halting exercises with the South Koreans would rapidly erode readiness and our ability to operate together.

The South Koreans were increasingly concerned about plans for US troops stationed on the peninsula. Were we planning a pullout?

The next morning, we boarded the E-4B at 5:00 a.m. to take off for the return flight to Beijing to pick up the team. As with all things related to taking care of Mattis, as a crew we were expected to be fine waiting for hours on the ground in Beijing, but there'd be hell to pay if we showed up a few minutes late. It was going to be a long day on the airplane.

The motorcade returned to the plane around 10:30 a.m. Everybody looked tired, but the team was in high spirits. All in all, the trip was deemed a success, though it was noteworthy that Chinese media launched a story quoting President Xi Jinping telling Mattis that, "Our stance is steadfast and clear-cut when it comes to China's sovereignty and territorial integrity."

Xi had followed up by saying, "We cannot lose one inch of territory passed down by our ancestors." The picture chosen for the article had Mattis beaming, while President Xi looked stoic and stern. According to Bloomberg News, Xi's comments were seen as "an unusually blunt warning."

Mattis was quoted as stating, "I'm here to keep our relationship on a great trajectory, going in the right direction, and to share ideas with your leadership, your military leadership, as we look at the way ahead." I worried that while Mattis was hoping to develop a lasting relationship, the Chinese were merely looking to use the secretary as a tool to demonstrate toughness. Perspective is also important. For Americans, a cabinet official's tenure is usually only a few years long. For the Chinese, a lasting relationship exists for decades.

We had an opportunity to meet in Mattis's cabin to discuss a bit more about his time in China. Overall, he viewed it as a success, though he directed the Policy team to prepare for a Navy cruiser and an aircraft carrier to navigate the Taiwan Strait as "a way to reinforce" the idea of "a free and open Indo-Pacific." As Mattis put it, "When the Liaoning [China's aircraft carrier] transited the strait, we didn't formally protest the action because they were in international waters." His point being that the same should hold true for US transits—China shouldn't protest the presence of US warships in international waters.

I made notes of the "toplines," or noteworthy language worthy of being reused in the future: Mattis had held positive, open, and honest dialogues in China. We had established a framework for a strategic relationship that's on a positive trajectory; and both the US and China remained committed to the complete, verifiable, and irreversible denuclearization of North Korea.

Reporters from our traveling press pool grilled Mattis during our return flight to Andrews Air Force Base. Mattis told them that "geography matters, which means the South China Sea." He also reinforced the importance of "collaborating with China where we can . . . We wouldn't be where we are on North Korea [the success of multiple United Nations sanctions] without China."

He emphasized the importance of monitoring Chinese actions. When it comes to how our two countries consider international waters, "The US hasn't signed the UN Convention on the Law of the Sea, but we still abide by it, while China signed it but doesn't abide by it."

It was a great point. As with most things in life—as I knew better with each passing day—actions speak louder than words ever can. The trip was a personal disappointment but there was no time to really think about it. We were already rushing headlong into our next crisis.

TWENTY-ONE

TOTALLY CONTROLLED BY RUSSIA

[A surprise attack], although it is rare, [is] less brilliant than a great strategic combination which renders victory certain even before the battle is fought.

—ANTOINE-HENRI JOMINI

Admiral Faller's first question during our morning catch-up meeting when we got back from China was, "Who the hell at the White House drafted the letters asking for an increase in NATO's military spending?"

While we were in China, President Trump had signed a letter to every NATO member regarding their level of commitment to the alliance solely in terms of their monetary contributions. The letter he sent to Norway so incensed its government that a copy leaked to the Norwegian press.

"As we look forward to the NATO Summit," Trump had written, "I appreciate Norway's action to increase its defense spending." So far, so good. "Norway, however, remains the only NATO Ally sharing a border with Russia that lacks a credible plan to spend 2 percent of its gross domestic product on defense." Uh-oh. It'd be hard for our allies to see the letter as anything other than another White House provocation.

Mattis said what everyone was thinking during that morning's Small Group meeting. "We have to get Pompeo through the next round of discussions with North Korea so he can start running the state department and messaging to the world. The rest of the administration is in complete disarray here."

Referring to the president's letters to NATO allies, he added, "We're really in a damage-control mode here . . . and we're going to reap what we sow from the tariffs on our allies and partners." Apprehension about the presidential summit was once again ratcheting up. Mattis summed up the situation nicely: "It's like we're going to declare war on our allies."

Yet we were receiving a consistent message of reassurance from the White House. It rang hollow, however, offered so soon after the surprises involving the North Korean summit and Space Force announcements.

Anticipating this situation, Mattis had pulled me into his office on June 18, after returning from a meeting with National Security Adviser John Bolton and Secretary Pompeo. "Bus, I'm concerned about where we're heading with the transatlantic alliance. Reach out to Stephen Miller at the White House regarding the president's remarks [for the upcoming NATO Summit]."

I nodded my head as Mattis continued. "Tell him we need to hold the transatlantic alliance together. NATO has got to be stable."

This was one of the few times I'd seen Mattis so visibly apprehensive. He continued, "The president has an opportunity to calm the waters and lower the temperature. Our allies enabled us to yield maximum success with our [North Korean] efforts and for a possible Syria withdrawal. We will want them there when we need them." I jotted it all down. "Yes, sir."

Mattis started to chew his lower lip and moved back over to his stand-up desk, lost deep in thought. Realizing that the meeting was now over, I turned and headed back to my desk to coordinate a call with Miller.

Miller, for his part, had previously assured me that the president would be "on message" during the summit. It was the same idea he now provided. The letters, he assured me, were merely meant for shock value. His message was clear: don't worry, the upcoming summit was still on track for alliance unity—to recognize the allies for their strides to increase spending under the watchful eye of the Trump administration.

Ambassador Hutchison at NATO wasn't convinced. She was on the front lines in Brussels, and in regular contact with our allies. She was concerned enough that she arranged to call Mattis the next day, on Tuesday, July 3. The timing worked well, as Mattis was scheduled to speak with his German counterpart, Defense Minister Ursula von der Leyen, before speaking with Hutchison, providing an opportunity to make his own assessment of NATO's concerns. At the appointed time, I took a seat on the couch in Mattis's office, just as Hutchison's phone call was connected.

Hutchison revealed that she'd just gotten off the phone with Bolton. "[Last] Friday's call between Trump and NATO Secretary General Stoltenberg was looking like a disaster," she shared. Trump was refusing to agree to sign the standard communiqué following the upcoming NATO Summit, because he still felt burned by his experience with the similarly titled document from last month's G7 meeting. He wouldn't sign a communiqué—period. That being said, things sounded better after her phone call with Bolton. He had provided her with reassurances that the White House wasn't going to significantly alter the status quo, the same message Miller had shared with me.

Hutchison and Mattis bounced ideas off each other. How could they position for success at NATO?

Hutchison offered two suggestions. She pointed out that "the president wants to excel at something other presidents can't claim . . . that he's correcting yet another Obama mistake." This summit could be a chance for Trump to "define his priorities to create a 'fit for purpose' alliance, which *will* be one of his legacies."

Her second suggestion was for the president to keep his national security strategy in mind. "He should think of NATO as a ready force at our command under the president's strategy," she suggested. I knew this would never fly with the allies. NATO is an alliance, not a standing force to be ordered about at America's whim, but I knew she was suggesting a desperate idea in the hopes of bringing Trump on board.

Mattis disagreed. "I'm worried that the president won't be

swayed by strategic merits, but I like your first point [making Trump feel unique]." He advocated emphasizing NATO's successes with counterterrorism and the reversal in the decline on defense spending, as evidence that "we're on the right path."

There remained an overarching concern that Trump might skip the summit altogether. Trump was scheduled to meet with Russian President Vladimir Putin immediately after the NATO Summit. His White House team told us that Trump was considering skipping NATO altogether and simply meeting with Putin instead. As Hutchison put it, "It would be a huge Putin victory if the president blew off the summit and proceeded to his meeting with Russia."

At the end of the call, Hutchison agreed to try convincing the allies into renaming the communiqué a "declaration." She and Mattis wanted Trump to think he was signing a different document. Only the title would change—everything else remained the same.

The Fourth of July provided a much-needed respite and a cause for celebration: "Old Man" Rivers was getting married. It was an honor to attend. Sarah and I were incredibly touched to see that Mattis—despite everything else on his plate—also arrived for the ceremony.

Sarah and I sat next to Nicole Magney, the other member of my speech team, and Mattis for the ceremony. Mattis did nothing to call attention to himself before departing shortly after the ceremony ended. It was a moving, much-appreciated gesture from someone with so many international concerns on his hands.

On Tuesday, July 10, we loaded once more onto the E-4B,

this time headed for Brussels and a rendezvous with the administration's latest manufactured crisis.

Mattis met with reporters shortly after we took off. Every question centered around NATO and Trump's follow-up summit with Putin. Was there anxiety in Europe? What were the chances that Trump would chastise allies again before embracing Putin at their own summit in Helsinki? Mattis had the best line regarding the purpose of the Trump-Putin summit. "It's like sex in the 1990s," he said. "It's all about instant gratification." Hilarious, but telling. The administration wasn't operating strategically, but rather looking for issues to provide immediate satisfaction.

Members of Mattis's core team and Policy shop assembled in his private cabin. Tom Goffus, the deputy assistant secretary of defense for NATO, assured Mattis that everything was set for the summit.

Mattis shook his head. "The president's letters have done real damage. I would have stopped them if I'd known about them. Pompeo didn't know . . . Bolton didn't know . . ." I was incredulous. Other than Stephen Miller writing them in private and sending them out, how could John Bolton not know? If anything, the offending letters had likely been drafted by a staffer at the National Security Council. It was alarming to realize the number of issues of national significance that were now occurring without a sufficient (or was it any?) amount of coordination or consideration.

After the meeting, I made my way back to the conference room. I was worried too. Tapping my fingers on the table, I decided to talk with Stephen Miller. Despite Miller's assurances that everything was fine, Trump's Twitter feed indicated that he was gearing up for a fight. I notified Faller of my intentions before using an in-flight phone to call back to the Pentagon switchboard.

The watch officer on the other end of the line picked up, saying, "OSD [Office of the Secretary of Defense] Cables," the name of the group handling our communications. I asked to be connected with Miller, who I knew had recently departed on board Air Force One for the president's flight to Brussels.

Cables patched me through to the White House Situation Room, who then connected me to Air Force One. Miller got on the line about five minutes later. "Good afternoon, General." *Huh?* "Hey, Stephen, it's Bus. I'm calling from Mattis's plane." "Oh, Bus. The Situation Room told me that General Snodgrass was on the line for me." It was a silly-enough mix-up to elicit genuine laughter from both of us. It's always good to keep a sense of humor, particularly during challenging times.

Miller confirmed for a third time that Trump was "going to be on message" at the summit. His only request was that Mattis continue to use language he'd used previously, along the lines of "Europeans can't expect Americans to care more about the safety of their children than they do"—a reference to both North Korean and Russian threats to European nations. As they stood much closer to these threats, NATO nations needed to increase their military posture rather than appearing to depend so heavily on ours. Mattis had carried that water on every previous trip to Brussels, which the White House well knew. We should be fine.

Mattis walked into the conference room just as I hung up the phone. Faller acted like a proud parent. "Sir, Bus just got off the phone with Air Force One. It sounds like everything's going to be okay." Mattis looked genuinely impressed. "You called Air Force One?"

I nodded, "Yes, sir. I wanted Stephen to confirm that nothing had changed with the president's message. He assured me that despite some public posturing, we should be okay." The boss looked relieved for the first time that week. "Well done. Thanks, Bus." It felt like a much-needed moment of personal redemption.

Too bad it didn't last long.

Life was great again for twelve hours. If we'd paid more attention to what Trump was saying during his recent rallies around the country, we'd have been better prepared for what was coming. After more than a month of bolt-from-the-blue surprises from the White House, I believe we were just desperate for a win. We *wanted* to believe that things were finally back on track—that things were going to work out just fine. We couldn't have been more wrong, and it led to the only time on Mattis's team that I felt genuinely remorseful over the part I played.

In our hotel that evening, Mattis called Secretary General Stoltenberg to reassure him that everything was going to be fine. Trump was just posturing for his supporters back home. Everything would be okay. We all went to sleep believing that to be the case.

The team woke early on July 11 to prep for Mattis's departure. I usually attended the NATO meetings, but today would be a madhouse with twenty-nine national leaders all in one location. I elected to remain at the hotel rather than add one more body to an already packed delegation.

Working from our comms room, it wasn't long before I saw

the president's tweet from the evening prior. "Many countries in NATO, which we are expected to defend, are not only short of their current commitment of 2% (which is low), but are also delinquent for many years in payments that have not been made. Will they reimburse the U.S.?" He'd sent several other tweets around the same time lamenting how "unfair" the NATO alliance was for the US.

I was watching C-SPAN from the communications room at the hotel at 9:00 a.m. when President Trump met with Stoltenberg for their breakfast together. Joining him were Pompeo, Mattis, Bolton, Hutchison, and White House Chief of Staff John Kelly.

Members of the press clustered at one side of the room so videographers could capture the entire US delegation together with the secretary general and his team. The mood was positive for about thirty seconds, until a member of the press asked Trump, "Which nations do you want to spend more on NATO in particular?"

It was the opening Trump had been waiting for, and he immediately lit into the alliance. "Many countries are not paying what they should. And frankly, many countries owe us a tremendous amount of money." Our delegation looked ill. Kelly reached for his pen, while Hutchison and Pompeo struggled to maintain wan smiles. Trump continued, "This has gone on for decades . . . no other president has brought it up like I've brought it up."

The president was correct on that point. But it wasn't necessarily the message he was bringing, but the manner and style of his delivery. NATO, long a bulwark against Russian aggression, cherishes the unbreakable public unity of its alliance. Trump's language was pointed, inflammatory, and, worse, playing out publicly in front of the cameras for the world to see.

Trump offered Stoltenberg an opportunity to respond. Stoltenberg seemed surprised, but his impromptu comments were eloquent and polished, an obvious attempt to appease Trump. "After years of cutting defense budgets," Stoltenberg told the reporters, "[NATO nations are] starting to add billions to their defense budgets. Last year was the biggest increase in defense spending across Europe . . . in a generation."

Trump interrupted, "Why was that last year?"

Stoltenberg responded, "It's also because of your leadership and . . . your message is having an impact" in convincing allies to add an additional $266 billion to the defense budgets by 2024. He then tried deflecting the conversation to Trump's upcoming meeting with Putin. "The leaders are also looking forward to your thoughts about the meeting with President Putin."

Trump jumped right back in. "Well, I have to say I think it's very sad when Germany makes a massive oil and gas deal with Russia where you're supposed to be guarding against Russia, and Germany goes out and pays billions and billions of dollars a year to Russia. So we're protecting Germany, we're protecting France, we're protecting all of these countries and then numerous of the countries go out and make a pipeline deal with Russia where they're paying billions of dollars into the coffers of Russia. So we're supposed to protect you against Russia but they're paying billions of dollars to Russia, and I think that's very inappropriate."

Mattis and Bolton were out of the camera frame. Hutchison and Pompeo's feeble smiles had long since evaporated, but Trump would continue holding court for another four minutes.

Back in the comms room, I was dying by inches. Mattis had assured Stoltenberg that everything was going to be fine, a message he based on my conversation with Stephen Miller. Mattis never said a word to me about it. He knew that I was merely passing along what I'd been told. My larger concern was that the boss had now confirmed that he no longer spoke for the administration. He was grossly misaligned with Trump. A similar malady had proven fatal to Tillerson during his final few months.

At NATO headquarters, Trump's breakfast remarks continued, culminating when Trump declared that because of the energy pipeline, "Germany, as far as I'm concerned, is totally captive to Russia." What air was left in the delegation now vanished, as an obviously shocked Hutchison shot nervous glances across the table to her counterparts. Kelly made it his purpose in life to find a sudden interest in the flags sitting off to his right.

It was another public flogging of NATO. While Trump supporters back home no doubt cheered and detractors jeered, the underlying point was that the alliance looked more fractured than ever.

Tom Goffus, our NATO expert, had been at NATO headquarters and provided insight to me regarding the first meeting between NATO leadership. President Trump was moving the goalposts on the 2014 Wales Pledge (for 2 percent of GDP to be spent on defense), insisting it should be increased to 4 percent to match US spending, an astronomical sum for many European nations. It was also highly misleading, as the higher 4 percent calculation Trump quoted included military pensions, not just our current military force. Our actual military spending was closer to 3 percent.

Overall, it was an alarming first day at the NATO Summit.

The next day, July 12, was no different. Trump surprised everyone by hijacking an 8:45 a.m. meeting intended to discuss the security of Georgia and Ukraine into an emergency session about defense spending. Mattis wasn't even in the room, having left for a sidebar conversation with a counterpart. Soon learning of the change in direction, he decided against rejoining the meeting and missed the entire conversation.

Text messages sped back and forth between our team at the hotel and NATO headquarters, with several of our delegates warning of a very real possibility that Trump would announce a US withdrawal from NATO.

Trump soon emerged from the meeting to call an impromptu press conference. Taking the podium at NATO headquarters, he announced that "everyone has agreed to substantially up their commitment . . . to up it at levels that they've never thought of before." Mattis was nowhere to be seen. The team at NATO made it clear to me that nothing of substance had changed. Trump had created an emergency, and then "solved" it by returning to the status quo and claiming victory.

Trump's press conference remarks were incredibly thin and barely conveyed any more information than a good-sized tweet. It was another patented Trump-manufactured crisis like we'd seen with the F-35 Joint Strike Fighter: claim that the US had gotten a bad deal, swoop in and make a lot of noise, then claim victory while the terms of the deal remained the same as before. In this case, the announcement was really that NATO members would increase their spending to 2 percent of GDP . . . the same deal that President Obama had secured in 2014.

A prediction made by *Fox News* political editor Chris Stire-walt before the summit proved all too prescient: Trump would "fly into Brussels like a seagull . . . defecate all over everything, squawk, and fly away."

NATO, like any large, monolithic organization, needed to make changes to adapt to changing circumstances—or even to correct past mistakes. Trump's actions, however, only created additional fractures in America's long-standing NATO relationships . . . and not for any measurable benefit.

It was a bad deal. "All show and no go."

The stress and strain were once again showing with the team. I watched as Mattis, a stoic leader with amazing self-control, finally blew a gasket during our final stop in Norway.

We were at the US embassy for what is called a "country team meeting," where each director at the embassy met with Mattis to brief on their area of expertise. Those of us on Mattis's travel team usually listened in, as the economic, security, political, and military insights were always fascinating and directly applicable to other visits in the future.

Today didn't start well, however, as multiple members of the embassy team decided to "table drop" information during the meeting. Despite weeks of coordination leading up to this meeting, the Norway team had withheld information so that they'd look smart in front of Mattis when he arrived. It's an entirely understandable human desire—keep a little something in reserve for when the boss shows up.

Except Mattis hates it. It cuts against his deeply held belief regarding "transparency and alignment." If everyone is communicating beforehand, then there should be no surprises at the actual meeting. Any surprise indicates that his team didn't perform their due diligence, only sowing doubt in Mattis's mind. Never a good place to be.

That's exactly what happened with Ambassador Ken Braithwaite and his team. As each new functional director spoke, they started sharing important new tidbits of information that they hadn't previously reported. Mattis grew more and more agitated, until he did something I'd never witnessed before: he kicked everyone out of the ambassador's own conference room.

"I need everyone to step out so I can update my remarks with all the excellent new information you have provided here today." It was his passive-aggressive streak showing through. Embassy staff looked pleased. Those of us with Mattis knew what he was really saying—*thanks for screwing me.*

TWENTY-TWO

ENDGAME

There's a great deal of talk about loyalty from the bottom to the top. Loyalty from the top down is even more necessary and is much less prevalent. One of the most frequently noted characteristics of great men who have remained great is loyalty to their subordinates.

—GENERAL GEORGE S. PATTON

My fate on board Team Mattis oscillated rapidly as we returned from Brussels on July 14. I noted with wry humor that my own status on Mattis's team continued to ebb and flow in sync with Mattis's relationship to Trump. Somehow, I'd become an inadvertent barometer for Mattis's moods—a storm warning only further predicted by my relationship with Faller and Sweeney.

It had become abundantly clear in June that my position was in a tough spot. Simply rolling over and letting senior advisers hang whatever language they wanted on Mattis's speeches was a recipe for failure. I'd tried this path a few times, and the result was predictable—Mattis holding me accountable, not the person making the changes. As Mattis himself routinely said to us, "If you mix bad processes with good people, the bad processes will win nine out of ten times."

I also tried standing my ground on the speechwriting process, believing it was my job to retain responsibility for Mattis's "voice," as I had done successfully during my first year on the team. When that didn't work, I started looking for a third option, one where everyone could win.

There was one glaring flaw in the way Mattis's front office operated: no civilian had successfully exited his direct orbit to go for another job in the Pentagon (or in the administration). Conversely, a number of civilians had been forced to exit his office to seek greener pastures elsewhere.

Under normal circumstances, talented men and women would be brought into the secretary's office to mine salt for twelve to eighteen months before they were spun back out in the Pentagon to assume a different leadership role. The benefits were twofold. People were rewarded for the long hours, hard work, and the dedication they had committed to the secretary. It also provided positive incentives for others to accept the toughest jobs.

That's not how things operated with Mattis, and by extension his chief of staff, Kevin Sweeney. It's also likely one of the reasons why we retained a military-heavy office: you worked until you dropped or rotated out, then someone fresh was brought in to take your place. As Mattis once jokingly told me, "You find your horse and ride them. When they drop, you shoot them and find another horse." Plus, there just wasn't a lot of interest from civilians looking to join our team.

I believed I could break that cycle, successfully exiting to another Pentagon job. As a recently retired naval officer, I had now completed an additional three months with Mattis as a relatively senior civilian political appointee in a rank known as "GS-15 Step 10," or the highest level before being appointed as a member of the senior executive service.

It was in June 2018 that I'd had an opportunity to chat with Jim O'Beirne, the director of the White House Liaison Office located in the Pentagon. His was a small group of political appointees tasked with identifying talent and filling vacancies within the Pentagon. To hear O'Beirne tell it, we were still hurting for quality candidates to come in from industry or academia to assume leadership roles. During this same conversation, O'Beirne had asked how long I'd been with the secretary. "Coming up on fifteen months," was my reply. He cocked his head thoughtfully. "A normal rotation would be about a year and a half. Would you be interested in taking another job in the Pentagon?" I felt like I was being thrown a lifeline.

Retiring from the Navy had been a bitter pill to swallow. In Navy parlance, before joining Mattis's office, I'd been "on the path" of upward mobility in the military. Selection for aircraft carriers was a deal-breaker for my family, so I'd played the hand I was dealt by declining it and subsequently retiring.

Now O'Beirne was offering an opportunity to help Mattis enact his vision for the department, but in a leadership role instead of my current supporting role. Part of me also liked being the first civilian to successfully complete a tour with Mattis and move to a different job, a signal complementing his reputation. *If you go to work for Mattis, you'll work harder than you have in your life . . . but he takes care of his people.* It felt like a great outcome for everyone.

The rest of the process went smoothly. O'Beirne requested my résumé to better see where I might fit. On June 28, he copied me on an email to Mike Duffey, now the chief of staff for Under Secretary of Defense Mike Griffin. Duffey was responsible for staffing the Pentagon's newly formed Research and Engineering component. O'Beirne's email to Griffin read, in part:

> Even a brief examination of his attached resume will demonstrate that this is a brilliant young man with distinguished scientific credentials (in education) paired with formidable wartime experience, a synergy not often encountered.
>
> I could envision him making a significant contribution as an appointee in the world of high-tech research and engineering either as a special assistant to either of your incoming Directors or even as a potential DAS [deputy assistant secretary] as you build out your organization.

I appreciated O'Beirne's kind words, and was honored that he was providing both mentorship and a pathway forward. After fifteen months with Secretary Mattis, I knew that a person was either all the way in or all the way out when it came to working on his team. Bosses tend to dislike surprises. The last thing I needed was to have word spread that I was considering other options, so I immediately informed Sweeney about the opportunity. Another job was also on the table: a leadership role with

Dr. Will Roper, a talented scientist working as assistant secretary of the Air Force for acquisitions.

I caught Sweeney in his office. The conversation was straightforward. "Afternoon, Chief," I said. "A couple opportunities have presented themselves to me, and I want to share them with you before I consider exploring them."

Sweeney was surprisingly receptive, saying, "Sure. What's on your radar?" I shared both prospects with him, and followed up immediately with, "I understand if you need me to continue manning my oar. Happy to stay as long as you and the team need."

Sweeney was quite supportive. "You should hear what they have to say," he said of Griffin and Roper. "Let me know how it goes and we can take it from there." With Sweeney's blessing, I responded to both Griffin and Roper that I'd be available to interview.

On July 18, Duffey, Griffin's chief of staff, made time for me to visit his office and talk about the upcoming interview. He also wanted to assess what roles might be a good fit for me.

Duffey expressed support and produced a Research and Engineering (R&E) leadership team organizational chart. Duffey mentioned that a deputy assistant secretary role would be appropriate given my experience, background, and corporate knowledge gained from working alongside Mattis and Deputy Secretary Shanahan.

Duffey noted that some positions were earmarked for industry leaders with deep experience in science and technology, but there were four leadership roles that were broader in nature. He said that a couple were already spoken for but volunteered that "Deputy Director for Research, Technology and Laboratories would be a great fit." I liked the description he shared with me: responsibility for leading the defense department's research laboratories and an opportunity to guide our efforts to transition to the latest technology. It would be a return to my engineering roots while helping directly support the national defense strategy. The conversation was positive, a great springboard for the next day's interview with Under Secretary Griffin.

I had already put together a one-inch binder full of study material to prepare for meeting Griffin. While helpful, it turned out it wasn't directly applicable to the interview. Griffin seemed already convinced to hire me, informing me five minutes after I walked in the door how he wanted me on board.

"Look, you've had a successful twenty-year career as a leader in the Navy. Your advanced engineering degrees give you credibility. You wrote the National Defense Strategy, so you're intimately familiar with what we're trying to accomplish, and you've spent the last year and a half working for Mattis. Am I missing anything? I could really use your help. Frankly, I could have used you months ago. How soon can you get here?"

Roper expressed a similar sentiment regarding joining his Air Force team. I was deeply honored by and enthusiastic about both opportunities. In the span of a few days, Sweeney had endorsed me to pursue leadership positions, I had interviewed, and both organizations wanted to bring me on board. It was an embarrassment of riches.

I caught up with Sweeney the next day to let him know about both offers. He remained incredibly supportive. When I asked which job he recommended I take, his gut reaction was to choose Griffin. "Bus, you could work for Roper and do some really good things. But Research and Engineering is a new organization. If you work for Griffin, you'll be writing the history books as you help him form the very first team." I agreed but told him I'd like to think on it. Could I give him my decision the following day?

Sarah immediately noticed that I was on cloud nine when I walked in the door that evening. She'd watched me simmer in the pressure cooker for nearly a year and a half. Now I was being given a chance to do what I loved most—develop and lead a high-performance team, just like I had as the commanding officer of a fighter squadron in Japan.

I told Chief about my decision to join Griffin's team at Research and Engineering on Saturday afternoon. "Bus, I think you made the right call. The secretary and I discussed your move this morning." I thanked Sweeney for his mentorship and for the opportunity. "I won't let you or the secretary down, sir." He chuckled. "You'll do a great job, Bus. Enjoy the rest of your weekend—go celebrate with the family."

My next email was to Griffin, Sweeney, and O'Beirne. "Dr. Griffin," it read, "thank you for the offer and your vote of confidence . . . I'm honored to accept the position of Deputy Director for Research, Technology, and Laboratories." Griffin replied to all of us two hours later, "Guy, we'll be delighted to have you!"

Sarah and I decided to follow Sweeney's advice to let loose, so we loaded the kids up for a visit to Baskin-Robbins for some ice cream.

The rest of the process was straightforward. I was already a political appointee with all the right security clearances. O'Beirne saw nothing standing in my way. I expected a quick move to Griffin's office.

I was looking forward to my new role but adamant about ensuring that Mattis and the team were left in good shape. Growing up, my dad had always reminded me to "leave the campsite better than I found it," a recommendation I planned to follow. My original office in the "D-ring," which I retained for a quiet place to write, had been a messy disaster when I inherited it. I cleaned it out and tidied it up for the next person. My desire to leave the job better than I found it also meant ensuring there was no shortfall in Mattis's speechwriting effort.

On Monday, I notified Rivers and Magney, my two speechwriters, of the impending move. Both were happy for me but a little nervous about the workload. Working for Mattis was fast-paced, and we'd be losing a third of our horsepower. "Don't worry," I said. "I've printed off the list of every event on Mattis's calendar for August. I won't leave until we've drafted speeches for the next month and a half's worth of events."

We got to work on the speeches. It was a tough start to the week, but I was on top of the world, walking in the door at home each night with a spring in my step. Well, for at least the first few days. My dream turned into a nightmare on Wednesday, July 25, less than a week after accepting the position with Griffin.

I had a long-standing plan for time off in Seattle the following week to attend a leadership conference. Since I'd be out of town right before showing up at Research and Engineering, I'd asked Duffey for a meeting to discuss ways to show up ready to succeed on my first day. He'd asked me to come by his office at 11:15 a.m.

Just before 10:30, Mattis materialized in front of my desk. I was leaning down, busy putting some items into a cardboard box, when I noticed he'd stopped. I glanced up.

Mattis looked exhausted. He'd recently had a minor surgical procedure above his left eyebrow, leaving him with an angry red incision, which only reinforced his tired demeanor. Strangely, he didn't say a word. He just stood there. Staring at me. *This is odd,* I thought.

I broke the silence. "Good morning, sir."

He didn't say anything at first, his expression indecipherable. "So, you're leaving us . . . ," was all he said.

While I kept a poker face, inwardly I was confused. I hadn't spoken with Mattis directly about my upcoming move, but Sweeney reassured me that he'd kept him up to date. I wasn't looking for any fanfare, especially since I'd had my award ceremony three months before, but he wasn't offering a hand to say "Congrats" or "Well done, Bus."

He was just watching me. Studying me.

"Yes, sir. Dr. Griffin asked me to come and provide some leadership at R&E. Thank you for the opportunity." Mattis paused before saying, "Build a good team when you get there."

Then he turned, walking back down the hall to his office.

I knew Sam, our intelligence representative whose office was situated next to where I sat, had likely overhead the conversation so I poked my head in and said, "Uh, that seemed off." Sam thought I was fine. "He's obviously tired. He probably just hates losing you." But the apprehension wouldn't go away. Sometimes you know in your gut. *Something just shifted.*

As if on cue, Duffey emailed me six minutes before I was due to meet with him. His email read, "Guy—can we postpone for 45 minutes?" Then at 12:20 p.m., he asked for another hour's delay. He next called me at my desk. "Bus, can you come by at sixteen hundred?"—military parlance for 4:00 p.m. *What is going on?*

I finally made it in with Duffey just after 4:30 p.m. "Sorry to reschedule you like this. It's been a crazy day. You can obviously tell we need your support over here." I chuckled. "No problem, Mike. Thanks for making the time—I know it's your most precious resource. It's late in the day so I'll cut to the chase. I'll be gone all next week, but what can I do to prepare so that I walk in here on 'day one' ready to support Griffin and the team?"

Duffey folded his hands on his desk. "Okay, we need to talk before we go any further." *Uh-oh, here it comes.* "I really hate to do this, but I'm going to have to rescind the offer that we made you."

I was floored. Absolutely floored. "What do you mean?" I asked. He looked morose. We'd known each other since I first arrived at the Pentagon, and I could tell he hated to be the bearer of bad news. "We can no longer offer you the position," he said. My head was spinning.

Duffey continued, "I want you to know that this is not Griffin's desire, but I'm also not at liberty to say where this is coming from." *That's a weird statement to make.* During our conversation, he told me that someone had blocked my move. But who? Duffey had been ordered to keep me in the dark.

"Mike, look, I made major life changes based on this offer.

Sarah and I just put down $10,000 on a home this weekend, since we knew we were going to be staying in the area. Let me go chat with Sweeney. He can override anyone who's trying to turn this off." Mike just looked at me blankly before saying, "You can try. I don't think the decision will change."

Mike didn't have much more to offer. He felt bad and shared that he'd suffered an eerily similar fate earlier in his job, which is why he was currently sitting as a chief of staff and not running his own team.

I was becoming irritated. I'd served Mattis honorably for close to a year and a half. My military career had been derailed. Now my opportunity to serve in a leadership capacity was being pulled back? "Mike, I've already closed out my job in Mattis's office. It'd be untenable to stay there." Duffey just held his hand out, palms facing upward, a sign of powerlessness. "I'm sorry, Bus, there's nothing else I can share with you."

I looked at my watch. If I hustled I could catch O'Beirne before he went home. He'd been one of my most vocal advocates for this opportunity, even going so far as helping me begin to assemble a "kitchen cabinet" of advisers. I had planned to learn from people with decades of experience in the Pentagon bureaucracy to help me make the best and most positive impact in my new role.

O'Beirne would know what to do.

Luckily, he was still in his office. O'Beirne was a straight shooter. "Look, Sweeney is the one that stabbed you in the back. He called Duffey and directed him to kill the offer. This is one of the most underhanded things I've ever seen, and I'm going to fight for you." I was grateful that Jim wanted to help, but I was uncertain that anything would change. If Sweeney had killed the offer, it was most likely dead.

I tried to reach Sweeney but couldn't get him on the phone, so I called Sarah. It was gut-wrenching. "Babe, I don't know what to tell you. Chief just pulled the job. We might lose the house." She was a trooper, just like she'd been throughout our entire marriage. "I'm so sorry. Why don't you come home and we can talk about it when you get here." I hung up and stared at the wall for about five minutes before closing up shop and heading home.

The next day I was out of the office for a meeting in Annapolis. It was the best thing that could have happened, as several close friends of Mattis's were present at the gathering, including former deputy secretary Bob Work, General John Allen, and Vice Admiral Pete Daly. All three said I had to go directly to Mattis on this one. Daly, a longtime mentor who'd actually placed me in the job with Mattis, said I had to go all in.

"Bus, you kept your powder dry when you were selected for aircraft carriers. You have no choice now. You have to talk to Mattis." Work agreed, "There's no way that Mattis knows what's going on—he'd never let this happen to one of his people, especially after all you've done." Even Michael Bayer, chairman of the Defense Business Board and one of the mentors O'Beirne had arranged for me to work with, emailed that I should speak directly with Mattis.

Their take was unanimous—confront Mattis. Nothing good would come from meeting with Sweeney.

That night, I carefully crafted an email to Mattis. Trying to catch him in the hallway would be a fool's errand, and Sweeney held tight control over access to his office. An email would undoubtedly reach him. Just in case Mattis didn't see it in his work account, I copied his personal email account and copied Sweeney as well. In my email I requested to speak with Mattis regarding my appointment, writing in part, "Sir, I know you care deeply about those who have dedicated themselves to supporting you, and can only believe that Wednesday's actions were taken without your knowledge, which is why I raise this issue with you now." I hit send at 9:35 p.m.

The next morning Sweeney emailed me at 5:38 a.m., writing simply, "See me this morning." It was a predictably guarded response, but I needed to talk to O'Beirne first to determine my options moving forward.

I happened to be sitting in O'Beirne's office around 7:30 a.m. when Navy Captain Hal Mohler, Mattis's executive secretary, walked in. It was like a scene from a cartoon. Mohler wasn't expecting to see me, so he just looked back and forth between O'Beirne and me for about five seconds before he focused all his attention on me.

"Bus, Chief is upset. He told me to come over here to tell O'Beirne he's going to fire you. Sorry." At this point nothing could surprise me. Jim and I just looked at each other. I spoke up first. "Okay, thanks, Hal. I appreciate your sharing with me." Mohler turned and walked back out the door.

O'Beirne offered his support. "This may be the time where I need to fall on my sword. I haven't talked with Mattis since taking this position, so this would be a good opportunity to do so. Besides, you're a political appointee from the White House . . .

Sweeney can't just fire you like that." I shrugged, saying, "Well, staying on the team with Sweeney isn't going to happen. I figured Kevin might overreact, so let me step across the hall and submit my resignation letter before this goes any further."

I walked over to my secondary office in the "D-ring" and shut the door. I'd known I was taking a risk by going around Sweeney to email Mattis, so I'd written my letter of resignation and signed it the night before. I wrote, in part, "It has been an honor to serve alongside you during this pivotal time in our Nation's history. Your steady hand as Secretary has put the Department on a path towards genuine renewal, with a promise of a military that can be far more lethal than the one you inherited. Thank you for your unyielding pursuit of this goal. As a recently retired Naval officer, I can assure you that your message resonates on the flight line, at the waterfront, and on the front lines."

I hit send on my email to Mattis, including a few other senior leaders and friends in the Pentagon.

Then nothing happened. Security didn't swarm my office to escort me out with a cardboard box in hand. After sitting in my office for thirty minutes, I decided to make my way around the building to say goodbye to some of the senior leaders I'd enjoyed working with the most.

I was walking back to my office when Sweeney saw me in the hallway. Smiling broadly, with a saccharine voice he said, "Bus, there you are! I'd love to chat if you have a few minutes." I continued toward him. "Sure thing, Chief. Happy to."

We walked past reception and into his office, located just inside Mattis's suite. Sweeney held up a hard copy of my resignation.

With an incredulous voice he, oh-so-innocently, asked, "Bus, what's going on? You're resigning? Why?"

It was one thing to have the knife slipped slowly into my back, but lying to me was too much.

"Chief, this is bulls—t. You're lying straight to my face. I was in with Jim [O'Beirne] when Mohler came in to say you were trying to fire me." His demeanor changed immediately. Gone were the over-the-top pleasantries and smiles. With a completely normal voice, he said, "Okay, we should talk."

I'd had enough. "No thanks, Chief. I don't want to work for an office that treats its people this way. I'm done."

I turned and walked out.

Although I'd remain on the books for another week, my second Pentagon tour was effectively over. I spent the rest of the day saying goodbye to friends before grabbing the rest of my things and heading home.

Sarah walked in the door about a half hour after I did. "Well," I said, "that's that. I just resigned from my position with Mattis." She gave me a tight hug, saying, "Well, know that I'm incredibly proud of you. I know how tough this year has been, but you hung in there and never gave up. There's a lot to be said for that." I squeezed her a little tighter. "You too," I said. "You and the kids were there for me every step of the way. Thanks for the tireless support."

Sarah was right. Despite the hardships, it'd been one last incredible ride with the military in the Pentagon. Staying tough in the face of adversity didn't feel unusual. It's what I'd trained for my entire career. Although the challenges were different in Mattis's office—far more personal and tougher to "solve"—my response was the same. Stay mentally tough. Always give the job your very best.

It's the way we all operated, especially Mattis. You stay in the fight, giving the job your very best, until you can no longer do so.

And I wasn't the only one who would walk away, resigning in frustration.

TWENTY-THREE

HANGING ON

It's better to walk away than to tolerate nonsense.

—ANONYMOUS

On December 20, 2018, one day after Trump announced a unilateral withdrawal of US military forces from Syria against the best advice of his defense secretary, Mattis resigned.

His resignation letter highlighted the sharp differences dividing a president and his secretary of defense. Mattis wrote that "our strength as a nation is inextricably linked to the strength of our unique and comprehensive system of alliances and partnerships." Mattis pointedly wrote that America must "maintain strong alliances and [show] respect to those allies." He noted that his views on respecting our allies derived from over four decades of experience and careful study.

Catching press attention was this line: "Because you have the right to have a Secretary of Defense whose views are better aligned with yours on these and other subjects, I believe it is right to step down from my position."

Mattis's resignation reverberated around Washington, DC, in a way that no other senior official's departure had. Although Mattis offered to remain on the job until February 28, 2019, to provide time to nominate a new secretary, White House staff felt that Mattis was using his resignation letter to take a calculated public stand against Trump—a suspicion further amplified by the response from the public, members of Congress, and domestic and international news organizations. President Trump rebuked Mattis's offer, instead insisting that Mattis hand over the department to Deputy Secretary Shanahan before January 1, 2019.

Watching from a distance, I knew that the framing of Mattis's resignation as a spur-of-the-moment decision made in a final moment of passion was incorrect. Mattis had already decided to resign the previous summer. I had—quite literally—stumbled upon the meeting that led to his decision.

I had stopped in to see Mattis's scheduler to coordinate, asking, "Hey, how's it going? I need to sync with your schedule for the next couple of weeks."

She admonished me, for the second time, for being far too loud, stating, "Bus, jeez, keep your voice down. The boss is meeting with General Kelly." I glanced at Mattis's schedule, which I religiously printed and pasted into my notebook each day.

No meeting with John Kelly was listed.

"Uh, really? I don't see anything on here." She cleared up the mystery for me. "This is a private meeting. We deliberately kept Kelly off the schedule so no one, not even our staff, would know. We want to keep this under wraps."

Intrigued, I asked, "Really? What's going on?" She looked disheartened. "They're discussing departures. The boss is planning to leave this winter but Kelly is going to stay on at the White House." A few minutes later, I made my way back to my desk. Even though I was certainly aware of the heat Mattis was taking, I still hoped he would just gut it out, staying on the job to support the president—and the nation—with his dedication to the country.

Selfishly, I knew that if he left after only two years, he was far less likely to have a lasting impact on the military. The US military is an enormous organization. Effecting fundamental—and much-needed—change would take more time. Evidently, it was time he no longer felt he had.

Was Mattis's scheduler pulling my leg?

No. Mattis's long-range schedule in Microsoft Outlook confirmed her remarks: all of his scheduled events stopped in December 2018. Nothing moved forward into 2019 except a daily recurrence of an hour blocked each day for "Lunch / Reading Time."

It didn't take long before others around the secretary's personal staff started to catch on, especially those planning events months into the future. Several approached me in late summer, asking what I knew. I demurred. It wasn't my story to tell, nor would my telling it have improved morale.

Mattis treasures his legacy. I knew longtime friends and associates had emailed him during his tenure, asking him to consider leaving the Pentagon. They expressed concern that staying on too long meant that he'd fully embraced an administration's policies that ran counter to his values and beliefs.

I thought it honorable that Mattis had designed a smooth, coordinated exit. He could have easily walked out the door far earlier. Instead, he chose to stay in the fight, remaining until Washington, DC, invariably slowed down during the winter break.

As I'd watched Mattis from a distance for the final four months, I'd enjoyed my freedom. The change in lifestyle was immediate. No steady stream of emails overflowing my in-box. No late-night phone calls to hurriedly edit a set of remarks for the White House. I was free. The last year and a half had been a pressure cooker with the temperature and pressure cranked up to maximum. Now, as I reflected on what to do next, all I wanted to do was sleep, eat healthy food, and lace up my running shoes to hit the road for some quality runs. It felt amazing to see the children in the morning before school—and know that I'd also be able to see them before bed each night. Or to be free to take Sarah out for lunch "just because."

But even as I enjoyed my new lease on life, I had been tracking what was going on in the Pentagon, counting down the months until Mattis's departure. Sometimes being too close to events is a disadvantage. Stepping back allows you to see things from a wider perspective. And that's how it was, at my home in Virginia, with friends in the Pentagon and at the White House keeping me apprised of the latest developments. Unfortunately, Mattis had remained under fire and, as each day's headlines now made ever clearer, President Trump continued to further resist his counsel. I knew Mattis was working overtime to make as positive a difference as he could with the time he had remaining.

Yes, Trump had every right to ignore Mattis's recommendations. Trump was the president. Mattis was merely one of his appointed cabinet secretaries. Mattis owed Trump his best advice in private, but once Trump decided, Mattis needed to support the president publicly. If he couldn't, then he needed to resign. It was a careful balance he'd been managing during his entire tenure.

What bothered me during these final few months were Mattis's public statements in *support* of policies that I knew he personally loathed. Near the top of the list was the deployment of US troops to the southern border with Mexico in the fall of 2018.

That spring, Mattis had deployed the National Guard to the southern border to help stem the flow of illegal immigrants into the country. He had issued vague statements of support, merely saying that securing America's borders was an important priority—an extremely political statement that really said nothing at all. All nations care about securing their borders. The issue here was determining the military's role in a domestic matter.

Moreover, during a visit to troops deployed to the southern border in November, Mattis defended their deployment as "good training." Worse, he later stood outside the Pentagon telling the press that America's military "doesn't do stunts." Having listened to him discuss the previous deployment, I knew that's *exactly* what he thought the situation was—a political stunt.

Trump's use of several thousand troops on our Mexican border diverted precious resources from legitimate military operations. The Posse Comitatus Act of 1878 clearly prohibits military forces from enforcing domestic policies within the United States. Their presence at the border, ostensibly to install barbed wire to deter a migrant caravan from Central America, was the very definition of a "political stunt" to support the November 2018 election cycle. With the elections over, the White House had ceased warning about the caravan. But the troops remained.

Mattis was now caught up in his own graveyard spiral, expressing public support for a policy he didn't agree with, bending his personal and professional beliefs to support the president.

Then, in early December, Trump announced he was naming US Army General Mark Milley to replace General Dunford as the next chairman of the Joint Chiefs of Staff. That was noteworthy for a couple reasons.

First, Mattis had backed General David Goldfein, the senior officer in the US Air Force, for the role—to the exclusion of every other potential candidate. I was aware that Mattis had told Admiral John Richardson he wouldn't be named to the job. Although Mattis liked Richardson, who had worked for him at US Central Command, the ship collisions that occurred on Richardson's watch were too much. Similarly, Mattis had always had a somewhat contentious relationship with Marine Corps Commandant General Robert Neller. The same held true for General Milley. Mattis felt the Army had "grown fat," and had commented in private that Milley himself was too hefty. To Mattis, optics mattered. He demanded that all branches of the armed forces be in top fighting shape. That meant you also had to look the part.

Second, choosing the chairman of the Joint Chiefs of Staff—as well as other senior military leaders—ranks among the most lasting, meaningful decisions a secretary of defense can make. It affords the secretary an opportunity to chart the course for each service and for the department itself. Senior military officer assignments offered Mattis an opportunity to leave a mark for the next few years, a chance to pick individuals whose values mirrored his own. Yet Trump stripped him of that power.

Trump's selection of Milley was both a slight and a repudiation, another indicator of Mattis's waning influence. It also greatly undercut General Dunford, the current chairman, and his authority. When teams know a new boss is in the wings, they gravitate to that person, not necessarily the old boss. Milley's priorities as chairman were suddenly of great interest. The White House also began to shift to Milley, not Dunford, for advice and decisions.

One last significant event ultimately set the timing for the exact moment of Mattis's resignation: Trump's announcement that he was withdrawing, "effective immediately," American military forces from the counterterrorism fights in Syria and Afghanistan. Like most Trump announcements, he issued it via Twitter, writing, "We have defeated ISIS in Syria, my only reason for being there during the Trump presidency."

Mattis judged our rapid withdrawal as a betrayal of the Coalition to Defeat ISIS that he'd helped build, an abandonment of the Kurdish fighters who had been instrumental to retaking

ISIS-held territory, and waving the white flag of surrender in Afghanistan. These were intensely personal issues for Mattis— you don't abandon your international friends. You don't retreat.

———

Before Mattis departed on December 31, he transmitted his final message to the military:

MEMORANDUM FOR ALL DEPARTMENT OF DEFENSE EMPLOYEES

SUBJECT: Farewell Message

On February 1, 1865, President Lincoln sent to General Ulysses S. Grant a one sentence telegram. It read: "Let nothing which is transpiring, change, hinder, or delay your military movements, or plans."

Our Department's leadership, civilian and military, remains in the best possible hands. I am confident that each of you remains undistracted from our sworn mission to support and defend the Constitution while protecting our way of life. Our Department is proven to be at its best when the times are most difficult. So keep the faith in our country and hold fast, alongside our allies, aligned against our foes.

It has been my high honor to serve at your side. May God hold you safe in the air, on land, and at sea.

James N. Mattis

Mattis then turned the reins over to his deputy, Pat Shanahan, who now became the acting secretary of defense. Part of their formal transfer of power included handing off responsibility for America's nuclear arsenal.

Mattis departed the Pentagon to spend the next few weeks at a nondescript office building in Crystal City, Virginia, closing out his affairs in Washington, DC. Mattis had managed to pull off a smooth exit from the Trump administration. Or had he?

Two days later, on Wednesday, January 2, Trump gathered his senior administration officials and White House staff for their first executive meeting of the new year. Now sitting at Trump's left was Acting Secretary of Defense Pat Shanahan, just thirty-six hours into replacing Mattis.

Trump launched into his remarks, describing 2019 as an exciting year for America. He relayed that the administration had notched many successes during the preceding two years—a recently passed criminal justice reform bill, the appointment of two Supreme Court justices and numerous federal court judges, a reduction in regulations, the passage of sweeping tax cuts, a restored budget for the military, and progress with North Koreans regarding their nuclear stockpile.

Trump paused a moment, regaining enthusiasm as he moved into a lengthy description of the requirement to build a wall to ensure effective border security. Despite the challenges, "the military had been fantastic," he said, in supporting his controversial decision to send active-duty military forces to the US-Mexican border.

Members of the media took the opportunity for a few questions. One in particular caught Trump's attention. Why had the president been able to defeat ISIS, while in Afghanistan the Taliban, a Sunni Islamic fundamentalist political movement, remained a challenge?

President Trump shifted in his chair. His eyes narrowed.

Let's "talk about our generals. I gave our generals all the money they wanted. They didn't do such a great job in Afghanistan. They've been fighting in Afghanistan for *nineteen years*. General Mattis thanked me *profusely* for getting him 700 *billion* dollars. He couldn't believe it. General Mattis thanked me even more the following year when I got him 716 *billion* dollars. He couldn't believe it! Because our military was depleted."

Trump grew more animated, waving his hands. His voice adopting a mocking tone.

"But General Mattis was *sooo* thrilled. Well, what's he done for me? How has he done in Afghanistan? Not too good. Not too good. I'm not happy with what he's done in Afghanistan. And I *shouldn't* be happy. But *he* was very happy. He was very thankful when I got him 700 billion dollars, and then the following year, 716 billion dollars.

"So, I mean, I wish him well. I hope he does well. But as you know, President Obama fired him . . . and, essentially, so did I.

"I want results."

Trump's rebuke was a stark departure from Mattis's reception when he arrived in Washington two years previously, when Trump declared Mattis to be "the living embodiment of the Marine Corps motto *semper fidelis,* always faithful. And the American people are fortunate a man of this character and integrity will now be the civilian leader atop of the Department of Defense."

Mattis's tenure lasted 710 days, about half a year less than the average secretary of defense, although the average is skewed by three defense secretaries with incredible longevity: Robert Mc-Namara (7 years, 39 days), Donald Rumsfeld (7 years, 29 days for both tours), and Caspar Weinberger (6 years, 306 days). However, Mattis managed to outlast many other senior leaders in the Trump administration. John Kelly would survive in the administration for two days more than Mattis. The only high-profile administration officials who seemed to accomplish a graceful exit were UN Ambassador Nikki Haley and White House Press Secretary Sarah Sanders. Both received a warm send-off from President Trump, and he has had only positive comments about them.

Mattis delivered several high-profile accomplishments during his nearly two-year tenure: the defeat of ISIS's physical caliphate; publication of a wide-ranging and long-overdue defense strategy; and a two-year budget deal from Congress to restore funding to help rebuild—and augment—America's military strength.

Charles Stevenson's book *SECDEF: The Nearly Impossible Job of Secretary of Defense,* a careful evaluation of those who have run the Pentagon, groups defense secretaries into three types of leaders: Revolutionaries, Firefighters, and Team Players. Revolutionaries are "bold innovators who sought to change the Pentagon in far-reaching ways." Firefighters are those "diverted from the tasks they considered most important in order to deal with immediate problems." Team Players, the most common role, are "supportive members of the administration, helpful in how they handled their jobs and in how they worked with their colleagues."

At this early stage of reflection, seven months after his departure, Mattis is squarely in the Firefighter camp. William Cohen, another Firefighter and a mentor to Mattis, served as the twentieth secretary of defense during Bill Clinton's presidency. Stevenson describes Cohen as being "inevitably drawn into the controversies of the period and forced to try to keep them from tarnishing the administration." He performed admirably, and "with the fires successfully extinguished or contained, he left the Pentagon in the wake of praise and satisfaction."

Mattis provided a valuable service to the nation, our international allies and partners, and the members of the department he led. Just as important, Mattis effectively translated the president's desires into ethical, well-executed outcomes. In the summer of 2018, Trump called and directed Mattis to "screw Amazon" by locking them out of a chance to bid for the $10 billion networking contract known as "JEDI." Mattis demurred. Relaying the story to us during Small Group, Mattis said, "We're not going to do that. This will be done by the book, both legally and ethically."

He never ran to the press to leak an explosive tidbit. Instead, Mattis worked to align the military's actions to legally pursue the outcomes he knew Trump wanted to achieve. Mattis pursued the legal and ethical path, a careful balancing act when weighing loyalty between three important constituents: the president, the Constitution, and the defense department.

Many in Mattis's immediate orbit departed shortly after he did.

Kevin Sweeney left the Pentagon to return to Norfolk, Virginia.

Mattis nominated Faller for his third star in April 2018.

Shortly thereafter, Faller was promoted to four stars and command of US Southern Command in Florida.

Dana White departed the day after Mattis, with an active DOD inspector general investigation proceeding into allegations of misconduct and abuse of her position to elicit personal favors from members of her staff.

Special Assistant Will Bushman continued on in the office with acting secretary of defense Pat Shanahan, providing much-needed continuity, before departing for an advisory position in Personnel and Readiness.

My time in the Pentagon reminded me of an old movie called *Grand Hotel*. In the film there is massive business fraud, a fatal illness, a jewel robbery, and a murder. But the movie ends with one character ironically remarking, "The Grand Hotel. Always the same. People come . . . people go. Nothing ever happens."

At the Pentagon, people came. People went—including me. But, unlike in *Grand Hotel,* a lot really did happen. A lot of lessons were there to learn.

You just had to know where to look.

EPILOGUE

The media coverage surrounding Mattis's resignation peaked in the days following his December 20 announcement. CNN cited the resignation as a rare "no confidence vote" from a cabinet secretary regarding the president he served. The biggest question remained: What did Mattis's resignation foreshadow for the Pentagon? Will the line drawn by a traditionally apolitical—and traditionally highly respected—institution hold?

These questions are more pressing because we live in a dangerous world.

Not since the Cold War has a long-term strategic competition between nations presented the most dangerous threat. But Russia is once again rattling its saber. China is aggressively contesting the long-standing US-led international order. North Korea and Iran threaten security in their respective regions. Despite coalition-led forces reclaiming ISIS's territory, terrorism will remain an ever-present menace requiring continual vigilance.

In some ways, we have grown complacent. For too long we have pursued a status quo approach to how we organize, train, and equip the military, focused on incremental improvements to already outdated systems. If we are to preserve the peace for decades to come, we must fundamentally shift to a force that is agile and responsive, able to move "at the speed of relevance."

However, there is a high risk of failure.

As a student at TOPGUN many years ago, I learned that the most critical portion of any mission wasn't its preparation or even the flight itself—no matter how stressful or dangerous it might have been. It was the debrief conducted after we had landed and all our gear was removed.

As fighter pilots, we flew faster than six hundred miles per hour, traveling ten miles every single minute. Things happen fast. Invariably, our near supersonic speed distorted our perception of what had happened during the heat of battle. At its worst, our confusion resembled the old joke of the eyewitness telling the police, "I saw the whole thing, officer. What happened?" The post-flight debrief was our opportunity to analyze videotapes and "truth data" to determine what *actually* happened, formulate "lessons learned," and contemplate how to fly better the next day.

But lessons are only one part of the equation. Using those lessons to predict outcomes—to fly better the next day—is far more essential.

As chief speechwriter and communications director, I occupied a unique perch to observe the majority of Secretary Mattis's time in office. My desk was in his front office. I traveled extensively with him, attended senior-level meetings, and worked closely with many key Pentagon, administration, and international officials. My job required me to observe Mattis closely, to understand his worldview in order to write for him, and to focus solely on his success.

My time in the Pentagon fostered a strong belief that successfully transitioning our military to provide the security America needs isn't a foregone conclusion. Success requires clear priorities, a willingness to challenge the status quo, and a change in the department's long-held mind-set. This can only occur with strong secretary-level leadership and the longevity required to see it through.

As this book headed to the Pentagon for review, Pat Shanahan had set a new record for longevity as an acting secretary of defense—nearly six full months. Then in June 2019, Shanahan was forced to withdraw from consideration as a possible defense secretary nominee following alarming personal revelations, thrusting the department once more into uncharted territory. Mark Esper, the secretary of the Army, then stepped into the role of acting secretary of defense.

By July 1, eighteen senior Pentagon positions were vacant or filled by temporary leaders. More uncertainty ensued. On July 7, Admiral Bill Moran, the most senior uniformed naval officer, whom the Senate had already confirmed to be the next chief of naval operations, abruptly resigned three weeks before he was due to take office.

A third acting secretary of defense, Secretary of the Navy Richard Spencer, took the helm on July 15. The law required Esper to vacate the role he was under consideration for. In general, friends serving in the Pentagon described a disordered situation, with no one able to speak with confidence regarding the military's long-term priorities. This chaotic environment no doubt emboldened our nation's adversaries while continuing to alarm our allies and partners. The seven months of uncertainty finally ended on July 23, when Esper was confirmed as the twenty-seventh secretary of defense.

Esper's confirmation was an important step forward, but sixteen leadership spots below him remained unfilled. How can the military set priorities without a full complement of leaders at the helm? How can the Pentagon "gain full value from every taxpayer dollar" or "deliver performance at the speed of relevance" unless leaders—at all levels—are swiftly identified, nominated, and confirmed for their roles in the department of defense?

Trump has proclaimed that, "I like acting [officials] because I can move so quickly. It gives me flexibility." But the reality is that acting officials create uncertainty in the departments they lead. This is amplified in the case of Defense, a department already missing 25 percent of the normal complement of political appointees. Despite proclamations to the contrary, the Pentagon has found it just as difficult to recruit high-quality senior leaders, especially with Mattis no longer there to provide "top cover."

Worse, the US military's longstanding apolitical nature is under fire. On June 11, Shanahan released two memos reminding defense department personnel of their apolitical role in the wake of efforts by the White House to compel US Navy leaders to "hide" the USS *John McCain*—a destroyer based in Japan—from Trump during his visit to the naval base in Yokosuka. A week later, Secretary of the Navy Richard Spencer was so alarmed that he, too, issued a third memo reminding sailors that "as military professionals, we are an apolitical body."

Despite this chaotic environment, the Pentagon continues to conduct daily operations around the globe. Ships are still putting out to sea, aircraft are taking to the sky, and troops are in the field. We should expect no less—yet another testament to the tireless efforts of the men and women serving in the Department of Defense. It's what they're trained to handle from the first day on the job: uncertainty, surprise, and an ever-changing operational environment.

But as skilled and dependable as the rank and file are, professionals will always need strong leadership to continue to keep America safe. So, what important lessons can we learn from Mattis to inform future secretaries of defense?

First is the importance of unwavering focus on big-picture success. Among Mattis's many strengths was his self-discipline, an awe-inspiring ability to maintain singular focus on the task at hand. This intensity ensured a consistent, strategic approach at the highest levels of the Department of Defense. It served as the "North Star" for those in lower rungs of the organization and fostered alignment throughout the department. But the department will require longevity on the order of a Robert McNamara, Caspar Weinberger, or Donald Rumsfeld to make the changes required to transform the military.

Second is the requirement to foster unity of effort—teamwork—within organizations. A former congresswoman from South Carolina shared something profound with me. As we discussed our disparate backgrounds, I expressed surprise at some things I'd seen during my DC tenure. Chuckling, she advised me that my military background simply ill-equipped me to understand politics. "In the military," she said, "you spent your entire career maximizing everyone's strengths to build the best possible team. In politics, it's the opposite. You want to know as much as possible about everyone else's weaknesses so that you can apply pressure to get what you want."

There will always be tensions between senior-level teams who work together—different priorities, equities, values, and expectations. This is especially true when translating between military and civilian offices. Building a small, competent team underpinned by trust in one another is a requirement. Trust is paramount. In a leadership position, take care of the people who work tirelessly on your behalf.

Finally, we must reinvest in our long-standing allies and partners. America has long benefited from the web of alliances it helped to create from the ashes of a post–World War II world. These alliances have—to a large extent—preserved democratic interests and preserved peace for more than seven decades.

America's cooperation with allies and like-minded partners enables us to accomplish far more than we can alone. Attacking this most fundamental of strengths risks the rapid erosion of our position as a global leader and the partner of choice for myriad other nations. We are already witnessing this decline. European nations now look increasingly inward as they question US resolve. Indo-Pacific nations are reassessing the regional balance of power as China accelerates its rise. Nations appear increasingly reluctant to align with the US on issues that we deem important.

The Trump administration has yet to face a significant military crisis overseas. With adversaries increasingly willing to challenge the US, will allies and partners—who have been publicly lambasted for the previous three years—still be there if we need them?

Trump did, however, get the military "parade" he had long sought during the 2019 Fourth of July celebration in Washington, DC.

As for me, I believe Ryan Stoddard put it correctly when I first contemplated joining Mattis: "If you want the good life, stay put. Mattis tends to burn out his staff. But if you're up for the challenge, I doubt you'll ever find a job more rewarding than this one."

He was right. Working for Mattis was certainly the most exhausting tour of my career—a tour that challenged me mentally, physically, and emotionally. But the experience proved to be rewarding every step of the way.

Now I've lived it. The experience was different from anything I'd expected—working alongside a widely respected military leader in one of the most challenging positions within a chaotic administration.

An old Chinese curse supposedly says, "May you live in interesting times."

I certainly did.

ACKNOWLEDGMENTS

Everything of significance I have accomplished throughout my career has been possible only through the tireless effort and support of friends, family, and coworkers.

This book is no different.

In Peggy Noonan's *What I Saw at the Revolution*, she describes writing her first book as "an exciting trauma." I understand what she means. Her statement feels especially apropos when writing about firsthand experiences so soon after serving in uniform. I wanted this book to be enlightening but apolitical as I shared the experience of serving alongside Secretary James Mattis.

This was possible only because of a tight network of senior leaders, fellow military members, and friends who dedicated countless hours to helping me reflect on my experience. Collectively, they provided additional insight into the inner workings of the Pentagon and White House and provided sanity checks as I worked through the manuscript. There are too many to mention by name, but Tom Bodine, Chris Nelson, Fred Rainbow, Charlie Sierra, and Dave Waidelich were particularly generous sounding boards.

I also appreciate those who have already lit the path ahead with their own memoirs or historical books. Books by Peggy Noonan, George Stephanopoulos, Walter Isaacson, General Colin Powell, Cliff Sims, and Admiral Elmo Zumwalt were regular references as I sought to discover my own voice after years of channeling someone else's.

Mattis mentioned on more than one occasion the importance of getting multiple sets of eyes on a piece of work, reminding me that "even Ernest Hemingway had an editor." I've been lucky to author my first book under the watchful eye and ready assistance of Bria Sandford. She, along with Helen Healey, Tara Gilbride, Stefanie Brody, and Nina Rodriguez-Marty, worked to make this project the success it has become. I was also lucky to find Matt Latimer and Keith Urbahn, my agents, who were there every step along the way as this manuscript went from concept to reality.

I owe my deepest gratitude to my family.

To my mother, Sherri Olsen: thank you for providing tireless feedback on multiple revisions of the manuscript. More importantly, thank you for never hesitating to tell me when you thought I was veering too far from my apolitical approach.

To Sarah: this book could never have happened without your support and supreme patience. Our constant conversations over many months resulted in a book that is far better than I could have ever written on my own. Thank you for always making time to pick up a pen to perform line edits, even when you'd seen the same chapter three times in a row. You inspired me to want to write a book that will stand the test of time, and a book that I'll be proud for our children to read in the future.

Lastly, to the many men and women I've been honored to work alongside during my time in uniform: thank you for serving as a steady reminder of the values that make America's experiment in democracy so critically important.

America will always need patriots.

These references have shaped the thinking of many senior leaders and members of the military. Each one serves as a guidepost for those holding the line in our nation's defense.

Constitution of the United States of America
The Federalist Papers
Meditations, Marcus Aurelius
Grant, Ron Chernow
Washington: A Life, Ron Chernow
The Lessons of History, Will Durant and Ariel Durant
Fighting Talk: Forty Maxims on War, Peace, and Strategy, Colin Gray
The Histories, Herodotus
Kissinger, Walter Isaacson
Leaders: Myth and Reality, General Stanley McChrystal, Jeff Eggers, and Jason Mangone
Sea Stories, Admiral William H. McRaven
Military Innovation in the Interwar Period, Williamson Murray and Allan Millett
SECDEF: The Nearly Impossible Job of Secretary of Defense, Charles A. Stevenson
History of the Peloponnesian War, Thucydides
The Guns of August: The Outbreak of World War I, Barbara Tuchman

NOTES

FIRST PRINCIPLES

ix **"I, James Norman Mattis"**: James Mattis, "Watch Gen. James Mattis be sworn in as secretary of defense," accessed March 3, 2019, www.youtube.com/watch?v= -vZuuyDh5lw.

ix **"We in the Department of Defense"**: James Mattis, "Defense Chief Mattis Gives West Point Commencement Address—Full Speech," May 27, 2017, accessed March 6, 2019, www.youtube.com/watch?v =vuc90nCnYHc.

INTRODUCTION

xiii **Officially, Mattis had gone:** Grace Segers, "James Mattis resigns as defense secretary," updated December 20, 2018, www.cbsnews.com/news/james-mattis -resigns-as-defense-secretary-today -12-20-2018/.

xiv **The letter minced few words:** James Mattis, resignation letter, accessed February 21, 2019, www.theatlantic.com/ideas /archive/2018/12/read-text-james -mattiss-resignation-letter/578773/.

CHAPTER 1

2 **"immediate action items"**: NATOPS Flight Manual Navy Model FA-18A/B/C/D 161353 and Up Aircraft, September 15, 2008, V-12-1.

3 **Set each throttle:** NATOPS Flight Manual, V-12-4.

6 **Would I be interested:** Author phone call with Major Melissa Lewis, March 23, 2017.

7 **seven thousand books:** Amanda Macias, "The extraordinary reading habits of Defense Secretary James Mattis," CNBC, September 15, 2018, www.cnbc.com/2018/09/13 /defense-secretary-james-mattis -extraordinary-reading-habits.html.

8 **Navy decided to position:** The US Navy places officers using a system of detailers (who work with the sailor) and placement officers (who work to answer the command's personnel needs). Here, I am referencing a series of conversations that started on September 16, 2016, with Commander Geoffrey Bowman, my placement officer. Bowman, over the course of ten days, placed me into a job in Norfolk, Virginia, that

would ensure I was not selected for the
nuclear-powered aircraft carrier career path,
thereby preserving me for selection of a
carrier air wing. Source: Commander
Geoffrey Bowman emails, received on board
USS *Ronald Reagan*, September 12–28, 2016.

9 **"the good life, stay put"**: Phone call with
Commander Ryan Stoddard, March 26,
2017.

10 **Mattis carried a copy**: Michael Doyle,
"Advice Gen. Mattis' favorite philosopher
might give to Donald Trump," McClatchy,
December 2, 2016, www.mcclatchydc.com
/news/politics-government/article118417708
.html.

10 **led the interview**: Interview with Deputy
Chief of Staff Tony DeMartino, Fran
DuFrayne, and Major Melissa Lewis in the
Pentagon, April 6, 2017.

11 **joining Team Mattis**: Leaving my job in
Norfolk to join Secretary Mattis would place
me into what is known as a "joint job," or a
job receiving joint credit as required by the
1986 Goldwater-Nichols Act. Joint credit
would make me eligible for the nuclear
power career path. The job in Norfolk was a
"de facto" disqualifier for aircraft carriers, as
I would not have the time required to
complete the aircraft carrier career path and
joint credit.

11 **More than a few officers**: One of the most
vocal officers was then-Rear Admiral Bruce
Lindsay, my boss at Naval Air Force Atlantic.
He had replaced Sweeney as commander of
Carrier Strike Group 10 in August 2014.

12 **A few days later, Tony called**: Phone call
with Tony DeMartino on April 10, 2017.

12 **"the secretary of defense wants this guy"**:
Phone call with Commander Geoffrey
Bowman, April 12, 2017.

13 **a geographic bachelor**: This was not unusual
for members of Mattis's personal staff.
Several team members lived apart from their
families, finding lodging in the Washington,
DC, area to support Mattis, with all
expenses coming out of pocket (non-
reimbursable).

CHAPTER 2

15 **"this morning's town hall"**: Mattis's remarks
to the Office of the Under Secretary of
Defense for Personnel and Readiness, April
26, 2017.

15 **his father was a merchant mariner**: Katie
Lange, "Meet James N. Mattis: 10 facts
about the new DOD secretary," DoD News,
January 24, 2017, www.army.mil/article
/181147/meet_james_n_mattis_10
_facts_about_the_new_dod_secretary.

16 **"nothing new under the sun"**: Geoffrey
Ingersoll, "General James 'Mad Dog' Mattis
Email About Being 'Too Busy to Read' Is a
Must-Read," May 9, 2013, www
.businessinsider.com/viral-james-mattis
-email-reading-marines-2013-5?r
=US&IR=T

16 **"You stay teachable"**: Jena McGregor,
"The avid reading habits of Trump's
secretary of defense, James 'Mad Dog'
Mattis," *Washington Post*, December 1, 2016,
www.washingtonpost.com/news
/on-leadership/wp/2016/11/23/the-avid
-reading-habits-of-trumps-potential
-secretary-of-defense-james-mad-dog
-mattis/?utm_term=.df20cb1ee638.

16 **named Nathan Fick**: Nathaniel Fick, *One
Bullet Away: The Making of a Marine Officer*
(New York: Houghton Mifflin Harcourt,
2006), 118.

17 **"We're doing it in the Marines"**: Tom Ricks,
"As Kelly Eyes the Door, A Look Back At
Him And Mattis Firing A Colonel In The
Iraq War," Task & Purpose, July 3, 2018,
https://taskandpurpose.com/john-kelly
-mattis-iraq-war-firings.

17 **Christmas Day to visit Marines**: Friends
widely shared this story, which has multiple
internet sources.

18 **"In 2006, he said"**: Tom Ricks, *Fiasco: The
American Military Adventure in Iraq* (New
York: Penguin Books, 2007).

18 **"You go into Afghanistan"**: "General: It's 'fun
to shoot some people'," CNN International,
February 4, 2005, http://edition.cnn.com
/2005/US/02/03/general.shoot/.

18 **"Be polite, be professional"**: Madeline
Conway, "9 unforgettable quotes by James
Mattis," *Politico*, December 1, 2016, www
.politico.com/blogs/donald-trump
-administration/2016/12/james-mattis
-quotes-232097.

18 **"Engage your brain"**: *Politico*, December 1,
2016.

18 **"There is only one 'retirement plan'"**: Tom
Ricks, "Fiasco," *Armed Forces Journal*, August 1,
2006, http://armedforcesjournal.com/fiasco/.

19 **"There are hunters"**: Tom Ricks, "Fiasco."

19 **"If you can't eat it"**: Stan Coerr, "#Essays on War: Mattis," *The Strategy Bridge*, November 28, 2016, https://thestrategybridge.org/the-bridge/2016/11/28/essays-on-war-mattis.

19 **"Always carry a knife"**: Widely cited on the internet; no primary source found.

19 **"What keeps you awake at night?"**: Transcript: Defense Secretary James Mattis on "Face the Nation," May 28, 2017, www.cbsnews.com/news/transcript-defense-secretary-james-mattis-on-face-the-nation-may-28-2017/.

19 **the nickname he actually preferred**: James Mattis, Air Force Association speech, September 20, 2017.

20 **the "Tailhook certification"**: Lieutenant Colonel J. N. Mattis, Tailhook certification letter, January 12, 1993.

21 **His remarks, later reprinted**: James N. Mattis, "The Meaning of Their Service," *Wall Street Journal*, April 17, 2015, www.wsj.com/articles/the-meaning-of-their-service-1429310859.

21 **Mattis nicknamed him**: The nickname was created by Secretary Mattis's scheduler, and widely used by Mattis and others in the front office.

28 **"Give me a pack of cigarettes"**: Mattis used the same line, widely reported by the media.

28 **"appoint 'Mad Dog' Mattis"**: Donald Trump, "Trump announces he will appoint Gen. James Mattis to secretary of defense," YouTube, December 1, 2016, www.youtube.com/watch?v=xoTIJrkeKb8.

CHAPTER 3

31 **I read with interest**: Mark Perry, "James Mattis' 33-Year Grudge Against Iran," *Politico*, December 4, 2016, www.politico.com/magazine/story/2016/12/james-mattis-iran-secretary-of-defense-214500

33 **"referred to them"**: James Mann, "The Adults in the Room," *The New York Review of Books*, October 26, 2017, www.nybooks.com/articles/2017/10/26/trump-adult-supervision/

34 **"How do you work with senior leadership?"**: Question posed to Mattis during an all hands call with US Africa Command

personnel in Stuttgart, Germany, February 16, 2018.

35 **earned a silver star for valor**: M1a1 Abrams Tanks in action Iraq-73 Easting, http://dragoonbase.com/video/m1a1-abrams-tanks-in-action, accessed February 5, 2019.

36 **"The best service"**: Omar Bradley, http://www.military-quotes.com/omar-bradley.htm, accessed April 4, 2018.

37 **Trump had sprung a bombshell**: Fox 10 Phoenix, "President Trump At Pentagon Ceremonial Swearing-In of Secretary of Defense James Mattis," YouTube, January 27, 2016, www.youtube.com/watch?v=GbPMogg-eXI.

37 **Just six months earlier**: Helene Cooper, "Trump's Signing of Immigrant Ban Puts Pentagon in Uncomfortable Light," *The New York Times*, January 28, 2017, www.nytimes.com/2017/01/28/us/politics/trump-immigration-ban-muslims-military.html.

39 **His severance package**: Kate Kelly, "Goldman's $285 Million Package for Gary Cohn Is Questioned," *The New York Times*, January 25, 2017, www.nytimes.com/2017/01/25/business/dealbook/goldman-sachs-gary-cohn-285-million-departure-package.html.

40 **"If you think this war"**: Rowan Scarborough, "Border security hawk Gen. John Kelly attracts Trump Cabinet interest," *The Washington Times*, November 27, 2016, http://www.washingtontimes.com/news/2016/nov/27/john-kelly-trump-cabinet-mention-a-border-security/

CHAPTER 4

42 **we knew what we wanted**: The Secretary's Action Group kept a long-range planning calendar, tracking major events and opportunities twelve months into the future. This planning style meant we were usually operating far out in front of the White House, National Security Staff, and Department of State.

43 **Mattis had listed three**: Committee on Armed Services, US Senate, stenographic transcript for James Mattis confirmation hearing, January 12, 2017, www.armed-services.senate.gov/imo/media/doc/17-03_01-12-17.pdf.

43 **codify Mattis's priorities:** Using these three priorities, I authored Mattis's October 5, 2017, memorandum for all defense department personnel. I was pleasantly surprised that he made no changes, merely signing the memorandum and writing "Charge!" next to his signature.

47 **two types of organizations:** This is a sentiment that Mattis would routinely share during Capstone, a professional development course for rising one-star generals, admirals, and senior executive service equivalents.

52 **"I would never have imagined":** James Mattis speaking at the US Military Academy in West Point, New York, May 27, 2017, YouTube, James Mattis, "Defense Chief Mattis Gives West Point Commencement Address—Full Speech," May 27, 2017, accessed March 6, 2019, www.youtube .com/watch?v=vuc90nCnYHc.

CHAPTER 5

54 **"We have much great news":** Donald Trump, "President Trump's first full cabinet meeting," YouTube, June 12, 2017, accessed February 12, 2019, www.youtube.com /watch?v=6ARgUIpM6f0.

55 **"Thank you, Mr. President":** Various speakers, "Trump must be praised during June 12, 2017 Cabinet Meeting," C-SPAN, June 12, 2017, accessed February 12, 2019, www.c-span.org/video/?c4673387/trump -praised-june-12-2017-cabinet-meeting

56 **"Mr. President," began Mattis:** C-SPAN.

59 **"it's costing us too much money":** CNN transcript of Wolf Blitzer interview with President Donald Trump, July 11, 2018, http://edition.cnn.com/TRANSCRIPTS /1807/11/wolf.02.html.

59 **"we have a treaty with Japan":** Jesse Johnson, "Trump rips U.S. defense of Japan as one-sided, too expensive," *The Japan Times,* August 6, 2016, www.japantimes.co.jp /news/2016/08/06/national/politics -diplomacy/trump-rips-u-s-defense-japan -one-sided-expensive/#.WJq-8xKGNPV.

60 **America's "ironclad commitment":** Theme of Mattis's remarks to South Korean acting president Hwang Kyo-ahn of South Korea and Japanese prime minister Shinzo Abe during his February 2-4, 2017, visits to both nations.

60 **"a message that Tillerson":** H. R. McMaster and Gary D. Cohn, "America First Doesn't Mean America Alone," *Wall Street Journal,* May 30, 2017, www.wsj.com/articles /america-first-doesnt-mean-america -alone-1496187426.

61 **an alarming speech:** Donald Trump, "Watch: President Trump's speech at NATO HQ," YouTube, May 25, 2017, www.youtube .com/watch?v=4glfwiMXgwQ

63 **"Security is the foundation of prosperity":** James Mattis, speech at the Shangri-La Dialogue, Singapore, June 2, 2017, dod .defense.gov/News/Speeches/Speech-View /Article/1204264/shangri-la-dialogue/.

64 **"return on invested capital":** This is a slide I created in cooperation with the Joint Staff J5 (Strategy, Plans, and Policy) Directorate. It depicted the current laydown of US forces arrayed around the globe as compared to host nation forces, demonstrating that the US received a good return on its security investment.

64 **"NATO remains critical":** Donald Trump, "President Trump in Poland," Warsaw, Poland, July 6, 2017, www.whitehouse .gov/articles/president-trump-poland/.

64–65 **we were scheduled to brief Trump:** This meeting was held in the seventh floor dining room of the state department.

CHAPTER 6

69 **Trump had declared:** Justin Worland, "Trump Announces Withdrawal From Paris Agreement," Time, June 1, 2017, https:// time.com/4801134/paris-agreement -withdrawal-donald-trump-rose-garden/.

71 **"disagree on the fundamentals":** This was said behind closed doors, but he also used a variation of this saying publicly. E.g., Ellen Mitchell, "Mattis called reports he contradicted Trump on North Korea 'ludicrous,'" *The Hill,* August 31, 2017, https://thehill.com/policy/defense /348792-mattis-calls-reports-he -contradicted-trump-ludicrous.

71 **on a near-hourly basis:** This directive from Mattis consumed an extraordinary amount of time. My counterpart was Colonel Francis Park, assigned to the Joint Staff J5.

72 **"very well against ISIS":** Tim Hains, "Replay: President Trump Arrives at Pentagon for 'Grand Strategy' Meeting With Sec. Mattis," *Real Clear Politics,* July 20, 2017, www .realclearpolitics.com/video/2017/07/20

/replay_president_trump_arrives_at
_pentagon_for_grand_strategy_meeting
_with_sec_mattis.html.

73 **President Trump crossed his arms:** Mattis
shared these sentiments publicly, including
the 2018 Shangri La Dialogue in Singapore.

74 **America's two fundamental powers:** An
excellent example of this speech: Staff
Writer, "Mattis opens up about face-to-
face meeting with terrorist who tried to kill
him," Popular Military, September 27, 2018,
https://popularmilitary.com/mattis-opens
-face-face-meeting-terrorist-tried-kill/.

75 **Japan footing the bill:** This move had been
discussed publicly for more than a decade:
Justin McCurry, "Japan to pay 60% of costs
of moving US troops to Guam,"
The Guardian, April 24, 2006, www
.theguardian.com/world/2006/apr/25
/usa.japan.

76 **"One Belt, One Road":** Zheping Huang,
"Your guide to understanding OBOR,
China's new Silk Road plan," *Quartz*, May
15, 2017, https://qz.com/983460/obor
-an-extremely-simple-guide-to
-understanding-chinas-one-belt-one
-road-forum-for-its-new-silk-road/.

78 **"I'm ready for a trade war":** Trump didn't
officially pursue tariffs against China until
January 2018.

CHAPTER 7

83 **"Enough words have been spoken":** James
Mattis, "CVN-78 USS Gerald R. Ford
Secretary Mattis introduces President Trump
Commissioning," BusinessUSAToday, July
22, 2017, www.youtube.com/watch?v
=0kdwauLQR4M, accessed on March 4,
2019.

84 **"After consultation with my Generals":**
Donald Trump via Twitter, series of three
tweets posted July 26, 2017, https://twitter
.com/realDonaldTrump/status
/890193981585444864.

84 **Mattis sent a memo:** James Mattis, "Accession
of Transgender Individuals into the Military
Services," Office of the Secretary of Defense,
June 30, 2017.

85 **General Dunford released guidance:** Robert
Burns and Catherine Lucey, "Gen. Joseph
Dunford says transgender policy unchanged
for now," July 27, 2017, www
.washingtontimes.com/news/2017/jul/27

/pentagon-caught-flat-footed-on-trumps
-transsexual-/.

86 **word of Priebus's sacking:** Dylan Matthews,
"Report: Reince Priebus literally got kicked
out of the presidential motorcade," July 28,
2017, www.vox.com/2017/7/28/16060352
/reince-priebus-motorcade-air-force-one
-departure.

86 **"I am pleased to inform you":** Donald Trump
via Twitter, July 28, 2017, https://twitter
.com/realDonaldTrump/status
/891038014314598400.

88 **"a fox loose in the henhouse":** The actual
quote McCain used was "I have to have
confidence that the fox is not going to be
put back into the henhouse."

89 **the department's "third offset strategy":** Bob
Work, "Remarks by Deputy Secretary Work
on Third Offset Strategy," as delivered by
Deputy Secretary of Defense Bob Work,
Brussels, April 28, 2016, https://dod
.defense.gov/News/Speeches/Speech
-View/Article/753482/remarks-by
-d%20eputy-secretary-work-on-third-offset
-strategy/.

90 **"that was out of control":** Josh Lowe, "F-35:
U.K.'S Fighter Jets Won't Function Fully but
their Cost Has Almost Doubled: Report,"
Newsweek, July 17, 2017, www.newsweek
.com/f-35-planes-uk-defense-637556.

91 **smaller-than-normal speech team:**
Traditionally, the speech team had seven or
eight people: four speechwriters, two to
three researchers, and an administrative
assistant. On Mattis's team, I was leading a
team of three—a total that included me
as well.

92 **a special, undercover trip:** My trip to
Kissinger Associates was on August 10,
2017, coordinated through Meredith Potter
from Kissinger's office.

CHAPTER 8

96 **my first international trip:** We departed
Andrews Air Force Base on August 19,
2017. Stops included Jordan, Turkey, Iraq,
and Ukraine. We returned to Andrews on
August 24, 2017.

97 **the E-4B "Nightwatch" plane:** US Air Force
Global Strike Command Public Affairs
Office, Official E-4B Fact Sheet, current as
of November 2016, www.af.mil/About-Us
/Fact-Sheets/Display/Article/104503/e-4b/.

97 **secretary's private cabin:** An excellent and official guided walkthrough can be found on YouTube, posted by Horizontal Rain, "Guided Tour Inside the E-4B NAOC Doomsday Plane," September 30, 2013, www.youtube.com/watch?v=maZdUtB0ojs.

99 **final version of the strategy:** I finished the entire strategy package for key congressional members in October, handing the completed package off to Mattis's executive secretary for signature and transmittal. The effort began in earnest in June 2017 and lasted for months. Mattis discussed with Trump, Tillerson, and others to coalesce around the final military strategy in advance of Trump's August announcement.

102 **"America First, America Only":** Wikipedia, "America First (policy)," https://en .wikipedia.org/wiki/America_First _(policy).

106 **watch President Trump's speech:** Donald Trump speech announcing South Asia Strategy, www.youtube.com/watch?v= w9ClUhJDx7A, accessed March 3, 2019.

CHAPTER 9

107 **"Hey Bus, here you go":** Overseas travel to India and Afghanistan September 24–28, 2017. Only a small contingent would continue on to Afghanistan with Mattis. Most of us remained in Qatar until the contingent returned, then we all boarded the E-4B to return home.

108 **I took the speech:** This was a speech I wrote for Mattis to deliver at a joint press conference with Indian Minister of Defense Nirmala Sitharaman. I also made changes to another speech Mattis would deliver in Afghanistan alongside President Ghani and NATO Secretary General Jens Stoltenberg the following day on the South Asia Strategy. Mattis wanted Stoltenberg in Afghanistan to emphasize the importance of the allied effort through NATO's Resolute Support Mission.

110 **Stoltenberg summed up:** Transcript of Joint Press Conference with Secretary Mattis, Secretary General Stoltenberg, and President Ghani in Kabul, Afghanistan, September 28, 2017, https://dod.defense.gov/News /Transcripts/Transcript-View/Article /1328746/joint-press-conference-with -secretary-mattis-secretary-general -stoltenberg-and/.

111 **Trump had addressed:** Transcript of Donald Trump speech to the United Nations, September 19, 2107, www.the-american -catholic.com/2017/09/19/trump-un -speech/.

113 **McMaster wanted to speak to Mattis:** On September 28, 2017, during our flight from Qatar to Andrews Air Force Base in Maryland.

115 **"I'll need you with me":** The meeting with McCain was September 29, 2017. Mattis's testimony on the South Asia Strategy occurred on October 3, 2017.

CHAPTER 10

122 **McCain made it clear:** Transcript from US Senate Armed Services Committee (SASC) hearing on political and security situation in Afghanistan, October 3, 2017, www.armed -services.senate.gov/imo/media/doc/17-82 _10-03-17.pdf.

123 **But that success:** SASC transcript, 2.

124 **focused exclusively on Afghanistan:** SASC transcript, 13.

126 **During a campaign stop:** Donald Trump's remarks at Sunrise, Florida, campaign stop on August 10, 2016, *The Guardian*, www .theguardian.com/us-news/video/2016 /aug/11/donald-trump-president-obama -is-the-founder-of-isis-video. Accessed February 26, 2019.

127 **"I don't want to broadcast":** Jacob Pramuk, "Trump: I don't give a specific ISIS plan because I don't want enemies to know it," *Yahoo Finance*, September 7, 2016, https:// finance.yahoo.com/news/trump-dont -specific-isis-plan-020335606.html.

127 **their 2014 proclamation:** Staff writer, "ISIS jihadists declare 'Islamic caliphate'," *Al Arabiya News*, June 29, 2014, https://english .alarabiya.net/en/News/2014/06/29/ISIS -jihadists-declare-caliphate-.html.

127 **Obama administration initiated:** Robert Farley, "Trump Takes Too Much Credit on ISIS," FactCheck.org, March 22, 2018, www.factcheck.org/2018/03/trump-takes -too-much-credit-on-isis/.

127 **On his first day in office:** Emma Reynolds, "What Trump's first day in office will look like," November 16, 2016, www.news.com .au/finance/work/leaders/what-trumps -first-day-in-office-will-look-like/news -story/2a5c9126d550397aeff441585f026f8d.

128 **"slowed decision cycles"**: Mattis remarks at a Department of Defense press briefing on a campaign to defeat ISIS, May 19, 2017, https://dod.defense.gov/News/Transcripts /Transcript-View/Article/1188225 /department-of-defense-press-briefing -by-secretary-mattis-general-dunford -and-sp/.

129 **"President Trump directed the Department"**: Mattis remarks at DOD press briefing.

130 **"the destruction of ISIS"**: Mattis remarks at DOD press briefing.

130 **"crush ISIS's claim"**: Mattis remarks at DOD press briefing.

130 **campaign's diplomatic element**: Tillerson and Mattis consistently coordinated and messaged a whole government approach to defeating ISIS, as they did with most issues.

130 **the coalition had retaken**: Mattis remarks at DOD press briefing.

130 **last stronghold in Raqqa**: Wikipedia, "Battle of Raqqa (2017)," accessed April 7, 2019, https://en.wikipedia.org/wiki/Battle_of _Raqqa_(2017).

131 **Under the terms of**: Wikipedia, "Joint Comprehensive Plan of Action," accessed July 7, 2019, https://en.wikipedia.org /wiki/Joint_Comprehensive_Plan_of _Action.

132 **"My number-one priority"**: Tim Hains, "Obama Meets With President-Elect Trump: My Number One Priority Is to Ensure He Is Successful," RealClear Politics, November 10, 2016, www.realclearpolitics .com/video/2016/11/10/watch_live _president-elect_donald_trump_meets _with_obama_at_white_house.html.

132 **Iran's version of "Mad Dog"**: For a good primer of General Qassem Soleimani, see Dexter Filkins, "The Shadow Commander," *The New Yorker*, September 30, 2013. Filkins wrote a similar piece profiling Mattis. www.newyorker.com/magazine/2013/09 /30/the-shadow-commander.

132 **Iran was complying**: Leslie Wroughton, "U.S. says Iran complies with nuke deal but orders review on lifting sanctions," Reuters, April 18, 2017, www.reuters.com /article/US-iran-nuclear-usa-tillerson- idUSKBN17L08I.

133 **letter to House Speaker Paul Ryan**: Wroughton.

133 **recertified Iran's compliance**: Scott Neuman, "State Department Certifies Iran's Compliance with Nuclear Deal," July 17, 2017, www.npr.org/sections/thetwo-way /2017/07/17/537793465/state-department -certifies-irans-compliance-with-nuclear -deal.

133 **"Yes, senator, I do"**: Transcript from US Senate Armed Services Committee (SASC) hearing on political and security situation in Afghanistan, October 3, 2017, www.armed -services.senate.gov/imo/media/doc/17-82 _10-03-17.pdf, 50.

133 **"If we can confirm"**: SASC transcript, 56.

134 **"We'll have a recommendation"**: *Politico*, "Full text: Rex Tillerson's press conference transcript," October 4, 2017, https://www .politico.com/story/2017/10/04/full-text -rex-tillersons-press-conference-transcript -243450.

134 **"the Iran Deal was one of the worst"**: Remarks by President Donald Trump on Iran Strategy, Diplomatic Reception Room, White House, October 13, 2017, www .whitehouse.gov/briefings-statements /remarks-president-trump-iran-strategy/.

135 **"negotiate with Little Rocket Man"**: Donald Trump tweet on October 1, 2017, https://twitter.com/realDonaldTrump/status /914497787543735296.

135 **when NBC reported**: Carol E. Lee, Kristen Welker, Stephanie Ruhle and Dafna Linzer, "Tillerson's Fury at Trump Required an Intervention from Pence," NBC News, October 4, 2017, www.nbcnews.com /politics/white-house/tillerson-s-fury -trump-required-intervention-pence -n806451.

135 **"address the main headline"**: "Full text: Rex Tillerson's press conference transcript," *Politico*, October 4, 2017, www.politico .com/story/2017/10/04/full-text-rex -tillersons-press-conference-transcript -243450.

135 **"this is what I don't understand"**: Tillerson's press conference transcript, *Politico*, October 4, 2017, www.politico.com/story/2017/10 /04/full-text-rex-tillersons-press -conference-transcript-243450.

135 **"General Mattis and I"**: Tillerson's press conference transcript, *Politico*, October 4, 2017, www.politico.com/story/2017/10 /04/full-text-rex-tillersons-press -conference-transcript-243450.

136 **"I think it's fake news":** Randall Lane, "Inside Trump's Head: An Exclusive Interview with the President, and the Single Theory That Explains Everything," *Forbes*, October 10, 2017, www.forbes.com/donald-trump /exclusive-interview/#2427f47abdec.

136 **Senior Leaders Conference at the Pentagon:** Held in the Nunn-Lugar Conference Room across from the secretary of defense front office. The meeting included members of the Joint Chiefs of Staff, combatant commanders, and senior civilian leaders.

CHAPTER 11

138 **called the Dark Ages:** Good insight into the Dark Ages at the Service Academy Forum, www.serviceacademyforums.com/index .php?threads/dark-ages.16406/.

140 **returned from Asia:** Weeklong trip to Asia: October 22–24 in Philippines for ASEAN Defense Ministers meeting, October 25–26 in Thailand, and October 27–28 in South Korea for Korea Security consultative meeting.

140 **next weeklong overseas trip:** November 5–7 in Helsinki, Finland, for Northern Group, November 8–9 in Brussels, Belgium, for NATO Defense Ministerial and Defeat ISIS Coalition meetings, and November 9–10 in London, England.

141 **"Unless things change":** Phillip Rucker, "White House Chief Kelly: 'Unless things change, I'm not quitting. I'm not getting fired,'" *Washington Post*, October 12, 2017, www.washingtonpost.com/news/post -politics/wp/2017/10/12/white-house -chief-kelly-unless-things-change-im-not -quitting-im-not-getting-fired/?noredirect &utm_term=.be3c8558ab8f.

144 **a Henry Kissinger move:** As described by Walter Isaacson in *Kissinger* (New York: Simon & Schuster, 2005).

CHAPTER 12

152 **crucial of Mattis's tenure:** Meeting on the 2018 National Defense Strategy held in Mattis's office.

154 **ship collisions the Navy suffered:** T. Christian Miller, Megan Rose, and Robert Faturechi, "Fight the Ship," *ProPublica*, February 6, 2019, https://features.propublica.org/navy -accidents/uss-fitzgerald-destroyer-crash -crystal/.

155 **"Tell McMaster we won't wait":** Trump's State of the Union address to Congress was scheduled for January 30, 2018.

156 **protests over a political speech:** Susan Svrluga and Alejandra Matos, "Student protesters burn American flags at confrontation over Trump victory," *Washington Post*, November 9, 2016, www.washingtonpost.com/news /grade-point/wp/2016/11/09/student -protesters-burn-american-flags-at -confrontation-over-trump-victory /?noredirect&utm_term=.c87631e1e201.

159 **"America's security, prosperity, and standing":** Remarks by President Trump on the administration's National Security Strategy, White House transcript, December 18, 2017, www.whitehouse.gov/briefings-statements /remarks-president-trump-administrations -national-security-strategy/.

159 **"our national strength":** Trump remarks on National Security Strategy, December 18, 2017.

160 **Nadia Schadlow, one of McMaster's:** Schadlow's visit occurred in Mattis's office on January 10, 2018.

CHAPTER 13

173 **a long whitepaper:** Guy M. Snodgrass, "Keep a Weather Eye on the Horizon," *Navy War College Review*: Vol 67, Number 4 (Autumn), Article 7.

CHAPTER 14

178 **"This is a defense strategy":** Remarks by Secretary Mattis on the National Defense Strategy, January 19, 2018, https://dod .defense.gov/News/Transcripts/Transcript -View/Article/1420042/remarks-by -secretary-mattis-on-the-national-defense -strategy/.

180 **"Restoring American Power":** John S. McCain, "Restoring American Power," http://fedne.ws/uploads/011617_mccain _defense_budget_whitepaper.pdf.

181 **Speaker of the House Paul Ryan:** Paul Ryan and John Hamre, "Defending Defense: A Conversation with Speaker Ryan on Military Readiness," CSIS, January 18, 2018, https://csis-prod.s3.amazonaws.com /s3fs-public/publication/180118_%20 Defending_Defense_with_Speaker_Ryan _on_Military_Readiness.pdf?Uoib2r SxeXf_mTdbjuDah6xWKxESaLFZ.

182 **closed-door briefing:** This meeting was held in the secretary's dining room.

182 **"the Republican retreat":** The meeting was held on February 1, 2018.

186 **"I am heartened":** Press briefing by Press Secretary Sarah Sanders and Secretary of Defense James Mattis, White House transcript, February 7, 2018, www.whitehouse .gov/briefings-statements/press-briefing -press-secretary-sarah-sanders-secretary -defense-james-mattis-02072018/.

CHAPTER 15

189 **"As you can see":** CNN Newsroom, "McMaster: Russia Meddling 'Incontrovertible,'" CNN, February 18, 2018, http://transcripts.cnn.com /TRANSCRIPTS/1802/18/cnr.19.html.

189 **"General McMaster forgot":** CNN Newsroom, "McMaster: Russia Meddling 'Incontrovertible,'" CNN, February 18, 2018, http://transcripts.cnn.com /TRANSCRIPTS/1802/18/cnr.19.html.

189 **"effective at the end":** Statement by Secretary of State Rex Tillerson, Reuters Video, March 13, 2018, www.reuters .com/video/2018/03/13/tillerson-says -goodbye-to-step-down-marc?videoId =408675199.

191 **enabled Mattis to operate:** A pull-aside with Mattis and Dana White, following a phone call with NATO Secretary General Stoltenberg.

CHAPTER 16

199 **"good to see you":** "US defence secretary welcomes 'devil incarnate' John Bolton to Pentagon," *Guardian News,* YouTube, accessed April 3, 2019, www.youtube .com/watch?v=Jd0fVREENzM.

204 **coordinated an opportunity:** Phone call with Stephen Miller and Matt Pottinger.

206 **"I am writing directly":** Secretary Mattis memorandum, "Be Peerless Stewards of Taxpayers' Dollars," March 26, 2018, www .govexec.com/media/gbc/docs/pdfs _edit/peerlessstewards-3.pdf.

207 **Faller risked being forcibly retired:** Craig Whitlock, "Investigations Admiral tapped for promotions despite dinners with 'Fat Leonard'," *Washington Post,* September 24, 2018, www.washingtonpost .com/investigations/admiral-tapped -for-promotions-despite-dinners-with

-fat-leonard/2018/09/24/d499c62e -bb79-11e8-9812-a389be6690af _story.html?noredirect&utm_term= .290e6a15c05f.

CHAPTER 18

226 **we had flown to Brussels:** Our trip to Brussels, Belgium, and London, England, June 6–9, 2018.

228 **"reversed the downward trend":** Transcript of press conference by Secretary Mattis at the NATO Defense Ministerial, Brussels, Belgium, June 8, 2018, https://dod .defense.gov/News/Transcripts/Transcript -View/Article/1545079/press-conference -by-secretary-mattis-at-the-nato-defense -ministerial-brussels-b/.

228 **for Mattis's participation:** For a primer on Britain's Trooping the Colour ceremony, see https://en.wikipedia.org/wiki/Trooping _the_Colour.

229 **Twitter post seized my attention:** Photo by Jesco Denzel, a copy of which can be found at www.thelocal.de/20180610/trump- destroys-trust-with-g7-tweets-germany.

230 **"very dishonest and weak":** Donald Trump tweet posted June 9, 2018, https:// twitter.com/realDonaldTrump /status/1005586562959093760.

230 **"I have instructed":** Donald Trump tweet posted June 9, 2018, https:// twitter.com/realdonaldtrump/status /1005586152076689408.

231 **"stopping the war games":** Ian Schwartz, "Trump: We Will Stop 'Playing The War Games' with South Korea," RealClear Politics, June 12, 2018, www .realclearpolitics.com/video/2018/06/12 /trump_we_will_stop_playing_the_war _games_with_south_korea.html.

233 **"the exercises with South Korea":** White House transcript of press conference by President Trump, Capella Hotel, Singapore, June 12, 2018, www.whitehouse.gov /briefings-statements/press-conference -president-trump/.

233 **our Large Group meeting:** Meeting held in Nunn-Lugar Conference Room.

235 **phone call with Japanese defense minister:** Phone call was held in Mattis's office.

236 **"Space Policy Directive 3":** This policy directive can be found at www.whitehouse .gov/presidential-actions/space-policy

-directive-3-national-space-traffic
-management-policy/.

236 "I strongly urge Congress": Rebecca Kheel,
"Mattis opposes plan to create new military
branch for space," *The Hill*, July 12, 2017,
https://thehill.com/policy/defense
/341650-mattis-opposes-space-corps-plan.

237 "reclaiming America's heritage": White
House transcript of remarks by President
Trump at a meeting with the National Space
Council and signing of Space
Policy Directive 3, June 18, 2018, www
.whitehouse.gov/briefings-statements
/remarks-president-trump-meeting
-national-space-council-signing-space
-policy-directive-3/.

CHAPTER 19

242 **Mattis's fourth trip:** June 24–29, 2019, with
stops in Alaska, Beijing, China, and Tokyo,
Japan.

242 **article by Courtney Kube:** Courtney Kube,
"Mattis is out of the loop and Trump doesn't
listen to him, say officials," NBC News, June
25, 2018, www.nbcnews.com/politics
/donald-trump/mattis-out-loop-trump
-doesn-t-listen-him-say-officials-n885796.

245 **Senior Civilian Offsite:** Meeting was held
on March 8, 2018.

245 **distributed a collection:** A copy of this
collection can be found at www.scribd
.com/document/416095033/Secretary
-Mattis-s-Philosophy-and-Guidance.

248 **first exclusive interview:** Teddy Fischer, "Full
transcript: Defense Secretary James Mattis'
interview with The Islander," *The Islander*,
June 20, 2017, http://mihsislander.org
/2017/06/full-transcript-james-mattis
-interview/.

249 "That means you're living": Paul Szoldra,
"Mattis to Sailors: 'You're Not Some P—y
Sitting on the Sidelines,'" Task & Purpose,
August 15, 2017, https://taskandpurpose
.com/mattis-navy-sailors-pussy-sidelines.

252 **Gates had also pointed out:** Robert Gates,
Duty: Memoirs of a Secretary at War (Knopf:
New York, 2014), 109.

CHAPTER 20

261 **Alaska for Beijing:** June 24–29, 2018, trip to
Alaska, China, and Japan. I met with Mattis
the morning of June 25, 2018.

265 "Our stance is steadfast": Bloomberg, "Xi
Jinping Warns U.S. That China Won't
Surrender 'One Inch' of Territory," *Time*,
June 28, 2018, https://time.com/5324571
/china-xi-jinping-james-mattis-south
-china-sea/.

265 "a great trajectory": Bloomberg, https://time
.com/5324571/china-xi-jinping-james
-mattis-south-china-sea/.

CHAPTER 21

269 "As we look forward": Alf Bjarne Johnsen
and Julie Vissgren, "Donald Trump til Erna
Solberg: Norge må oppfylle toprosentmålet,"
VG, June 26, 2018, www.vg.no
/nyheter/innenriks/i/WLAavj/donald
-trump-til-erna-solberg-norge-maa
-oppfylle-toprosentmaalet.

276 "Many countries in NATO": Donald Trump
tweet on July 10, 2018, https://twitter
.com/realDonaldTrump/status
/1016729137409486853.

276 "Which nations do you want": "Trump
and Stoltenberg get into tense exchange at
NATO summit," *Washington Post*, July 11,
2018, YouTube, www.youtube.com
/watch?v=Vpwkdmwui3k/.

CHAPTER 23

298 "our strength as a nation": Staff, "Read:
James Mattis's resignation letter," CNN
Politics, December 21, 2018, www.cnn
.com/2018/12/20/politics/james-mattis
-resignation-letter-doc/index.html.

302 "doesn't do stunts": Alex Horton, "Mattis,
who used a Hollywood actor as a stand-in
spokesman, says the military doesn't 'do
stunts,'" November 1, 2018, *Washington Post*,
www.washingtonpost.com/national
-security/2018/11/01/mattis-who-used
-hollywood-actor-stand-in-spokesman
-says-military-doesnt-do-stunts/?utm
_term=.4cebc717d3d1.

304 "We have defeated ISIS": Donald Trump
tweet on December 19, 2018, https://
twitter.com/realDonaldTrump/status
/1075397797929775105.

306 "the military had been fantastic": White
House transcript of remarks by President
Trump in cabinet meeting, January 2, 2019,
www.whitehouse.gov/briefings
-statements/remarks-president-trump
-cabinet-meeting-12/.

307 **"talk about our generals"**: White House transcript, www.whitehouse.gov/briefings -statements/remarks-president-trump -cabinet-meeting-12/.

307 **"But General Mattis"**: White House transcript, www.whitehouse.gov/briefings -statements/remarks-president-trump -cabinet-meeting-12/.

307 **"the living embodiment"**: Jessica Taylor, "Trump Touts Military Strength in N.C. on Second Stop of 'Thank You' Tour," NPR, December 6, 2016, www.npr.org /2016/12/06/504632155/trump-touts -military-strength-in-n-c-on-second -stop-of-thank-you-tour.

308 **"bold innovators who sought"**: Charles Stevenson, *SECDEF: The Nearly Impossible Job of Secretary of Defense* (Potomac Books: Washington, DC, 2006), 21.

308 **"diverted from the tasks"**: Stevenson, 75.

308 **"supportive members"**: Stevenson, 119.

309 **Trump called and directed**: Mattis shared that "POTUS does not want Amazon to win the contract," emphasizing that he was told "they [Amazon] are not to win this".

310 **Dana White departed**: Dareh Gregorian, "Top Pentagon spokeswoman resigns on New Year's Eve amid internal probe," NBC News, December 31, 2018, www .nbcnews.com/politics/politics-news /top-pentagon-spokeswoman-resigns -new-year-s-eve-amid-internal-n953421.

EPILOGUE

313 **eighteen senior Pentagon positions**: Barbara Starr, "18 senior Pentagon roles filled by temporary officials or vacant," CNN, www .cnn.com/2019/07/01/politics/pentagon -vacancies-list/index.html.

314 **I like acting**: Brian Naylor, "An Acting Government for the Trump Administration," NPR, April 9, 2019, www.npr.org /2019/04/09/711094554/an-acting -government-for-the-trump-administration.

314 **Shanahan released two memos**: Sam LaGrone, "Acting SECDEF Shanahan Reminds Pentagon to Stay Apolitical Following 'McCain Situation,'" USNI News, June 11, 2018, https://news.usni .org/2019/06/11/acting-secdef-shanahan -reminds-pentagon-to-stay-apolitical -following-mccain-situation.

315 **"as military professionals"**: Faith Karimi, "The Navy issues a memo on political activities after a scandal involving the White House," CNN, June 28, 2019, www.cnn .com/2019/06/27/politics/navy-issues -memo-trnd/index.html.